CREOLE ITALIAN

SOUTHERN FOODWAYS ALLIANCE
STUDIES IN CULTURE, PEOPLE, AND PLACE

The series explores key themes and tensions in
food studies—including race, class, gender, power,
and the environment—on a macro scale and also
through the microstories of men and women
who grow, prepare, and serve food. It presents a
variety of voices, among them those of scholars,
journalists, and writers of creative nonfiction.

SERIES EDITOR
John T. Edge

SERIES ADVISORY BOARD
Brett Anderson | *New Orleans Times-Picayune*

Elizabeth Engelhardt | University of North Carolina
at Chapel Hill

Psyche Williams-Forson | University of Maryland
at College Park

CREOLE ITALIAN

Sicilian Immigrants
and the Shaping of
New Orleans Food Culture

JUSTIN A. NYSTROM

The University of Georgia Press

ATHENS

© 2018 by the University of Georgia Press
Athens, Georgia 30602
www.ugapress.org
All rights reserved
Designed by Kaelin Broaddus
Set in Minion Pro by Graphic Composition, Inc.

Most University of Georgia Press titles are
available from popular e-book vendors.

Printed digitally

Library of Congress Cataloging-in-Publication Data

Names: Nystrom, Justin A., 1970– author.
Title: Creole Italian : Sicilian immigrants and the shaping
   of New Orleans food culture / Justin A. Nystrom.
Description: Athens : The University of Georgia Press,
   2018. | Series: Southern Foodways Alliance : studies in
   culture, people, and place | Includes bibliographical
   references and index.
Identifiers: LCCN 2017058468 | ISBN: 9780820353562
   (hardcover : alk. paper) | ISBN: 9780820353555 (pbk. :
   alk. paper) | ISBN: 9780820353579 (ebook)
Subjects: LCSH: Sicilians—Food—Louisiana—New
   Orleans—History. | Sicilian Americans—Food—
   Louisiana—New Orleans—History. | Cooking,
   Italian—Sicilian style. | Cooking, Creole. |
   Immigrants—Louisiana—New Orleans—History. |
   New Orleans (La.)—Social life and customs.
Classification: LCC F379.N59 1849 2018 | DDC 641.59763—
   dc23
LC record available at https://lccn.loc.gov/2017058468

For Jess

Contents

Acknowlegments

Contemplating the people and moments who propelled me over the last decade to write this book, I'm reminded of a collection of mementos and found objects that somehow made their way into a keepsake box in a sock drawer. Collectively these observations tell the story of how the story got told.

In the beginning there were the conversations with Peter Massony, who I only half-jokingly call my adoptive uncle. His stories of growing up Italian in New Orleans fired my imagination to craft a narrative of a people who contributed so much a place I love. I continued to find myself circling back to place and people with updates on what I'd found and where I planned to head next. The idea of using food as a lens onto this world I owe entirely to the creatively verdant year that I spent at the Center for the Study of Southern Culture at Ole Miss. Without running into John T. Edge and his contagious enthusiasm for the Southern Foodways Alliance, this book might never have taken shape. And without the inspiration of filmmaker Joe York, I would not have come to embrace oral history in a way that is now so important to my career.

Launching into the real work brought me into contact with the American Italian Cultural Center and its devoted curator Sal Serio. He introduced me to the vast and largely untapped oral history collection created by the center's visionary founder Joe Maselli. At the New Orleans city library, my old friend Greg Osborn made it possible to pore through untold criminal court cases, periodically coming over with the ever helpful "have you seen this?" I find myself indebted to others who made critical oral histories possible, including Elizabeth Williams from the Southern Food and Beverage Museum, who introduced me to Joe Segreto. Becoming friends with Joe, who cared deeply about history, not only enriched my life but also helped me find many other people to talk with about these histories. Likewise, my former student Allegra

Tartaglia brought me to see her grandmother, Rose Uddo Testa, and her friend Adele Chopin Uddo, which led to a phenomenal interview and an even better meal of eggplant parmesan. I must also thank archivists Kevin Williams and Sean Benjamin at Tulane and especially Bruce Raeburn, Lynn Abbott, and Alaina Hébert of the Hogan Jazz Archive.

Good folks, most of whom who I've never met in person, have been quite generous with images or documents, including Michael Dauenhaer, Sophia Segreto, Colin Hulin, Vincent Mariano, and Ronnie Sciortino.

A true friend is someone who will patiently read a draft of a manuscript, and nobody fits this bill better than my Loyola colleague Mark Fernandez. Others, like Jack Davis and Gene Bourg, offered particularly useful insight into aspects of New Orleans that I had not before considered. Likewise, Jason Berry gave thoughts on style and approach. When it came time to publish, it seemed only fitting that I send it off to John T. Edge again, along with Pat Allen at UGA Press. Locally, our departmental assistant Crystal Ramey kept me on the rails while the team at Georgia, including Rebecca Norton and my gifted and long-suffering copyeditor Ellen Goldlust, and SFA's Sara Camp Arnold made this a much better book than it otherwise might be.

Last but hardly least, throughout all of this my wife Jess put up with this project. I still laugh at us working together in the same room and my interrupting her with "did you know . . . ?" And she answering, "let me guess, this is about lemons." Ten years and two little boys later, our collaboration continues to flourish.

CREOLE ITALIAN

Uncovering the Sicilian Past in the Creole City

When people—especially those of Italian descent—hear the phrase *Sicilian New Orleans*, they often think of Mosca's, that Westbank mecca of old-school Italian cuisine; the muffuletta; or perhaps a corner grocery store in Mid City. They also often think of the Mafia. In short, they possess a patchwork of memories rather than a coherent understanding of the city's Sicilian past. The fact that my parents were born and raised in Chicago, a city that celebrates the ethnic diversity of its immigrant people, doubtlessly attuned me more than others to the Sicilian influence in New Orleans. For me, the city's European immigrants—German, Irish, and Sicilian, leavened by significant Jewish contributions—gave New Orleans the feel of one of the great urban spaces found in the North. Today I remain awestruck that such a crucial thread of the city's fabric has received so little systematic exploration. This book tells that dramatic story of the Sicilian experience in New Orleans.

Interpreting Sicilian New Orleans through the business and culture of food evolved organically. Tracing the contrails of cultural lore to their origin almost always led back in some form to the planting, harvesting, transportation, marketing, preparation, and consumption of food. Sicilian immigrants cut sugarcane, sold groceries, ran truck farms, operated bars and restaurants, and manufactured pasta. The more I burrowed into the topic, the clearer it became that Sicilians had much to do with shaping the city's crucial relationship with food and that food played a pivotal role in the migration and assimilation of the Sicilian people. As a consequence, this project chronicles how the business of food, broadly conceived, dictated the reasoning, means, and outcomes for a large portion of the nearly forty thousand Sicilian immigrants who entered the United States through the Port of New Orleans in the nineteenth and early twentieth centuries and how their actions and those of their descendants helped shape the food town we know today.

My journey to make sense of the Sicilian past in New Orleans began in 2010 as a study of corner grocery stores run by Sicilians, a key touchstone of local ethnic memory. I realized that these corner stores could not be explained without winding back the clock to the early nineteenth century and exploring the reasons why Sicilians began leaving the Mediterranean and coming to the Gulf Coast. This led in turn to an exploration of Sicily lemons, transoceanic shipping in the age of sail and steam, the economics of sugar, and the physical and cultural *terroir* of Sicily itself. My narrative came to encompass global economics, environmental processes, and transformative technologies—and oysters. Only by knitting together these factors could I begin to explain the impact of different food products on the people who harvested, shipped, wholesaled, retailed, prepared, and consumed them, much less the cultures that developed around the various stages in this process. And although there are moments where I discuss Sicilian cuisine, readers hoping for nostalgic prose drowned in red sauce like grandmother made will need to look elsewhere. This book tells the story of how food became the medium through which Sicilians came to New Orleans, shaped the culture that they found, thrived as a people, and became American.

In this work, I dissolve simplistic perceptions of the Sicilian migration as a cultural and economic monolith—the familiar tropes about the Italian American experience constructed by twentieth-century popular culture. Sicilians came from a range of social and economic classes and engaged in a similarly wide array of commercial and cultural activity on this side of the Atlantic. Such diversity translated into a breadth of influence in society, culture, and economics, and the Sicilian migration played a pivotal role in shaping New Orleans culture in both ways that are readily visible and others that require deeper inspection. In short, while we know that Sicilian immigrants made important contributions to the local culinary style, they had a far greater—but less obvious—structural impact. Sicilian importers, wholesalers, farmers, grocers, saloon men, restaurateurs, and nightclub operators quietly capitalized, built, and innovated much of the city's food apparatus and made it feasible for New Orleans to become the most interesting food city in the nation.

The term *Creole Italian* (or *Italian Creole*) was a neologism of pioneering New Orleans food writer and historian Richard Collin, who began using it in the mid-1970s to describe the restaurants of this particular culinary idiom in his insightful and sometimes acerbic reviews. Collin, whose restaurant column and important *New Orleans Underground Gourmet* drip with perception and understanding of New Orleans demography and history, coined the term to describe a culinary fusion of Italian ingredients and preparations with Creole dishes. Yet I use the phrase here almost entirely in the spirit of irony, a form of resistance to the unimaginative lexicography that finds New Orleanians setting the word *Creole* as the keystone in an interpretive arch that bridges all that is culturally worthwhile about the city. This practice often stems from the need to market New Orleans's charms to outsiders, a process that almost always cheapens moments where the term might rightfully apply. *Creole* is at its best as the agent of cultural nuance; at its worst, it is the leading signifier of New Orleans exceptionalism. The desire to see *Creole* in all things arguably has long robbed the city of the potential for a richer cultural self-image.

The city's cultural and historical myopia is not entirely the fault of the current or even several previous generations but has done much over the years to obscure the contributions of the city's diverse ethnic groups, among them the Sicilians. Creole cultural pervasiveness has colored the city's perception and historiography since at least the middle of the nineteenth century, taking wing as a defensive impulse against the threat that Anglo-American and immigrant cultures posed to Francophone survival. As a case study for taking an offense-as-the-best-defense strategy in the face of cultural marginalization, the terrain-staking actions of the city's Creole elite can only be judged as wildly successful. Yet in the historical demography of nineteenth-century New Orleans, *Creole* as an ethnic category does not even constitute a sort of plurality. In 1850, the first year that the U.S. Census kept track of such things, 42.8 percent of the city's population was foreign-born. Yet the notion of New Orleans as a "Creole city" has persisted—indeed, it is the rock on which Irish, German, Anglo-Protestant, and Sicilian cultures have seemingly broken themselves for the past two centuries. In a rite of self-conscious cultural perpetuation, this conception has been the dominant gene in a family tree whose deep-set roots hide its ethnic diversity.[1]

In spite of the broad mythic space carved out by the idea of "Creole" and the rampant perpetuation of the city's studied Gallic affectations, at its core New Orleans is inevitably an immigrant city shaped by successive waves of outsiders. Indeed, the arrival of thousands of southern Italians between 1835 and 1914, with 90 percent of them coming from Sicily, combined with the steady in-migration of rural African Americans in the century following the Civil War, has probably done more to lend New Orleans its "unique" flavor in the last four or five generations than any other cultural or demographic trend. Although the city declined in rank relative to the rapidly urbanizing Upper Midwest, the New Orleans population more than doubled between 1860 and 1920, a key fact in evaluating the motivations that gave life to the city's many declension narratives. Not until 1960 (or as former mayor Maurice "Moon" Landrieu insists, 1958) did Orleans Parish enter a steady decline in population.[2]

Second only to Creole exceptionalism in its purposeful shaping of historical memory in the city has been the decades-long conscious construction of the antebellum period as the city's golden age, an implicit if unwitting celebration of the slaveholder's perspective so pervasive that even those who might otherwise reject such assumptions fall victim to its illusive power. I was invited to sit on a panel, "Before Katrina: The Decline of New Orleans from the Civil War to the Twenty-First Century," at the 2013 annual meeting of the American Historical Association. The panel was predicated on the fallacious notion of New Orleans's steady decline since the Civil War, an intellectual assumption bound by threads of culture and memory to the subtly powerful ideology of the Lost Cause. This was the first time that I consciously and publicly called this assumption into question, articulating a growing belief in the need to construct a modern narrative that reflects all of New Orleans's people. A greater openness to the plurality of our shared historical narrative may finally be upon us, however. In 2015, the Historic New Orleans Collection's *Purchased Lives* exhibit attracted record numbers of visitors, challenging them to ponder the endemic nature of the internal slave trade's presence in the city's urban landscape despite the effects of a sustained program of civic erasure. Another indicator of a spreading reappraisal came with the 2014 opening of a slavery museum at Whitney Plantation. The contentious ongoing debate over the place of Confederate monuments in New Orleans and elsewhere has revealed the brittle edges of change, but it is clear that hoopskirt fantasies are no longer paradigmatic.

The same preservationist impulse that emerged in the 1920s French Quarter and birthed the fabrication of an antebellum architectural fantasy devoid of its slave underpinnings also steadily obliterated traces of the Sicilian immigrants who had taken root there in the last quarter of the nineteenth century. Devoid of the imperative to construct a glorious past and to the dismay of nascent preservationists, Sicilian immigrants accelerated the industrialization of the French Quarter, while the poorer among them crowded into the neighborhood's run-down structures. The studied antebellum illusion in place today, codified by the Vieux Carré Commission, has left little trace of the former "Italian Colony" that thrived before the era of modern tourism. For this reason, this volume frequently refers to place-names in contemporary New Orleans where Sicilians lived, worked, and built their social and economic networks. Their inclusion has been intended not only to help connect the narrative to physical geography but also so that this study will promote the incipient maturation of the city's historical consciousness and the ongoing renegotiation of the relationship between place and past.[3]

A thoughtful investigation of the Sicilian migration and its impact on New Orleans also seems particularly relevant in today's postdiluvian era, a time of dramatic and fundamental change in the city. The pain of this ongoing transformation has been exacerbated by the historical disconnect represented by the lived experience of those New Orleanians who came of age in the city in the late 1970s and early 1980s. Their youth may have borne witness to a long-deferred black political empowerment, but there is no denying that oil-bust New Orleans, punctuated by the financial disaster of the 1984 World's Fair, entered a period of long economic stagnation attended by a steady outmigration of jobs and residents. Members of this generation, now entering their sixties and seventies, reflect fondly on the cheap rents and vibrant anachronism-loving local culture that thrived here, skyrocketing crime rates of that era notwithstanding. The 1990s amplified notions of New Orleans exceptionalism and unwittingly reinforced Lost Cause narratives by doubling down on its Paradise Lost trope for reasons that were different yet somehow the same. Living amid such economic stagnation, the city's residents gazed warily at the hustling metropolises of Charlotte, Atlanta, and Houston, jealous of their wealth but inwardly thankful that New Orleanians possessed too great a cultural sensibility to so unwisely succumb to such terminal sameness. Yet as much as the city's inhabitants like to tell themselves that their city is not like every other place, it is fundamentally a city like any other in that it is governed by thousands of daily human interactions, with the flow of commerce pulsing through its veins. It deserves a systemic analysis that holds such romanticism at arm's length.[4]

With every passing day, the pre-Katrina epoch recedes into memory. Crime and studied anachronism may be with us yet, but many of the political and cultural assumptions that governed New Orleans for a generation or more before the storm have dissolved under the implacable pressure of human agency. Such pressures include escalating real estate prices driven by the arrival of moneyed outsiders and Airbnb, tourists crowding the sidewalks of

Magazine Street, and hipsters orbiting Sixth Ward second-line parades like a cloud of mosquitoes as well as quieter yet no less profound demographic shifts in ethnicity and class. While upsetting for some, these transformative events are more in step with the historical processes that have characterized development in the city since Bienville first claimed the river's muddy bank for France. For most of its life, New Orleans has been in ethnic, social, and cultural motion. The story of how Sicilians, an earlier tribe of newcomers, came to the city and left their imprint offers a historical analogy for today.

This project has transformed my understanding and appreciation of New Orleans. The city is most relevant, both in scholarship and in life, where we can describe its past in terms that are universal rather than those that paint it as exceptional. I was unprepared for and shocked by the comparatively threadbare nature of the historiography of twentieth-century New Orleans. Save for a handful of important works and a body of scholarship primarily about music, historians have been intellectually derelict in systematically exploring the city that we know today as opposed to the one that resided in the distant past. Although we cannot blame this omission entirely on the deep-set tendency toward New Orleans exceptionalism, the phenomenon plays an undeniable role. That we enjoy rich scholarship on specific aspects and eras of the city's past yet know almost nothing at all about others had much to do with my decision to write this narrative.[5]

I am hardly the first historian to observe this intellectual tendency to essentialize among those who write about the city. More than forty years ago, geographer Peirce Lewis observed wryly that "for a city of its size, age, and prominence," New Orleans enjoyed "an uncommon scarcity of serious scholarly work." More specifically, Lewis contended that historians and literary figures "have paid more attention to gumbo and hoopskirts, to scarlet women and duels at dawn, than to the harder realities of economics, geography, political science, or demography." Although a number of important works have appeared since Lewis's 1976 remarks, New Orleans still lacks a comprehensive study of the port and its commerce despite the fact that it is one of the world's greatest entrepôts. The single-most-influential migration to the city since 1865—that by Protestant African Americans—has received little exploration beyond the literature about the Robert Charles riot of 1900, impressionistic treatments of Louis Armstrong's Central City boyhood, and contemporary cultural studies of second lines. There is not even a credible single-volume history of New Orleans, doubtless in part because of the conspicuous lack of twentieth-century monographs on which such a synthesis might rest.[6]

Likewise, the literature on the Sicilian experience in New Orleans has fallen into one of a handful of categories that collectively create an episodic narrative that strangely parallels the topic's popular imagination. Receiving by far the most attention has been the 1891 lynching that followed the acquittal of the Sicilian defendants accused of murdering New Orleans chief of police David Hennessey. Gunned down near his home on a rainy fall night in 1890, Hennessey was almost certainly killed by men belonging to one of two competing Sicilian longshoreman gangs in whose long-running blood feud he had injudiciously interfered. Reformist mayor Joseph Shakspeare seized on the incident to feed discontent toward immigrant-friendly Democratic "Ring" political opponents and used the city's pliant newspapers to incite a mob that ultimately broke into the city jail and murdered eleven of the Sicilians inside. Scholars have explored what we may learn about race, "whiteness," and ethnicity from this event, while others have proffered it as evidence of the birth of the American Mafia. Studies of the role of organized crime in twentieth-century New Orleans have consisted almost entirely of grossly unsupported pop conspiracy histories that claim to link Carlos Marcello with the Kennedy assassination.[7]

Other, more sober work, like the remarkable social histories written by Donna Gabaccia and Jean Ann Scarpaci, has endeavored to understand the economic and cultural forces that drove the Sicilian peasantry across the Atlantic, but both Gabaccia and Scarpaci apply a sweeping approach to a narrow moment in time. Likewise, sociologists Anthony Margavio and Jerome Salomone have made a serious bid to document the Italian immigrant experience to Louisiana in broad social and economic contexts, but they examine a narrow chronological band of blue-collar migrants. The musical impact of New Orleans Sicilians has garnered some attention, particularly the important contributions of the controversial Nick LaRocca and the enormously influential Louis Prima, though neither figure has been the subject of a scholarly study truly worthy of his significance. Astonishingly, almost nothing scholarly has been written about jazz legend Sharkey Bonano or other Sicilian musical greats. Like twentieth-century New Orleans itself, the list of unexplored topics in Italian New Orleans is shockingly long.[8]

In the past decade, scholars have increasingly used food as a lens for understanding society, particularly with regard to immigrants' contributions, and this volume will help further the maturation of this field.[9] The literature about food and Sicilian New Orleans, however, is even thinner than the already scant bibliography of serious ethnic study in the city. Beyond some fine journalis-

tic treatments of notable restaurants such as Mosca's, we find largely celebra-
tory and impressionistic cultural pieces on cherished culinary traditions but
few works that probe the core historical processes that gave those traditions
life. St. Joseph's altars, though scarcely mentioned here, have enjoyed pictorial
treatment and cultural analysis if not scholarly exploration. And then there is
the discussion, at turns equally ubiquitous and unproductive, about who "invented" the muffuletta sandwich.[10]

My previous work in tracing the whereabouts of African Americans and
other marginalized people in the chaotic decades that followed the Civil War
supplied a ready historian's toolkit for exploring the lives of Sicilian immigrants to New Orleans.[11] I gathered a great deal of fragmentary primary source
material among government documents such as tax, vital statistics, and census records. Court cases and city directories as well as newspapers—especially
advertisements—helped piece together the lived experiences of people who
often are underrepresented (or not represented at all) in the traditional bas-
tions of elite white history, the archives. I also consulted personal scrapbooks,
menu collections, photographic images, and maps. In a few instances, spa-
tial analysis yielded more clues by aggregating bits of data across the physical
landscape.

Other sources came to me whole, living and breathing, to tell their story.
All work rests on the shoulders of those who have gone before us, and in this
instance no figure was more crucial than a pioneering civic visionary, Joseph
Maselli, a New Jersey native who came to New Orleans during World War II,
married a local Italian girl, and became fabulously successful as a liquor distributor. Snubbed by the Metairie Country Club, Maselli devoted himself to
his adopted community and particularly its Italians, whose significance his
outsider status may have enabled him to more readily recognize. Maselli recorded dozens of oral histories between 1975 and 1980, recognizing that the
immigrant generation was dying off and using his estimable charm and warm
personality to encourage these men and women to open up about their lives.
One of my great thrills in conducting research for this project was recording
my own oral histories with the descendants of Maselli's interviewees—or, in a
couple of instances, with the interviewees themselves.

My narrative unfolds across seven chapters that explore the mid-
1830s through the 1970s. I begin by describing how nineteenth-century transformations in global commodities, transportation technology, and geopolitical

realities of labor and economy drove the first wave of Sicilian migrants from the Mediterranean to the Port of New Orleans. Sicilian communities exist where they do in the United States today because of the island's long-forgotten trade in citrus, particularly lemons. Those Sicilians who came to New Orleans beginning in the 1830s were a maritime people who found success in the city's bustling steam-driven economy. Diversifying into tropical produce and investing in oceanic steamers in the 1880s ultimately enabled this merchant elite to serve as the padrones (labor agents) for a far more numerous migration of their poorer countrymen. Drawn initially by the false promises of the sugar growers, Sicilian peasants found salvation in storekeeping and saloons as well as the more financially stable world of truck farming, for a time transforming southern Louisiana into the produce hub of the Mississippi River Valley.

The second chapter traces the profound Sicilian imprint on the development of restaurant culture in nineteenth-century New Orleans. Oysters, fish, turtles, and wild game from Louisiana's aqueous landscape defined the period's culinary expectations far more than did the Gallic preparations traditionally defined as "Creole." The mechanics of this local system of food procurement and consumption found no greater appreciation than among the maritime Sicilian subculture hailing from Ustica, a tiny island sixty kilometers north of Palermo. First through oyster saloons and the once common industry of in-home catering, the *usticesi* positioned their nascent restaurants within the orbit of entertainment, alcohol, and gambling houses, most notably near hotels and at the lost pleasure zones of West End and Spanish Fort. Wildly successful as a class by the 1890s, the *usticesi* left a legacy that continues today in familiar landmarks such as Commander's Palace and Emeril's Delmonico.

Chapter 3 explores how the tension between Americanized elites and immigrant laborers led to spectacular intracultural violence in the young twentieth century. Mindful that the taint of peasant criminality might harm their fortunes, the prosperous second-generation importers and merchants of the Sicilian French Quarter moved to suppress the schemes of the Black Hand using tactics that deftly blended the Sicilian culture of vendetta with the New Orleans tradition of elite white vigilantism. Even as they wrestled with these threats from below, the members of the Sicilian merchant class invested heavily in the booming macaroni manufacturing business during the 1890s, transforming the Lower French Quarter into a hub of industrial food production and enabling the use of modern pasta factories to project the image of Sicilian immigrants as champions of American capitalistic progress. Meanwhile, the growing popularity of pasta outside the Italian community seemed to presage a broader embrace of its culture among non-Italians.

Much in the way that American diners today "discover" new ethnic cuisines, the growing popularity of pasta transformed American Italian cooking from the province of simple workingman's lunch houses in 1900 into some of the hottest fine dining in New Orleans by 1915. Chapter 4 explores how Italian restaurants' emerging ability to pull Sicilians into the American mainstream collided with the cultural phenomenon of jazz and the national morality crusade against vice. The ingredients of red gravy, jazz, and alcohol, combined with the land-reclamation projects that destroyed the competing pleasure landscapes of West End and Spanish Fort, fueled the rise of what became the entertainment zone of Bourbon Street. This transformation did not come without a cost, however. Between 1900 and 1919, Sicilians in New Orleans had made great progress in putting behind them old and largely unfair associations of Black Hand criminality while enjoying the surging popularity of their cuisine and a respect for their successful embrace of capitalism. Enforcement of the Volstead Act, however, caused Americans to broadly associate Italian immigrants with bootlegging and violent organized crime. The frequent arrest of Sicilian-born restaurateurs reinforced this notion locally. Yet the trauma of Prohibition also paradoxically fostered the economic and cultural maturation of the city's food and entertainment sector, shaping what became the modern New Orleans restaurant and nightclub scene. Those establishments that emerged in 1934, a time one might associate with the beginning of Bourbon Street's golden age, were wiser and tougher; most important, they also found ready sources of capital in profits gained through bootlegging.

Chapter 5 reconstructs the French Quarter before World War II as a site of Sicilian memory. This landscape has been largely erased by the "Creole" and antebellum prerogatives of civic organizations that have dictated a selective preservation of the Quarter's "historic character." The intersection of St. Philip and Decatur Streets, at the foot of the old French Market, served as the locus of Sicilian New Orleans, the crossroads of the region's food distribution network. Here, along the same working riverfront where thousands of Sicilian immigrants first landed in America, cargoes of food commodities from the Mediterranean and Latin America mingled with oyster luggers ferrying to market the yield of the region's salty estuaries as well as wagons burdened with produce grown in the countryside. All of it was connected to the great metropolis of Chicago by the dockside rails of the Illinois Central. In the storefronts along Decatur, retail grocers haggled with the street's prominent wholesalers over the price of imported cheese and olive oil. In precisely this landscape, the Provenzano-Matranga feud erupted and eventually left Chief Hennessey dead. It is where street vendors bought bananas, where local legends like Angelo Brocato and international corporations like Progresso Foods made their start. It is also the birthplace of the estimable muffuletta, whose ironic historical significance is that its skyrocketing popularity in the 1970s demonstrated that the long-held rhythms of this old Sicilian neighborhood had died and been replaced by a tourist economy.

Of the cultural institutions that have defined Sicilian New Orleans in the twentieth century, few resonate more broadly than the rise and ultimate disappearance of the neighborhood corner grocery, once a fixture on the city's landscape. Chapter 6 chronicles how the members of New Orleans's immigrant generation drifted away from agriculture, often finding work in the city by selling produce from a cart and ultimately realizing the dream of opening a grocery. For countless Sicilian-descended New Orleanians, the corner store marked a crucial step on an immigrant family's journey toward the American middle class. Although a handful of these groceries persist, most have long since succumbed to a combination of demographic decline, fundamental changes in the way Americans buy food, and the upward mobility of grocers' sons and daughters into white-collar occupations. Nowhere has the systemic transformation of food distribution had more dramatic effects, however, than in its former transactional hub in the Sicilian French Quarter. As the second and third generations of Sicilians moved into the suburb of Gentilly during the 1950s and 1960s, the institutions of this original ethnic neighborhood declined. In the early 1970s, the Decatur Street corridor and dormant riverfront yielded to economic realities and underwent transformation under the auspices of an ambitious municipal urban renewal program that reimagined the French Market as a tourist destination and recast the docks as a riverfront park. Today, what was once the Sicilian French Quarter has become the hub of gay New Orleans.

Chapter 7 explores the maturation and ultimate disappearance of the city's traditional-style Sicilian-run restaurants and their relationship with Italian cultural identity in twentieth-century New Orleans. The classic New Orleans Italian restaurant that emerged out of Prohibition entered its heyday in the postwar period. With the Marcello, Moran, and Segreto families wielding their greatest influence, the idea of Creole Italian finally came of age, with restaurants such as Mosca's, Sclafani, and Elmwood Plantation finding equal footing with the city's finest old-line Creole houses. Systemic changes to the restaurant industry beginning in the late 1970s, including a trend toward casual dining, growing interest in less traditional culinary renditions, and the replacement of the maître d' by the celebrity chef as the face of the restaurant, increasingly made this style of establishment obsolete. The oil bust of the 1980s and the decline of Carlos Marcello exacerbated cultural shifts and drove all but a handful of local mainstays out of business. Those who remain carry on as standard-bearers of ethnic pride while tapping into deep veins of nostalgia for a bygone era.

CHAPTER 1

Sicily Lemons and Sugarcane

The Backstory of Italian New Orleans

In his 1944 ethnic novelty hit "Please No Squeeza Da Banana," Louis Prima rhymes the protestations of "Tony," a street fruit peddler, as he confronts "Riley the cop," whose Hibernian manhandling of Tony's produce in search of freebies needlessly damages the goods. Giving voice to the fictional Tony, Prima sings:

> *You touch-a dis, you touch-a dat,*
> *You touch-a everyt'ing—*
> *You push-a dis, you push-a dat,*
> *You never buy notting!*
> *So please no squeeza da banana!*
> *If you squeeza, Officer, please,*
> *Squeeza da coconut!*

Prima's dialect-laden routine in "No Squeeza da Banana!" deflated and deflected anti-Italian sentiment that bubbled just under the surface of American society during World War II. Despite his self-deprecating and humorous tone, Prima's genius lay in his refusal to yield ground to xenophobia, choosing instead to showcase rather than diminish his Italianness. This soft approach also proved good for business, a point reinforced by a 1945 *Billboard* magazine ad for the song that deftly employed the same idiom: "Operators: I think this record will squeeza da nickels into da machinas something terrific! So pleasa no teasa da customers . . . let them hear—PLEASE NO SQUEEZA DA BANANA." Like other ethnic minorities, Italians had long since learned to laugh their way to the bank by the middle of the twentieth century.[1]

The fact that one might periodically hear a playful tune like "Please No Squeeza da Banana!" on an Apple Radio playlist in 2016 or perhaps on a Friday broadcast of WWOZ's *Louisiana Music Show* speaks to the endurance of Prima's connection with Italian American cultural memory, especially in his native New Orleans. New Orleanians of a rapidly disappearing generation remember well the street peddler of their youth, hawking bananas from a cart, an occupation recalled with hard-earned pride, representative as it was of the immigrant generation's first toehold on the financial ladder. Indeed, the banana man with his street cries and indomitable hustling occupies an important mythic space in the nation's immigrant experience, symbolic of the thrift and toil inherent in the struggle to become American. Perhaps it was inevitable, then, that his powerful cultural symbolism would come to obscure the fact that "Tony" was a social construction of remarkably recent vintage, a memory scissored out of time and pasted onto the historical subconscious, one without clear origins and that, on closer examination, raises more questions than answers. How did Sicilian immigrants became so fundamentally associated with the tropical fruit trade when bananas had become a mainstream part of the American diet only during the waning years of the 1890s, after the massive exodus of Sicilians across the Atlantic to North America had already begun? Moreover, bananas are not Sicilian or Italian, so how did these immigrants from the Mediterranean come to market commodities from Central America? Only by tracing the threads of logic to their origin may we uncover the fascinating but largely forgotten chain of human processes that sent millions of Sicilians to our nation's shores in the decades leading up to the Great War.

We must first acknowledge, however, that what we think we know about the history of Sicilian Americans is only a historical fragment formed during the middle decades of the twentieth century. Indeed, from Louis Prima to the *Godfather*, popular culture has done much to shape what Americans understand to be true about the history of Italian immigrants generally and Sicilians in particular, a memory paradigm familiar to anyone who comes into more than passing contact with it. Our first mental image finds the immigrant generation packed into the damp hold of an ocean steamer, a desperate lot traversing the Atlantic in search of a new life, however uncertain, that could not help but be superior to the sunny, dusty, backward, and poverty-stricken one that they left behind. As a class, they were poor, swarthy, Catholic, clannish yet gregarious, industrious, and irrepressibly voluble. In this country, their growing families populated the urban slums of the nation's teeming cities, where the men and boys crisscrossed neighborhoods peddling bananas and repairing shoes while the matriarch and her daughters sewed piecework in the dimly lit confines of their crowded apartment. Yet by the 1940s, toil, frugality, and the pooled energies of *la famiglia* had carried this aging first generation and their children to the pleasant bungalows of the nation's inner suburbs. Here, they gathered after mass for Sunday supper, an aromatic homage to red gravy followed by a lazy afternoon of cousins playing stickball in the yard and parents and aunts and uncles drinking Chianti while they dealt cards or washed dishes to the melodic tones of Sinatra and Prima drifting from the living room stereo. By the 1950s, the popular imagination saw Italians as the embodiment of the immigrant American Dream even as they preserved a distinct and inherently worthwhile culture, seemingly without effort.

Sicilians in America, however, have a deeper, more complicated past than this powerful twentieth-century construction lets on, a past whose origins lie in a long since vanished transatlantic trade in Mediterranean citrus. The wave of Sicilian peasants that eventually hit American shores at the end of the nineteenth century was proportionally so great that it obscured an earlier migration of the island's merchant class to the Gulf South and Eastern Seaboard. The steam-driven citrus fleet that these seafaring traders later built supplied the means by which millions of their countrymen fled their homeland. As in New York and Philadelphia, the first significant Sicilian migration to New Orleans began in the 1830s, when Mediterranean lemons began to be sold on the Mississippi River levee. Their debut coincided with a population explosion during which the metropolis grew by more than 120 percent in a decade. Indeed, New Orleans of the 1830s was so awash with German and Irish immigrants that few contemporary observers seem to have noticed these Italian-speaking newcomers save for the marketing of their golden cargoes. Yet like the modest headwaters of the great river that defines the city, the presence of these early Sicilian fruit merchants dictated much about the course of events to come, and the story of Tony, the peddler of bananas, begins with these merchants.

Palermo and New Orleans sat on opposite ends of the Atlantic World of maritime commerce in the nineteenth century. Both handled cargoes that were primarily agricultural or extractive, with ships bearing goods from Sicily often filling their holds in New Orleans with products destined for a third port before returning to the Mediterranean. While this circular global trade was certainly nothing new at the dawn of the nineteenth century, the riverine steam technology of the 1820s brought its effects to bear on increasingly remote inland corners of the world and did so at an unprecedented pace. The founding generation of Sicilian families in New Orleans and other American cities arrived here as a consequence of this commercial revolution: Sicily grew what was perhaps the most ideal trading perishable commodity in this transitional epoch in maritime history of deepwater sailing and brown-water steaming: the Sicily lemon.[2]

Indeed, no single commodity was more important to establishing Sicilians in North America than the lemon. Without the nineteenth-century trade in Mediterranean citrus, Sicilian merchants would have never come to dominate the important trade in tropical fruit, specifically bananas, that most Americans still associate with the Italian immigrant. Without the citrus fleet, there would have been no trade route or efficient means to transport hundreds of thousands of penniless Sicilians to places such as New York and New Orleans. But the heyday of the Sicily lemon was long ago, it was subsequently eclipsed by the stunning success of the banana, and it was ultimately obliterated by the machinations of California citrus growers; consequently, few Americans of Italian descent retain a meaningful cultural memory of the Sicily lemon or possess any notion of its significance.

For most of Sicilian history, lemons have been by far the island's most profit-able export. Muslim conquerors first cultivated citrus groves there in the ninth century, and over the next millennium, the island established a fruit trade with the kingdoms of Europe. Small quantities of Sicily lemons made their way to North America as early as Columbus's first voyage, but they did not constitute a substantial commerce until 1832, when a ship carrying a cargo comprised exclusively of Sicilian citrus sailed into New York Harbor. Other American ports, including bustling New Orleans, soon began receiving ships full of fruit. An 1838 advertisement by Thomas Spear, whose establishment was located at the corner of Gravier and Magazine Streets, promised "150 boxes of Sicily Lemons, in fine order." One Julia Street produce house announced the 1843 auction of 112 boxes of "Lemons! Lemons!! Lemons!!!" Before the Civil War, the burgeoning trade in lemons and oranges from Palermo and Messina ar-rived in New Orleans aboard both American and Sicilian vessels but almost always ended up being marketed by Anglo-American produce auction houses. After the war, however, Sicilians gradually took over the American side of the trade, controlling not only the shipping but also the unloading and marketing of citrus cargoes in New Orleans, New York, and in other important produce markets. "About 1880," one early observer of Gotham's port noted, "the third and last change in the methods governing the Italian fruit trade began with the establishment here of representatives by several of the large Italian houses." By the mid-1890s, Sicilians controlled almost the entirety of the Mediterranean citrus trade in America.[3]

We tend to think of the global marketplace in produce as a late-twentieth-century phenomenon that has brought us blueberries and asparagus from Chile and apples from New Zealand, but the story of the Sicily lemon reminds us that such trade is nothing new. At the turn of the twentieth century, the vast majority of lemons consumed by the Western world, including the United States, came from Sicily's Conca d'Oro (Golden Shell), the plain extending east from Palermo along the island's northern coast that received its name from the color of its famous crop. A millennium's worth of agricultural knowledge, near-perfect weather and soil conditions, and a geographical situation along one of the globe's busiest and most accessible trade routes had given Sicily this near-monopoly. Lemon trees on the island bloom year-round, a horticultural phenomenon that afforded growers the ability to meet varying consumer demands. In the age of sail, Sicily lemons generally appeared for auction in New Orleans in the spring and summer, when demand for the fruit was at its greatest, though the fruit could also be found at other times of year. In contrast, Louisiana's soil and especially its warm, damp climate produced lemons that ripened in the fall through early winter months and that thus competed with imported fruit only in a token and localized way. The varieties of lemon grown in Louisiana in the nineteenth century were much like today's Meyer lemon, which was introduced to the United States by horticulturalist Frank Meyer in 1908. As anyone who has sliced open a Meyer lemon can tell you, the sweet fruit contains more juice, is larger, and, most important from the perspective of global commerce, has a thinner rind than do conventional modern grocery store lemons. Although pleasant when consumed locally, such lemons feature delicate characteristics that give them a short shelf life and prevent them from being profitably shipped in a systematic way over long distances, especially prior to the Age of Steam and the advent of refrigeration.[4]

Sicilian harvesting patterns grew more regularized with the advent of steamship lines in the late nineteenth century, establishing delivery seasons in North America that closely paralleled the prime arrival times for Sicilian immigrants in American port cities. The key botanical characteristic that made Sicilian lemons so suitable for overseas trade was that they could be harvested while still green and with careful handling shipped far away. According to a contemporary account, the premium export fruit (*primo-flore*) blossomed in April and was ready to harvest by early October, when gatherers could ensure with "practiced hands" that fruit "not less than 3 inches in circumference" entered the marketplace. Harvesters then conducted a second gleaning of fruit for export during a "November gathering." The first crop was always the most valuable because it would keep long enough for use in spring or summer. Dockworkers in the key citrus ports of Palermo and Messina "carefully stowed in tiers" boxes made from wood grown in Trieste or Bangor, Maine, and filled with fruit, with each lemon wrapped individually in tissue paper and surrounded by "paper shavings to fill up interstices" as it "ripen[ed] on the voyage" to America. Between 1892 and 1894, New Orleans imported almost four hundred thousand boxes of lemons, while New York imported just shy of nine hundred thousand. Such disparity, however, is a matter of proportion, for the contemporary population of New Orleans was roughly one-tenth the population of New York.[5]

It may strain modern credulity to believe that lemons occupied such a place of commercial importance, but a glance inside the beverage section of any cookbook printed before 1910 reveals that most of the recipes, whether alcoholic or not, start with an instruction along the lines of "squeeze the juice from two dozen lemons." Soda fountains did not come about generally until the very late 1880s, and modern frozen concentrates for home consumption did not appear until after the Second World War. In addition, lemons were also the primary source of citrate (citric acid), an essential ingredient in canning, a practice that boomed in the late nineteenth century. Thus, lemons had enormous industrial importance in the turn-of-the-century United States. Though scientists ultimately developed a method to synthesize citric acid from sugar, the process did not gain popularity until the First World War made it difficult to acquire Sicily lemons. Lemon oil, used for cleaning products, was also an important by-product pressed from peels. Some oil was manufactured in Sicily, often by English-owned factories, and shipped as a finished product, but the Mediterranean island never fully realized its industrial potential. Official corruption at all levels of government and a mostly ungovernable lawlessness in the countryside complicated efforts to do business in Sicily and always stifled growth.[6]

Like their counterparts in Louisiana, agriculturalists in Florida and California began dreaming of cutting into Sicily's lucrative citrus industry as early as the 1850s, but a variety of factors inhibited their ability to do so in the nineteenth century. Quality control was a serious obstacle, especially during the early years of American citrus cultivation, when growers lacked the expertise and industry discipline to produce a crop able to compete with Sicilian imports. After walking through a San Diego market in 1888 and noticing Sicily lemons selling for nine dollars a box when the domestic variety only commanded between one dollar and two dollars, one observer asked vendors to explain the discrepancy. In every case, the answer was, "The Sicily lemon is *good*, the California lemon is *good*—for nothing." He had to admit the truth of this assessment "because the former had been properly sweated, properly selected, of uniform size and shape, and were systematically wrapped and packed; while the latter had not been sweated, were as hard as rocks, were of all sizes, from a walnut to a citron, many of them covered with scale and smut, not wrapped, and were thrown into the boxes in the most promiscuous manner." In its 1893 survey of the California fruit industry, the famous Royal Gardens of Kew damningly concluded that although the citrus trade was "in process of development," "even San Francisco imports largely from Sicily." Nineteenth-century Florida planters, like their compatriots in Louisiana, discovered that they could not simply plant a Sicily lemon tree in American soil.[7]

American growers finally vanquished the Sicily lemon during the second decade of the twentieth century, an effort that reveals the exploitative and xenophobic tactics employed by early twentieth-century American big business. These tactics, in turn, influenced the habits of Sicilians and all other immigrants who hoped to prosper on the shores of liberty. The bare-knuckle fight between competing California citrus growers and New York produce wholesalers began in the late nineteenth century, when the collusive power of the nation's great railroad tycoons to make and unmake dependent industries was at its height. Usurious rail rates combined with mediocre quality all but eliminated the prospect of profitability for California citrus. Early efforts to organize a growers' marketing cooperative succumbed to crushing pressure from Eastern produce and transit magnates, but in 1905, orange growers formed the California Fruit Growers Exchange, known today as Sunkist. The future conglomerate, "with the help of the expanding government horticultural bureaucracy," gradually enforced stringent quality standards and agricultural practices among growers while lobbying in the trust-busting atmosphere of the 1910s for relief from exorbitant freight schedules.[8]

Even with competitive shipping rates and a vastly improved product, the California lemon still had difficulty competing with its Sicilian cousin in a free-trade environment, primarily because of the efficiency with which the

Atlantic commercial shipping network linked the Eastern Seaboard to the Mediterranean and the established nature of produce houses in New York and New Orleans. Protectionism was the only solution. "New York City is controlled by importing and foreign steamship interests," observed the official journal of the American Tariff League. "Among all the importers," it continued, "none are more persistent and vicious in their assaults on American industry than the firms, nearly all with Italian names, which are engaged in importing Sicily lemons." Efforts to impose a tariff wavered during the 1910s, particularly in 1912, when a hard freeze destroyed most of the California crop and threatened to make prices skyrocket. Yet by 1921, the California growers had taken advantage of the protectionist atmosphere to secure a tariff with which the Sicilian trade could not compete in the long run. Despite the fact that in 1920 a box of Sicilian lemons "produced by cheap labor resultant from a low standard of living" cost 2.3 cents less in New Orleans than a similar box from California, the tide had turned. In 1937, California overtook Sicily as the world's largest producer of lemons.[9]

Yet long before Sunkist put the final squeeze on the Sicily lemon, the Mediterranean citrus trade had transformed the cultural composition of the Gulf South. In fact, the first Sicilian businessmen to make substantial fortunes in the Crescent City were maritime sorts who had engaged in the shipping, unloading, and marketing first of citrus crops and later of bananas from South America. These entrepreneurs rose gradually, paralleling the evolving mechanics of the nineteenth-century wholesale produce business. In the very early years, a ship carrying citrus might show up and sell its cargo for cash to all comers on the levee opposite the French Market. When the bark *Avola* arrived from Palermo in the summer of 1846, its captain sold citrus by the box to individual peddlers and retailers, with lemons fetching $4.00 per box and oranges commanding $4.50. In a business that already assumed considerable risk, however, this approach was entirely too perilous. New Orleans had been born out of the maritime commodities trade, so the city's established auction houses soon began handling significant quantities of Sicilian produce. In 1850, the thriving mercantile firm of Sykes, Hyde, and Company auctioned on the levee twenty-seven hundred boxes of lemons and one hundred bags of filberts brought to New Orleans by the brig *Azelia*. In January 1853, R. F. Nichols and Company promised that the bark *Rover* would arrive carrying not only thousands of lemons and oranges but also two hundred boxes of "real Sicilian" macaroni. Like their counterparts in other ports around the world, New

Orleans commission agents sent buyers to Palermo and other Sicilian market towns to purchase commodities and ship them to America. The system functioned best before the 1866 laying of a transatlantic cable made the ocean so much smaller.[10]

Sicilians grew increasingly involved in this trade not only by working on boats and peddling produce in the streets but eventually as retailers who purchased their stock at auctions on the levee. An 1860 newspaper advertisement describing the wares of R. Tramontana reflected the growing participation of Sicilian immigrants on the American side of Mediterranean fruit commerce. His thriving grocery and wholesale businesses on Fulton and Front Streets (near where the Morial Convention Center stands today) offered not only lemons but also "creole oranges," bananas, pineapples, and a wide variety of other nuts and fruits. In 1866 Tramontana paid $1,000 in duties on a wholesale shipment of groceries worth $38,412, a transaction that revealed his ascent from retailer to importer. It made sense that Sicilians would eventually take over the wholesale trade in Mediterranean produce. These newcomers were merely following the path blazed by members of other ethnic groups in New Orleans more than a century earlier. Like British nationals or New England transplants who had coordinated shipments of manufactured goods or Frenchmen who had imported wine, the Sicilians acted as commercial agents for their native land.[11]

The story of the Grande and Cusimano families reveals the familial and multigenerational nature of the gradual takeover of the Sicilian citrus industry by the island's émigrés. Giuseppe Grande left Palermo sometime in 1851 with his wife and two small daughters, almost certainly journeying to America on a ship full of lemons. He probably had some existing connection to the citrus trade, and on arriving in New Orleans, he, like Tramontana, became a fruit retailer. By 1872, Grande's business had grown so much that he was able to bring in the entire contents of the Italian brig *Duo Sorrelli* while receiving lemons, wine, and other merchandise from the bark *Carriete* alongside other Sicilian merchants, among them Tramontana and rising shipping tycoons Joseph Macheca and Santo Oteri. Grande's business expanded further when twenty-four-year-old Angelo Cusimano arrived in New Orleans from Palermo in 1876 and married Grande's younger daughter, Philomene, who was five years his senior. In short order A. Cusimano and Company had joined the ranks of the city's top produce importers. Indeed, a trade bulletin produced for the 1884–85 New Orleans Cotton Exhibition noted the size of the Sicilian fruit commerce and suggested it was "largely due to the pushing and enterprising house of A. Cusimano & Company." His import house maintained offices in New York, Boston, and Palermo and served as the New Orleans agents of Phelps Brothers, who conducted "the larger part of the business in imported fruits of the United States." Five Phelps steamers of about two thousand tons apiece and "built for fruit traffic exclusively" carried citrus from Palermo and Messina to New Orleans. Revolutions in shipping technology had enabled Sicilian immigrants of Grande's generation to operate on a scale and pace that would have been unthinkable when he arrived in New Orleans thirty years earlier.[12]

The arrival of the British steamship *Bessarabia* from Messina in February 1882 was emblematic of the sinews of trade that tied Sicily to New Orleans in the decade before immigrants began arriving en masse. It carried 6,855 boxes of lemons and 13,727 boxes of oranges (a ratio that reflected the lateness of the season). The produce came from both Palermo and Messina, two important growing regions in Sicily, and had been ordered by an array of commission merchants, the vast majority of whom bore such Sicilian names as Le Secco, Trapani, and Randazzo. The smallest delivery went to R. di Cristina, who received 44 boxes of lemons, while the largest went to Angelo Cusimano—5,849 boxes of lemons, 924 boxes of oranges, and 102 boxes of macaroni. The *Bessarabia* also brought 11,073 boxes of Messina oranges "to order," meaning that they had been loaded to fill up the empty spaces on the ship and that their purchase would be negotiated on the levee in New Orleans. In 1883–84, lemons alone constituted the port's third-most-valuable import, at $400,000 in value (far behind the $2.8 million in coffee and $1.3 million in sugar that passed through New Orleans). During the same period, bananas, which would by the end of the century eclipse the lemon trade's importance in New Orleans, accounted for $386,000 in commerce. Contemporary observers noted the "constantly expanding" trade of tropical fruit being handled by Oteri and Macheca.[13]

For about seventy years, the Sicily lemon held a special place in the commerce that linked the Mediterranean with the markets of North America. More important, the mid-nineteenth-century citrus trade made possible the formation of small but tightly knit ethnic communities in New Orleans, Philadelphia, New York, and other cities, and these ties of culture and blood enabled Sicilian immigrants to lay the foundations of mercantile dynasties that would last for generations. The steam-powered revolution in transatlantic shipping during the last two decades of the nineteenth century and first decade of the twentieth century regularized trade routes between Sicily and America's great ports and made possible the transportation of larger cargoes in much shorter times. Grande's 1872 shipment aboard the *Duo Sorelli* crossed the Atlantic in an astoundingly (and atypically) slow 113 days. A decade later, the *Bessarabia* made the same voyage in 29 days, a typical run for the mechanized era. Connections across the North Atlantic between ports such as Liverpool and Bremen regularly took half that time. Fuel-efficient high-pressure steam engines (first developed in the 1860s), screw propellers, and the abandonment of wood hulls in favor of stronger, larger, and proportionately lighter steel ones made oceanic shipping faster as well as considerably cheaper. These changes enabled Sicilian produce merchants to ship lemons along established trade channels in far greater quantities and at significantly lower expense.[14]

Most authors writing about the immigrant experience in New Orleans breezily note that the citrus trade brought the first wave of Sicilians to Louisiana before skipping ahead to a discussion of sugarcane laborers or the much more enduring twentieth-century agricultural commerce in bananas. Yet the gold standard of citrus, the Sicily lemon, not only brought the original Sicilians to New Orleans but established the trade routes that nearly all of their subsequent countrymen followed and formed the nucleus of those urban colonies where most settled. Had it not been for the Sicily lemon, Italian immigration to America would certainly have unfolded differently. This forgotten trade also speaks volumes to the curious lack of staying power possessed by certain aspects of cultural memory. Few New Orleanians of Italian descent today, let alone the general public, hold any cultural memory of the citrus trade, despite the fact that only 120 years ago it was one of the port's principal commodities.

The efficiency of the citrus trade between Palermo and Messina and ports of North America's Atlantic Seaboard and Gulf Coast ultimately enabled hundreds of thousands of Sicilian peasants to leave their homeland for the United States. In the Gulf South, the southern sugar planters' unending quest for a solution to their perceived labor problems induced many of these migrants to sail for New Orleans. Profitability in southern plantation agriculture relied heavily on the ready availability of a workforce of agriculturalists who had few other options and consequently proved willing to labor in silence, year in, year out, in exchange for subsistence wages. As economic historian Gavin Wright has pointed out, the South was a "low wage region in a high wage country." Before the Civil War, slavery had redirected all but the most determined or destitute immigrants to the North, and this pattern continued during southern agriculture's lean postbellum years.[15]

Undeterred by the unlikely prospect that immigrants would want to share in the slim fortunes of the region's agricultural poor and apparently no wiser after Chinese laborers hired to work in the cane fields in the late 1860s refused to stay on the land, planters turned toward destitute Sicily for workers. As early as 1881, the Louisiana Sugar Planters' Association formed a committee to encourage Italian immigration to the state, recognizing the potential in the rapid and inexpensive steamship commerce that had only recently become a reality in the Gulf South. The idea of importing agricultural labor from across the Atlantic on a seasonal basis was in many regards a revolutionary idea and would not have been possible before the advent of comparatively cheap and rapid transit between the Gulf of Mexico and the Mediterranean Sea.[16]

A system of contract labor evolved in which planters paid for Sicilian workers' passage in exchange for a commitment of work for a predetermined amount of time. Sicilian middlemen known as *padroni* frequently arranged these agreements, recruiting laborers from their home villages and providing logistical support to both worker and employer for a fee. Indeed, a number of these *padroni* had experience in the global citrus trade and made a natural transition into dealing in the commodity of labor. Moreover, they operated within the Sicilian context of nineteenth-century class-based leadership systems. Historian Donna Gabaccia has argued that the Provenzano and Matranga families, whose war to monopolize labor on the fruit wharves likely led to the 1890 murder of New Orleans police chief David Hennessey, also acted as *padroni*. "We do not know if one or both thought of themselves as bandit leaders, civil bosses, or working-class leaders," notes Gabaccia, but all of those roles were "familiar from the rural rebellions of their Sicilian homelands in the early 1890s." Like any sort of financial transaction involving parties in widely disparate positions of power, the *padrone* system could and did lead to abuses. So, too, could life on the plantation. The system effectively became illegal in 1905 when new federal legislation forbade this sort of labor agency, but thousands of Sicilian immigrants had already entered into contract agreements and found their way to Louisiana's sugar parishes.[17]

In retrospect, harvesting cane seems an unlikely solution to the problems Sicilians faced in their homelands, but at the time, the island's dire economic and social conditions contrasted sharply with the possibilities for a brighter future in Louisiana in the years leading up to the First World War. Southern

Italians referred to the decades after national unification in 1871 as La Miseria. "By the end of the nineteenth century," notes historian Humbert Nelli, "taxes in Italy were the highest in Europe and weighed especially heavily on those least able to pay, that is, on the *contadini* (peasants) and the *giornalieri* (or day laborers) of the South." Ecological pressures also dimmed the fortunes of the region's agricultural workers. An extended drought and higher temperatures reduced crop yields, while earthquakes and landslides brought more immediate ruin. Even pestilence in the form of the *phylloxera* plant parasite nearly destroyed southern Italian wine production. This crushing evidence of woe strikes a familiar note, ringing true in the oral tradition of the immigrant generation's descendants. In a nutshell, this *is* the story of the Sicilian migration.[18]

Almost precisely one month after unknown parties—widely suspected to be Italians—gunned down Hennessey on a dark stretch of Girod Street, an event that fostered a pervasively electric atmosphere of intense anti-Italian sentiment, the U.S. Custom House in New Orleans reported that 1,862 of the 2,029 immigrants who arrived at the port in October 1890 had come from Sicily. More than 75 percent of these newcomers were men, and the vast majority were destined for the cane fields. It was an alarming figure for New Orleanians already concerned about the presence of "Mafia societies" that supposedly functioned among the Sicilian dockworkers who unloaded cargo along the French Quarter's busy waterfront. Yet many of the white urban elites who fretted about the arrival of so many swarthy foreigners also participated wholly in and benefited from the economic model that had brought them to America. As the nerve center of domestic sugar production, weather, soil, and labor mattered as much in New Orleans as they did in the verdant cane fields of the surrounding parishes. Both the economic and social sentiments of the planter class seeped through in the report of the health inspectors who examined the 1,345 immigrants aboard the *Manila* after it arrived in 1902: "They are robust, healthy-looking people, *inured to work in the fields*, and, therefore very desirable laborers for the sugar and cotton regions of Louisiana, Mississippi and Texas, where the large majority of them are going." In other words, Italian peasants understood their place in the social hierarchy and thus made a suitable replacement for black labor.[19]

The Sicilians' experience with the planter class certainly paralleled the relationship between African Americans and southern white elites, but the differences in degree and duration are profound enough that they should caution us against suggesting that Sicilians suffered the same intensity of discrimination. For centuries under slavery, planters' mistrust of their black field hands was always mitigated by the inescapable need for their labor, and the same held true when the workers were Sicilian. While mutual dependence had always governed the racial and class dynamics of the agricultural South, discrimination against Sicilians in the 1890s blossomed from much shallower roots than did discrimination against African Americans. Even in the face of societal resistance, Sicilians had the possibility of following the right path and thus gaining broader social acceptance.

Given the social and economic historical contexts in which Sicilians arrived, they might have found their lot far worse had Anglo suspicions been more deeply set. The immigrant laborers entered the cane fields just as the fight for white supremacy in the South had entered its bloody concluding phase. In 1887, as the Sugar Planters' Association courted Italian labor, a combination of state militia and vigilantes slaughtered an unknown number of black sugar workers in the Thibodaux Massacre in retaliation for their labor activism, underscoring planters' urgent desire for a subservient workforce. For black southerners, the period between 1890 and the start of the First World War represented an era of unprecedented racial violence that took the form of riots and lynching. The Sicilians who suffered from mob vengeance in 1891 as well as those who died in similar episodes in the Gulf South during this era paid dearly for their cultural and personal associations, but white New Orleanians generally took a view of Sicilians that was much more nuanced than the binary antagonism directed at people of color. By the 1890s, some Sicilians had already ascended to the ranks of the city's commercial elite. Moreover, most of white America saw the criminality exhibited among the Sicilian working poor not as the product of some innate biological flaw but instead as the result of inadequate acculturation to American ways and as largely attributable to a limited number of malcontents. In contrast, many whites believed that a rapist or thief dwelled within in the heart of each African American male, a faith nurtured by centuries of racial subjugation and reinforced locally in New Orleans after the 1900 Robert Charles riot, an episode of spectacular antiblack violence precipitated by a deadly standoff between police and a well-armed African American fugitive.[20]

By the turn of the twentieth century, New Orleanians had grown accustomed to the early fall "immigrant season," its approach dictated by the agricultural timetables of citrus and sugar. As a result, the business of food production dictated not only *why* Sicilians came to Louisiana but also specifically *when*. The first picking of Sicily lemons in early October set in motion a process that resulted in a cargo of humans and citrus steaming west toward New Orleans. As successive gatherings of lemons and later oranges continued, more waves of immigrant ships would make their way across the Atlantic until spring, when both shipping and immigration from the Mediterranean to the Gulf South tapered off. The 1,862 immigrants who arrived from Italy in October 1890 accounted for almost half of all Sicilian arrivals in New Orleans for the year. Typical of the season's opening were the arrival of two steamers, the *California* and the *Sempione*, in the third week of October 1900 "bearing over two thousand simple children of Sicily." In May 1896, in one of the last citrus and immigrant shipments of the season, the *San Glorio* came to port "laden with 34,000 boxes of lemons and 600 tons of sulphur, with a supplemental immigrant cargo of 121 souls." Even though a ship might make the journey between Palermo and New Orleans in under thirty days, avoiding the passage during the heat of summer and the threat of hurricane season still made a great deal of sense. Moreover, the summer months brought disease. The last yellow fever epidemic to strike New Orleans came in 1905, and not until a decade later did the city put in place measures to prevent the recurrence of the illness.[21]

At the turn of the twentieth century, the sugarcane harvest, or *zuccarata*, as Italian-speaking immigrants called it, extended from October through January and thus coordinated well with the shipping timetables for citrus. And just as had been the case for the Sicily lemon, agricultural, geographic, and economic factors had to converge to make the sugar harvest successful. Not only do the peculiarities of sugarcane differentiate it from other forms of southern agriculture, but its demands are so enormous and thorough that it governs the lifestyles of everyone involved in its cultivation. Before tractors and specialized harvesting machines mechanized cane production in the 1950s and 1960s, almost everything on the planting side of sugar save plowing was done by hand. The earliest Louisiana sugar planters were large-scale slaveholders with a ready supply of cash and an even greater reservoir of credit. Both then and now, there is simply no way to engage in limited sugarcane cultivation.[22]

The paradoxical need to bring both technology and human toil to bear on an enormous scale had everything to do with sugarcane's unique harvesting timetable. From the moment that the machete-like cane knife hacked through the crop's dense, fibrous stalk, the precious juices contained within began to deteriorate, starting a clock whose every tick measured evaporated profits. Once the sugarcane had been loaded onto wagons, teams of draft animals would rush it to a grinding mill that crushed the stalks, wringing forth the precious juice. Sugarcane must also be harvested at its peak, when its sucrose content is the highest. In the nineteenth century, the need for rapid processing meant that every plantation had to have a sugarhouse with complex steam-driven machinery that easily made it the most valuable building on the plantation. Ascending the Mississippi River on a Sunday in the fall of 1834, John H. B. Latrobe looked on in disapproval at Christian masters who had "every man, woman, and child" working in sugarhouses as "long teams of oxen drew heavy carts loaded with the newly cut cane" for processing. In the fields, every available hand not employed at the sugarhouse labored eighteen hours a day to feed the great apparatus. The unrelenting tempo of "grinding season" remains just as much a ritual of fall in Louisiana's sugar parishes today as it was in the 1830s. The withering chaff of harvest time litters country roadsides, strewn by tractors pulling trains of cane wagons at full throttle toward the grinding mill in the annual race against time. Outside the mill itself, tractors and semitrucks full of cane queue up in a gravel lot to await their turn to unload while light gray clouds billow from the smokestacks and drift off into the crystalline blue skies of a Louisiana winter.[23]

The *zuccarata* attracted by far the largest group of Sicilians to Louisiana, although most did not remain in the sugar parishes. The earliest waves of immigrants contained overwhelmingly working-age men who aspired to salt away money to carry back to their families in Sicily. These "birds of passage" found plantation wages so low, however, that they did not permit any savings to accumulate. The immigrants could not know they had been caught in the jaws of an agroeconomic crisis decades in the making. Indeed, Louisiana's sugarcane growers sought out the cheapest labor possible precisely because the industry was under attack from almost every angle. Louisiana has always been less than ideal for sugar cultivation, lying on the very northern rim of the crop's climate zone. Yet just as protectionism enabled the twentieth-century rise of California citrus, it permitted Louisiana's sugar planters to become some of the wealthiest agriculturalists in mid-nineteenth-century America.

Cane sugar's halcyon days came to an abrupt end during the last decades of the nineteenth century, when technological advances, geopolitical realignment, and environmental crisis conspired to throw production into not only regional but also global collapse. Plant diseases plagued cane varieties all over the Americas, with the mosaic blight devastating Louisiana. Technological advances in planting brought production increases, but the resulting oversupply further depressed the global price of sugar. At the same time, German engineers began extracting sucrose from the sugar beet, a more forgiving crop that could be grown in a broader range of climates and that soon eclipsed the output volume of cane sugar production. The stake through the heart, however, was the final elimination of any hope for protectionism in 1894 by a Democratic Congress with a constituency comprised of agricultural exporters for whom lower trade barriers made more sense and northeastern sugar tycoons who imported raw cane syrup from American holdings in Cuba and Puerto Rico. Just how far had sugarcane fallen? In 1850, 90 percent of the world's sugar came from cane. By 1900, that figure stood at just 32 percent. It would be difficult to imagine a worse moment to embark on a career as a sugarcane field laborer.[24]

The mythology surrounding the Sicilian heritage of cane cutting is steeped in the concept of the American Dream and suggests that through thrift and determination, the members of the immigrant generation saved enough money to buy property and lay the foundation for a prosperous future. The historical record suggests a different reality. Gabaccia's research in the Sicilian peasant town of Sambuca reveals not only that little money ever reached the old country but also that many farm laborers returned in even worse financial condition, content to have the American experience behind them. At a particularly desperate point in the economic life of Louisiana sugar production, the *New Orleans Daily Picayune* noted that "two Italian steamers are now en route with lemons, but they are not bringing immigrants." Tracking down "Mr. Vincent of St. Philip Street," a shipping agent and important link in the *padrone* system, the reporter discovered that another ship, the *Montebello*, had left New Orleans with 429 Italians. "He attributes the general exodus to the failure of the planters to get their bounty and the consequent reduction of wages that followed necessarily. Some of the Italians could earn no more than 50 cents per day." Not until these immigrants drifted toward more remunerative forms of work on railroads, on truck farms, in logging camps, and in the metropolis of New Orleans did they put down roots in the Gulf South and accumulate sufficient capital to send for their families.[25]

Because so many Sicilians ultimately moved away from Louisiana's cane country, a lasting imprint of their passage through the sugar parishes that took place a century ago is often difficult to discern. In some places, however, the general public can get a better grasp of what life was like back then. About a half hour's drive west of New Orleans, U.S. 90 crosses the sinuous path of Bayou Lafourche. Satellite images of the Lafourche country show a tapestry of farm fields radiating out from the banks of the bayou, a waterway that begins at the Mississippi in Donaldsonville and flows through the last inhabitable ground at Golden Meadow before emptying into the Gulf of Mexico at Port Fouchon. Traveling north on Louisiana Highway 308 not only rewards the motorist with a scenic drive through the verdant countryside but also leads to the general store and interpretive site of Laurel Valley Plantation, a formerly prosperous sugar plantation that featured a major grinding mill and its own company railroad before bankruptcy and mosaic disease brought sugar production to a standstill. Still surrounded by cane fields, Laurel Valley is the nation's largest surviving nineteenth-century sugar plantation. A right turn down a gravel road leads to a collection of unpainted, tin-roofed shacks that comprised a community that locals in a less culturally sensitive time referred to as "Wop Field" before the last of the Italian laborers left in 1926.

"It was rough out here," observed Paul Leslie, a longtime history professor at nearby Nicholls State University and executive director of the Laurel Valley Store. Leslie lived for a brief while in one of the weatherboard laborer houses that had been "modernized" with insulation but not with indoor plumbing. During the winter of 1984, the weather was so cold that the thousand-gallon cistern that served the shacks froze like "one big ice cube." In the 1970s, Leslie directed an oral history program in which his students interviewed "about three hundred sugarcane workers," and they recalled that for special holiday meals, "they had spaghetti and meatballs . . . or they would have a baked chicken"; on one occasion, the plantation's owner ordered himself a lobster from New Orleans. When the Laurel Valley historical site attempted to produce a cookbook, according to Leslie, "we asked all these old people who lived here to give us recipes. And the only recipe that we got was white beans and rice." Leslie's research in the plantation's account books confirmed the lean dietary habits of Laurel Valley's laborers: their tables were supplemented only by what could be grown in their yards.[26]

One rural enclave that attracted large numbers of Sicilian former cane workers was the immigrant town of Independence, located in Tangipahoa Parish, north and west of New Orleans across Lake Pontchartrain. Here they found in the strawberry the sort of financial salvation that sugar never provided. As had been the case for the Sicily lemon, transportation networks, technological innovation, environmental factors, and societal change converged to yield an agricultural fortune. With fertile acreage crisscrossed by the Illinois Central; Baton Rouge, Hammond, and Eastern; and New Orleans and Nashville Railroads, Tangipahoa stood in an advantageous position to profit from the late-nineteenth-century innovations in refrigerated cargo handling that made possible the delivery of fragile berries to lucrative urban markets in the Upper Midwest. The 1901 introduction of a hybrid variety, appropriately named Klondyke after the Alaskan Gold Rush, put Tangipahoa Parish on the path to becoming the third-richest agricultural county in the nation just seven years later. The strawberry growers' success depended on the same style of cooperative action that had enabled Sunkist to achieve market supremacy in citrus. They formed a marketing association that ensured top prices and guarded against undercutting while guaranteeing distant buyers a uniformly high-quality product. To that end, strawberry growers used special sets of springs on their wagons at harvest time to ensure that the precious crop arrived at the auction house undamaged.[27]

Modern transportation, the establishment of industry standards, and pricing cooperatives were not the only similarities between citrus and strawberries. The parallels in networking, labor, and competition reveal the factors that governed the emergent modern twentieth-century produce market. The first president of the strawberry growers' association was Sicilian-born Joe Di-Buono, who had come to Independence by way of Chicago. An educated man, DiBuono used his familial connections in the Windy City in the same way that citrus agents had forged commercial ties between the Mediterranean and the Gulf. The harvest season also tied the fields of Tangipahoa Parish with New Orleans, with as many as five hundred Italian laborers boarding the Illinois Central every Monday morning between March and May and returning home the following Saturday afternoon. Profits remained high for several decades, until market pressure from California and Florida began cutting into Louisiana's generous margin in the late 1920s.[28]

Today, any visitor to a New Orleans farmer's market during the late winter or early spring is likely to have no trouble finding a discussion of the decline of Louisiana strawberries. It is an old conversation. Independence's strawberry production hit its peak in 1931, and crown-rot disease decimated the beloved Klondyke in the 1960s. By 1984, according to an agricultural history of the town, old-timers would often ask, "Where have all the berries gone?" A generation later, the harvest continues to shrink, despite the popularity of an annual

Strawberry Festival and at least two local breweries that produce a seasonal strawberry lager flavored with juice from Louisiana berries. Contributing to the problem is that the Tangipahoa Parish crop now differs very little, genetically speaking, from its hybrid cousin grown in Mexico or Central Florida. The only edge enjoyed by the local crop stems from the fact that berries picked closer to the point of ripeness are almost always better, yet the degree to which this benefits the Louisiana harvest depends a great deal on the weather. Recognizing the need to promote their culture at a time when "many of Independence's younger Italian-Americans find it necessary to move to nearby Hammond, Baton Rouge, or New Orleans for professional reasons," townspeople organized the annual Independence Sicilian Heritage Festival in 2008. Like many places in the rural South, Independence struggles to reinvent itself.[29]

A smaller contingent of Sicilian cane workers stayed in sugar country by finding prosperity outside farming. Just a short distance outside Raceland on Highway 308, along the margins of a large plantation once owned by a son of the antebellum sugar aristocracy, Alidor Robicheaux, stands the old Brocato's Store. In 1885, twelve-year-old Vincenzo Brocato traveled alone in the hold of a citrus vessel from the Sicilian town of Cefalù to New Orleans. Like many other members of his generation, he initially labored at a series of odd jobs including cutting cane. Brocato's position in the New World improved significantly in 1900, when he married fourteen-year-old Anne Bananto at the altar of St. Mary's Church in Raceland. Members of her family had saved enough money to become farmers and sugar growers on the western bank of Bayou Lafourche, and they brought the girl over from Palermo for what her granddaughter characterized as an "arranged marriage." The couple bought the building that housed their store in 1905.[30]

The Brocato family stayed in business there for nearly a century. In an age before Wal-Mart and a place without Piggly Wiggly, Brocato's had a general store on one side and a bar and grocery on the other. In the early years, Vincenzo would travel into New Orleans once a week to buy produce, including a giant stalk of bananas that he would hang from a hook in a darkened closet known as the Steam-a Banana Room. Brocato's delivered groceries by cart and later truck to plantations and crossroads as far away as Laurel Valley. The store was also an important part of the rural social scene: before and during World War II, the bar/grocery offered oysters on the half shell, music, and dancing.

As Sicilian custom dictated, Vincenzo and Anne's eldest daughter, Philomene—"Aunt Phee," as the younger generation remembers her—served as her parents' caretaker. When the girl reached marriageable age, her father hid her away from visiting salesmen lest she get the notion that she had any choice about her freedom. In the early 1920s, the couple's eldest son died when, according to family legend, Black Hand extortionists held up his mule-drawn delivery cart in front of a train speeding down the tracks of the Texas and New Orleans Railroad on the outskirts of Bowie, a former lumber town near by. Prior to World War II, younger siblings moved away to New Orleans, leaving Aunt Phee and one of her younger brothers to run the store. Until the day before she died in 2000, she arrived at the store every morning to sweep the floors, cut meat (with a giant cleaver on a tree stump), and keep the books. The store has since appeared in several movies, most notably the Ray Charles biopic *Ray*, but the family has sworn off Hollywood, choosing "to not ever rent it out again" after the production company made a mess of the Brocatos' memories. Today it sits buttoned up against the elements and intruders, a veritable time capsule, while the bones of those who once ran it rest across the bayou in above-ground vaults in the cemetery of St. Mary's Church. The family harbors the worthy goal of someday reopening the store as a museum, depicting a way of life that has long since disappeared from the Lafourche country.[31]

The citrus and sugar trades brought two very distinct groups of Sicilian immigrants to Louisiana. The earlier migration brought a wealthier, more educated urban class who sought to capitalize on the technology-driven marketplace transformations of the nineteenth century. The later generation, generally poorer, rural, and with fewer educational resources but much greater in number, fled the Sicilian countryside and its attendant hardships by hitching rides on the steamships that sailed along routes and at times determined by others. Both groups reacted to the rampant modernization occurring across the globe, some as masters, and others as servants. Their divergent circumstances and worldviews placed them on a collision course, and the bloodshed that followed formed part of the acculturation process in which immigrants shed their Sicilian past and forged a new Italian American identity. At the same time, rich and poor alike had to adjust to the peculiarities of the South's largest port city.

CHAPTER 2

A Road Paved with Oyster Shells

Sicilians and the Origins of Restaurant
Culture in New Orleans, 1830–1900

Nestled among the New Orleans Garden District's live oaks and across from the romantic decrepitude of Lafayette Cemetery, with its memorable turret and trademark turquoise and white striped awning, Commander's Palace looks every bit the part of the grand dame New Orleans restaurant. It's a place where old money and its three-martini lunch Uptown worldview collide with out-of-towners who enthusiastically sample an epicurean lifestyle either frowned on or simply unavailable in broad swaths of America. For several generations, Commander's has served as one of the city's unofficial culinary ambassadors to the rest of the world, a role it fulfills admirably. Though it is an old restaurant, its website is vague, bordering on coy, with regard to its history, much of which seems to have been cribbed in incomplete fashion through verbal lore. Tales of the 1920s, when "riverboat captains" and "sporting gentlemen" "met with beautiful women for a rendezvous in the private dining room upstairs," probably contain a grain of truth. Broader fame came in the 1940s and 1950s, when people like society writer and professional bon vivant Lucius Beebe began frequenting its gracious dining room. Yet Commander's metamorphosis into the landmark we know today really began in 1974 with the Brennan family. Their savvy management and eye for culinary talent that enabled chefs like Paul Prudhomme and Emeril Lagasse to become household names were part of the Brennans' gutsy transformation of the genteel but careworn Uptown restaurant into a worldwide destination. Despite its legendary past, there is no question that Commander's culinary golden age is now.

The restaurant wasn't always so fancy, particularly in its early years. On Christmas Day 1923, Commander's Palace invited readers of the *New Orleans Daily Picayune* to enjoy the restaurant's holiday menu. For the princely sum of one dollar, diners could select from among such specialties as ravioli, steaks, chops, and oysters. While definitely an agreeable neighborhood restaurant, Commander's Palace had yet to take its place among the city's renowned eateries. It is difficult to imagine this scenario while dining in the Garden Room at Commander's today, but a century ago, many things were different at 1403 Washington Avenue, including its operation by the sons of *usticesi* immigrants. Emile Commander had been born in New Orleans to Pietro Camarda and Josepha Venuto Camarda, who came from the tiny Mediterranean island of Ustica and who changed their names to Peter and Josephine Commander when they reached America. When Emile Commander opened his namesake business in the 1890s, it was as much saloon as it was restaurant. With such a glorious present, there is no marketing angle for the Brennans' flagship to trade on this Sicilian past, especially when the menu promises "modern New Orleans cooking" and "haute Creole." Yet Commander's belongs to the Sicilian legacy in New Orleans as much as macaroni or the corner grocery, even though it occupies almost no comparative space in our imaginings of the city's history.[1]

A prevailing amnesia exists regarding the Sicilian role in developing the city's restaurant culture beyond the obvious and substantially later contributions such as red sauce, pasta, and the muffuletta: like the importation of Sicily lemons, the Sicilian contribution to New Orleans's restaurant culture took place so long ago that no living person possesses firsthand memories of it. This story also unfolds across parts of the urban landscape that appear considerably different to us today than they did 125 years ago. We have no emotional connection with the way the shores of Lake Pontchartrain looked and felt before land-reclamation projects of the New Deal era obliterated or irrevocably altered places with such names as Spanish Fort and West End. Similarly, the post-1950 bulldozing of the nineteenth-century footprint of the Central Business District and the first block of Canal Street in the French Quarter to make way for parking lots, high-rise hotels, and office towers has forever unchained that sector of our urban landscape from its previous human habitation. Even the gambling houses of Metairie Road, their electric signs glowing in the night sky as they beckoned motorists from New Orleans for an evening of illicit booze and dancing, disappeared long ago, replaced by an unbroken stretch of strip malls, subdivisions, and semi-industrial sprawl. Mentions of these vanished establishments usually draw doubtful inquiring glances from all but the most historically aware New Orleanians.

The chronological distance and geographical transformations that separate our world from the one inhabited by the first generation of Sicilian immigrants to New Orleans is only partly to blame for the dissonance between the narrative buried in the historical evidence and what lives in the city's collective memory. Those Sicilians who belonged to the mid-nineteenth-century migration and assimilated into mainstream American culture by the turn of the twentieth century were less ardent preservers of heritage than those who came later and built a distinctive Italian American culture. Yet the obscurity of their role as part of the city's founding generation of restaurateurs may also result from the fact that their arrival and ascendancy coincided with a concerted effort by native-born intellectuals to preserve the image of Creole culture against the pressures of a modernizing world. The historical consciousness promoted by this generation of Creole authors, aided by a parallel nascent movement to market "Creole New Orleans" to tourists, left an indelible imprint on the city's collective memory. Nor have professional historians been immune to the allure of the remarkable staying power of this Creole paradigm. From a demographic standpoint, New Orleans has since the 1830s constituted far more of an immigrant city than a Creole one, yet the Creole question often dominates the historiography, yielding a dubious brand of Louisiana exceptionalism that is what we have found because it is most often what we have sought.[2]

Sicilians began arriving in New Orleans about the same time that the elements of restaurant culture in the city first emerged. Boardinghouses had served food at set times from very early in the eighteenth century, but the first sit-down restaurants, where meals might be had "at the shortest of notice," sprouted near hotels and resorts in the late 1830s. They were almost always adjacent to some form of live entertainment—theater, opera, dance halls, sporting events, and gambling. "Carry-outs," too, were quite popular in the nineteenth century and played a crucial role in the development of the restaurant. In an era when cooking took place over a wood-fired stove without running water or a reliable source of refrigeration, catering was understandably quite popular. Indeed, most early restaurateurs in New Orleans were caterers who transitioned to serving customers in public dining rooms. Although men from all ethnic backgrounds participated in this industry, a conspicuous number of them were members of this early wave of Sicilian émigrés.

The importance of hotels and the theater and the environmental determinism of seafood have received much less attention for their role in developing a dining culture in New Orleans than have efforts to describe the emergence of an Afro-Gallic "Creole" culinary style. Fresh seafood—particularly oysters, raw, stewed, and fried—defined early New Orleans restaurant fare. Seafood, wild game dishes, and the ubiquitous green turtle were the dishes that mid-nineteenth-century visitors to the city expected to eat. If this was "Creole" cuisine, it reflected creolization only in that it combined the pre-refrigeration yield of the local landscape with the growing urban demand for the availability of fresh food at irregular hours. The evolution of the "Creole" restaurant—as typified by the old-line eateries and their French-language menus inspired by late-nineteenth-century Creole self-consciousness, the haute cuisine of private home chefs, and Gilded Age dining splendor—is only one aspect of New Orleans's culinary heritage. Gorging on the natural bounty of southern Louisiana's aqueous landscape is another, and it is older and arguably more fundamental. It is not surprising that Sicilian immigrants, so active in maritime trading and the marketing of fresh foodstuffs during the antebellum era, would also branch into the nascent restaurant business. This early restaurateur class came to constitute another segment of the Sicilian elite of late-nineteenth-century New Orleans, joining the early importers, merchants, and handful of professionals. The houses that these restaurateurs built made important contributions to the culinary reputation of the city, and some of them remain with us today.[3]

The emergence of the American restaurant in the early nineteenth century was far more of an evolutionary than revolutionary process, and its mechanics merit our attention because they remind us that the nation's culinary landmarks arguably came about less from epicurean considerations than from other cultural, social, and economic factors. A cultural consensus, based both in lore and in a particular definition of what constituted a restaurant, credits the Delmonico brothers in New York with opening America's first true fine-dining establishment in the late 1820s. By midcentury, the name *Delmonico's* had become synonymous with dining excellence. Yet as important as culinary style was to the Delmonico brothers and others who opened and operated restaurants during that era, the widespread emergence of eateries depended even more on a gastronomic infrastructure capable of consistently supplying and setting a table and an equally steady stream of customers who were both willing and able to afford to dine out as an act of leisure. Ensuring this foot traffic required a vital entertainment sector in which the restaurant occupied just one position in the constellation of theaters, hotels, and saloons that fueled a city's leisure zones. Exquisite gustatory preparations might keep restaurants in business but did not cause them to open. Then as now, keeping restaurants afloat was a difficult proposition. That a city could sustain restaurants of any kind thus signaled that it had reached a new level of both cultural and economic maturity.[4]

A similar but perhaps more dubious mythology to that surrounding Delmonico's positions Antoine's as the first New Orleans establishment to offer dining "in the style that we currently recognize as restaurants." It is actually rather doubtful that when sixteen-year-old Antoine Alciatore "opened the doors to a small *pension* on Rue St. Louis" in 1840, he initially offered much more than the typical boardinghouse fare. The Antoine's myth stems from the notion that the New Orleans restaurant and Creole cuisine were two ideas that evolved in a symbiotic fashion, birthing the grand dame that today has become the city's longest continuously operating culinary institution. Yet it is difficult to ascertain the degree to which Antoine's French-language menu, so common in America by the *late* nineteenth century, was uniquely "New Orleans" as a signifier of "Creole" or simply of its Francophone customers. Or, like restaurants in cities all over America in the late nineteenth century, did Antoine's use of a French-language menu merely act as a conventional and expected signifier that Antoine's was a purveyor of haute cuisine? All three factors most likely played roles. By the late 1870s, when Antoine's began cultivating a national reputation for Creole fare, it had already become a tourist destination.[5]

Environmental bounty, market forces, and the cultural trends of a modernizing young urban America seem to have had more to do with the establishment of restaurants in New Orleans in the antebellum era than a distinct Creole culinary style. Indeed, the restaurant as an idea if not as a place was certainly already au courant in the minds of New Orleanians by the time Alciatore arrived in Louisiana. The incomparable boom times witnessed by the city in the 1830s produced wealth and aspirations of urban style, and the members of the merchant class regularly traveled to New York and the principal cities of Europe and thus were aware of what was taking place there. New Orleans may have been a frontier town in many respects, but it stood at the crossroads of global commerce. The emergence of the city's restaurants during the 1830s seems to have arisen from forces different from those that led to contemporaneous developments in New York—most notably, a desire among members of

New Orleans's leisure class to enjoy the sort of amusements at home that they had seen elsewhere.

The path to the first true restaurants in New Orleans wound its way past the better hotels and the caterers who provided food service for guests. The St. Charles and St. Louis Hotels would have offered varying degrees of cuisine to guests at set hours and offered banquet facilities for catered affairs, but doing so required advance planning. The Washington Hotel, built in 1831, stood on the shore of Lake Pontchartrain in a verdant setting known as Milneburg. If the hotel remained in existence today, we would find it standing near the lakefront campus of the University of New Orleans, surrounded by ground reclaimed from the lake in the 1930s. A century ago, however, Milneburg was a rural resort area well outside the developed limits of New Orleans and served as a commercial port and terminus of the Pontchartrain Railroad. One of the earliest steam excursion trains in the region, the Pontchartrain Railroad ran from the foot of Elysian Fields Avenue to the Washington Hotel, crossing "five miles in a quarter hour." A spring 1839 advertisement informed readers that the hotel's owner had hired Louis Canonge, a local caterer, to run the kitchen, adding confidently that "Mr. Canonge is too well known to require any comment." Although not a stand-alone restaurant, the Washington Hotel promised "breakfasts, dinners, and suppers . . . served up for private parties at the shortest notice." Offering meals "at the shortest notice" was the essence of the modern restaurant, a concept built on the idea of walk-up service.[6]

The previous fall, Canonge, "so extensively and so favorably known as a *Restaurateur*," had leveraged his reputation downtown and opened on Camp Street what is among several candidates for what we might credit as the first Delmonico's-style restaurant in New Orleans. While the establishment remained within the paradigm of the boardinghouse or hotel—the 1840 U.S. Census reveals that the building was home to Canonge and thirty-seven other single men—the core business of this establishment was the restaurant and its food. Unlike most boardinghouses, Canonge's restaurant offered dining to the general public: "Every thing that art, or skill, can supply to make it the most perfect thing of the kind in the city has been done." As with his work at the Washington Hotel, catering remained an important aspect of Canonge's business model: he was "prepared to supply private parties with elegant dinners in separate rooms, and will supply families at their own houses with every luxury his cuisine can afford." But perhaps what more defined the role of this restaurant was its position within a leisure and entertainment environment. Canonge's occupied space formerly occupied by the Arcade Bath House, next door to the Camp Street Theater, around the block from the St. Charles Theater, and squarely within the "American" sector of the city. On the second floor above the restaurant was a barroom with four billiard tables. The restaurant was distinguished by "its contiguity to the two theaters," noted the paper, "and the facilities it will afford not only to the neighbors but to visitors in general and to the play going community in particular, for many a thousand oysters will be there consumed by those who have laughed themselves hungry."[7]

We cannot, of course, know how Canonge's cuisine tasted. In fact, other than "many a thousand oysters," we do not even know what appeared on the menu of his restaurant. Other evidence even undermines his culinary skill: an April 1839 issue of the *New Orleans Daily Picayune* bemoaned the city's culinary offerings, complaining that the "2nd Municipality," where Canonge's establishment was located, lacked a restaurant "worth eating at." According to the author, "None but a mere digesting automaton, who eats for eating's sake—an animated sausage as it were—a butcher and sepluchre [sic] of the animal world—could put his legs under the mahogany of any house of the kind now in operation, and wish to come again."[8]

The oyster was just as important as theaters and hotels to the emergence of the restaurant in New Orleans and elsewhere. From New York to San Francisco, the oyster saloon was to nineteenth-century urban America what the fast-food joint is to interstate automobile travel today. Perhaps for this reason, authors who write about dining history seem reticent to classify oyster saloons as true restaurants, though old establishments such as the Union Oyster House, founded in Boston in 1826, have received some notice as such. Oysters played such a crucial role in the development of the New Orleans dining scene that their contribution cannot be so easily dismissed. The bivalve was certainly cheaper and much more plentiful in most coastal communities before the early twentieth century, when ecological degradation took its toll and wrought havoc on the beds of varieties that are now nearly extinct. Steam transportation and the creation of a market for ice in the 1820s made fresh oysters a profitable and popular commodity in America's interior, where only pickled and canned oysters had previously been available. Today's "oyster bar" was standard at any hotel in any major American city in 1850. In New Orleans, guests entering the doors of the St. Charles Hotel could pick from several oyster saloons adjacent to the lobby.[9]

The development of the first "cold chain" for perishable goods in the early nineteenth century made the availability of oysters possible in any corner of the nation linked by steam transportation. We now take the desirability of refrigeration for granted, but the harvesting of ice from lakes and rivers in cold climates and its distribution by ship and later rail to cities all over the nation and especially to lucrative markets in the Deep South simply did not exist before 1800. By 1850, ice had become indispensable in warm climates, where it not only kept drinks cold but also played a vital role in expanding the market for perishable goods. Since the price of a pound of ice depended on the distance between its points of production and consumption as well as the amount lost to melt as it sat in insulated icehouses, it is not surprising that the South would be home to the first ice-manufacturing plants after the technology became practical on a large scale after the Civil War. New Orleans quickly emerged as the region's largest producer of ice, but the public did not immediately feel safe consuming ice made by chemical means. The businessmen responsible for bringing the Louisiana Ice Manufacturing Company to the city in 1867 ran an ad in which the city's doctors assured prospective customers of the product's purity. It was, in fact, far cleaner than ice harvested from a variety of natural sources. By 1880, Louisiana Ice Manufacturing's plant churned out more than one hundred tons of ice a day.[10]

Thus, antebellum oyster saloons, a product of emergent technological and market forces, drew some of the first Sicilians into the restaurant business in New Orleans. Tied to the world of hotels and the sporting life, these immigrants came to play a key role in what we identify today as the city's food and entertainment culture. Already working in the comestibles trade with citrus, these immigrants branched out into other sectors of business, including preparing and selling oysters. A symbiotic relationship between ice-cold, glistening oysters on a tray and wedges of Sicily lemon occupies the mind's eye, but in reality, it is more likely that oysters represented a bustling sector of the food business and hustling immigrants seized the opportunity to get a piece of the action. Evidence of Sicilians involved in selling oysters appears as early as 1845, when a city directory showed men with Italian names operating five of the city's twenty-seven oyster stands. One of them, Antonio Terzula (or Terzuli), advertised in 1847 that he had upgraded his stand into a full-fledged oyster saloon at 93 Poydras Street, "adjoining the American Theater"; there, "Oysters of a superior quality can be had at all times, served up to suit the palate of the customer." Like runaway slave, real estate, and steamboat listings, newspaper ads for oysters were such a staple of antebellum cities that they often featured a cartouche of two halves of a freshly opened oyster next to the copy.[11]

In 1852, Terzula partnered with Antonio Agello, who ran an oyster saloon in the American Theater building, to open another oyster house and restaurant at 108 Poydras Street, only a few doors down from the original, which remained in business. Appropriately named Antonio's, the new location reflected both the growth of the oyster business and the presence of restaurant-style dining, advertising that management had "procured the BEST OF COOKS, and obliging attendants," and had branched out to serve all manner of game. The precise meaning of *procured* is unknown, but slave cooks were not uncommon in antebellum New Orleans. Only fourteen years earlier, the *True American* had thought it necessary to italicize (and misspell) such an unfamiliar word as *restaurant* for its readers when describing Canonge's work, a change that testifies to the pace of the development of public dining in antebellum New Orleans and elsewhere. By 1850, dining out was not simply for hotel guests or the wealthy, nor was it any longer the sole province of men. Upstairs, the two Antonios offered "a Saloon fitted up expressly for Ladies and Family parties," where they promised that "the strictest decorum" would be observed. Terzula and Agello thrived on Poydras Street until April 1854, when a massive fire destroyed the American Theater and reduced to ash many of the surrounding buildings, including the oyster operations of the two Antonios.[12]

Other members of the first wave of Sicilian immigrants proved far more enduring in the restaurant business. Giacomo "Jim" Astredo's 1839 arrival in New Orleans marked the beginning of a multifamily food and sporting-life saga that stretched well into the twentieth century, revealing how Sicilian immigrants shaped many aspects of the city's food and entertainment culture, among them restaurants, jazz, and alcohol as well as sportfishing and gambling. The road to all of these things was literally paved with oyster shells. The record does not reveal precisely when Astredo entered the oyster saloon business, but by 1851 he had built enough capital to open a restaurant, Jim Astredo's Oyster House, at Common and South Saratoga Streets, where customers could enjoy "the best Barataria and Southwest Pass Oysters." As with most Sicilian immigrants, Astredo's was a family operation. In 1846, twelve-year-old Anthony Astredo and his eight-year-old brother, Giovanni, known as John, sailed from Palermo to New Orleans, where they joined Jim, who was likely their uncle. Anthony seems to have started apprenticing at an early age, while John attended Soulé College and later Christian Brothers University in St. Louis.[13]

The Astredo brothers arrived in New Orleans in time for the final decade of the city's antebellum boom. A sweeping urban landscape painted by Marie Adrien Persac in 1858 provides us with an idealized snapshot of port activity on the eve of the American Civil War. Persac's painting offers an up-river view toward the city from the vantage point of what is now the Bywater neighborhood. In the foreground we see the tall masts of sailing ships loading and unloading overseas cargoes, while in the distance a fleet of shallow-draft paddle wheelers are bunched together in a flotilla of whitewashed planking and black smokestacks, nosed against the levee with gangplanks lowered to disgorge the riverine commerce of the Mississippi River Valley. Although a side-wheel packet ship in the foreground churns its way downriver, Persac's painting captures a specific and transitional moment in the city's waterborne commerce. In the late antebellum period, sailing vessels still dominated seagoing freight, while steam propulsion technology had advanced to such a degree that for the previous thirty years it had served as the standard means for transporting goods on inland waterways. Beginning about 1820, this technological equilibrium had allowed New Orleans to grow at a dizzying pace and to finally achieve its potential as the undisputed commercial locus for the Lower Mississippi River watershed. These forces of technology and geography had also enabled commission merchants, Sicilian and otherwise, to prosper immensely.[14]

While some of his countrymen built thriving enterprises trading goods imported from overseas such as citrus, olives, or nuts, young Anthony Astredo was one of several Italian-speaking merchants in New Orleans who saw opportunity in the rapidly expanding produce markets of the interior. While we only have a few clues as to his whereabouts between 1846 and the fall of 1854, it is clear that Anthony was comfortable with the modernizing world of steam-driven navigation. By the early 1850s he had begun working up and down the Mississippi's banks, selecting and purchasing domestic fruit—"Pears, Apricots, and Apples of a very superior quality"—as well as fruit trees for resale in New Orleans. Astredo forged both professional and personal ties outside the Sicilian community, and he married an Illinois-born woman.[15]

In the fall of 1853, amid advertisements for slave auctions, young Anthony Astredo announced the opening of his new oyster saloon, which operated seasonally during the cooler months when the bivalves were at their freshest and the dining room not impossibly hot. Offering "the best of cooks and obliging attendants," Astredo also "made arrangements so as to fully supply all demands for Game of all kinds, fresh," and assured that his saloon would "be in daily receipt of the best Oysters that Louisiana and its environs afford." As the operation grew, so, too, did the menu at Astredo's. A promotional newspaper article attested that "nowhere in that region are finer bivalvular delicacies to be procured in all the various styles of dressing them for epicurean palates." Not only did Astredo offer meals around the clock "and at the shortest notice," but his wine and liquor selection was "unsurpassed by any other establishment." As at Terzula's place, families and private parties could reserve a special up-stairs dining room. The well-traveled Astredo revealed his awareness of the emergent restaurant scene in the nation's principal cities by announcing that his fare was "served in New York style." His restaurant owed its presence less to culinary forms than to the availability of fresh ingredients such as seafood and game acquired in reliable quantities by a keen trader with a network of sup-pliers. Astredo's regional cuisine resonates with today's locavore trend, which constitutes an attempt to connect with the pre-mechanical-refrigeration world in which Astredo's oyster saloon operated.[16]

As a restaurateur, Anthony Astredo demonstrated a flair for showmanship, a necessary skill in the nineteenth-century city. A crowd gathered on the side-walk outside his oyster saloon one November afternoon in 1859 to stare in awe at an enormous fish hanging from a hook just outside the front door. It was a massive cherne, known more commonly today as an Atlantic wreckfish or rock bass, and according to the *Daily Crescent*, "the weight of this finny fellow was three hundred pounds." Such promotional stunts were typical of the era's patent medicine hucksterism. Astredo's saloon stood in the first block of Royal Street's river side, next door to the Old Post Office, an elegant domed structure built in the 1830s, and across the street from the Gem Saloon, where in 1857 the men of Comus organized the first Mardi Gras Parade. As other scholars have observed, the first few blocks of Royal Street past Canal during the antebellum period were a middle ground where restaurants, theaters, offices, retail, and the sporting life converged—the Bourbon Street of its era.[17]

Despite the success of his restaurant, Astredo considered himself first and foremost a caterer, a viewpoint common among those we would today call restaurateurs. This meant *catering* not only in the sense of serving at special events and banquets but also in the way that modern food service companies supply a steady streams of foodstuffs to hotels and cafeterias. Astute enough to understand the value of plying journalists with free food, Astredo sent the *New Orleans Daily Picayune*'s offices "a specimen of his catering . . . in the shape of a basket of large and tempting looking Cook's Bay oysters; and another of his cooking, in the form of a dish of those succulent luxuries, delicately fried."[18]

Unfortunately for Anthony Astredo, whatever good name he built up in the 1850s collapsed amid unspecified accusations about his fidelity to the Confederacy during the Civil War. He had been in one of the several ethnic militias at the war's start and participated in the failed river defense of the city. The last advertisement for his saloon ran in the *Daily True Delta* on May 3, 1862, just days after the Union captured the city, promising "extensive arrangements with parties at the North" that would enable him to reopen. These arrangements apparently proved inadequate: General Benjamin Butler ordered Astredo to leave the city, and he soon left for California. He never returned to his oyster saloon at 16 Royal Street, and the establishment folded.[19]

John Astredo inherited the wreckage of his brother's produce and oyster business after the war, and he struggled to find success as a caterer during the lean postbellum years. He became active in Democratic politics during Reconstruction, a move that served him well in the coming decades. In 1868, he joined the Jewell Guards, one of the many quasi-military political organizations of the era, and by 1876 he was the captain of the "Italian Legion" comprised of the "naturalized members" of the city's Tenth Ward. From this point forward, he became known in the community as Captain John Astredo, a title and rank that had nothing to do with his brief stint as a private in a Confederate militia and everything to do with his contributions to overthrowing Republican rule in Louisiana. Unlike that of his estranged brother, John Astredo's loyalty to the region was unquestioned.[20]

John Astredo's restaurant and leisure empire began in 1870 when he opened a new restaurant at the corner of Tchoupitoulas and Poydras Streets. By 1872, he had moved further uptown, opening the Excelsior Restaurant and Oyster Saloon across the street from the Magazine Market with business partner Manuel Delerno. "Their fried, broiled, roasted and scalloped oysters cannot be excelled," promised the *New Orleans Times*. The paper revealed that weight that the family name still carried in the city by reminding readers that "Col. John Astredo is the brother of Anthony Astredo, known as the Oyster King of this city." Three years later, about the same time that John Astredo became significantly involved in Democratic politics, he and Delerno moved the Excelsior into spacious new accommodations a couple of blocks further uptown at 2015 Magazine Street in a building still standing today. The new establishment served oysters and other delicacies similar to those found at a modern seafood place. An ad from that era implored prospective diners to "Rally! Rally! Rally!" for fish and soft-shell crabs that Astredo's savvy dealings with fishermen had placed "within the reach of all" at a mere $1.25 a dozen. Like Louis Canonge forty years earlier, Astredo referred to himself as a "renowned caterer," illustrating the continued importance of that job in the city's dining culture. "He furnishes meals at residences as usual—all prepared in the highest style of the art," promised the ad.[21]

When he opened his oyster saloon in the Magazine Market section of the Faubourg St. Mary, Astredo entered the orbit of New Orleans's nascent *usticese* colony, which clustered around the Central City corridors of Melpomene and South Rampart Streets and the portions of the Faubourg St. Mary that bordered on the old Irish Channel. In fact, New Orleans is home to the world's largest concentration of immigrants from the tiny Mediterranean island. How small is Ustica? Sixty kilometers north of Palermo, it encompasses only three square miles and is today home to fewer than fourteen hundred people. The Kingdom of Sicily transplanted families to Ustica from the island of Lipari in the mid-eighteenth century to crowd out the pirates who had previously used Ustica as a raiding base. One hundred years later, the descendants of these settlers began arriving in New Orleans in noticeable numbers. In 1879 they founded New Orleans's first Italian fraternal club, the San Bartolomeo Society, named for the patron saint of the *usticesi* and sworn to the mutual aid of those who left the island to find their future in the Crescent City. It continues to operate today. In the 1920s, Mussolini imprisoned noted philosopher Antonio Gramsci on the island along with hundreds of other dissidents, and it remained a penal colony into the 1950s. One prisoner from that time listed the island's residents as "mostly fishermen." Today, its clear turquoise waters and unspoiled countryside have made Ustica a tourist destination. When New Orleans humorist Ronnie Virgets traveled to the island in 2005 to trace the path of an ancestor who migrated to Louisiana in 1840, he found a sun-drenched idyll worthy of a spread in a travel magazine.[22]

The descendants of *usticesi* immigrants remember well the stories of their forebears and the relationship between the food business and their journey toward Americanization. According to Niccolino "Peter" Compagno, every Italian who came to New Orleans seemed to open a grocery or barroom of some kind: his great uncle, Antonio Compagno, joked that immigrants would walk straight from the riverfront to Magazine Street and open an establishment selling food in the first vacant place they came across. Antonio Compagno had come to New Orleans in 1861 from Ustica, and after working on the riverfront for some years, saved up enough money in the 1870s to open a grocery and barroom on the pie-wedge corner of Magazine and Felicity Streets in the city's Irish Channel neighborhood, not far from John Astredo's oyster saloon in the Magazine Market. The structure at 1601 Magazine Street today houses a florist and looks much as it did in 1904, when Pietro Compagno closed in the second-story gallery. Like many thriving Sicilian businessmen, Antonio Compagno sponsored family members to join him. His eldest grandson, Peter, came in 1883, followed shortly thereafter by Peter's brothers, Frank, Anthony, and Charles. When Antonio died in 1902, the business went to his New Orleans–born son. Peter and his brothers eventually bought out their uncle and helped each other establish bars and restaurants in different parts of Uptown, the last of which operated into the late twentieth century.[23]

The combination restaurant, grocery, and bar that Pietro Compagno ran at Felicity and Magazine in the nineteenth century was no more discernably Italian in its cuisine than any of the other oyster saloons operated by his countrymen. During the 1920s and 1930s, his son, Niccolino "Peter" Compagno, worked as a delivery boy for the store, following a procedure that had not changed fundamentally since the widespread appearance of the telephone in the 1880s. According to Peter, anyone living within eight blocks of the bar could phone in an order for oysters on the half shell and a bucket of cold beer: a tray "would have four, five dozen oysters on it, and they'd open them up, and I'd take it on my hand, and I'd deliver it to those people." A dozen oysters on the half shell cost a quarter in the 1930s, while the fried variety ran thirty-five cents. The Compagnos bought hundred-pound sacks of oysters from Martina and Martina Oysters (another Sicilian company) for ninety cents each; the Martinas would deliver one hundred sacks a week, piling them onto the sidewalk along Magazine Street.[24]

Another *usticese* family that achieved great success and whose lives intersected with the Compagno and Astredo clans on the late-nineteenth-century New Orleans dining scene were the Tranchinas. When they arrived on the levee in April 1867, forty-one-year-old Felice Tranchina and his boys, Terigi, age nine, and Giuseppe, age seven, joined an established *usticese* community in the Faubourg St. Mary. The Tranchinas soon moved from their fruit stand on Dryades Street to join fellow *usticesi* in more upwardly mobile pursuits in the Magazine Market section. Like the Astredo brothers, the

Tranchinas quickly Americanized their names, with Felice becoming Felix, Terigi becoming Terry, and Giuseppe becoming Joseph. In 1876, the year after Astredo and Delerno opened the Excelsior Restaurant, Felix Tranchina and another *usticese*, Felix Bertucci, opened an oyster saloon eleven blocks further uptown at 858 Magazine, a building on the corner of Ninth Street, across from the old Ninth Street Market, that still houses a restaurant today. Joseph and another younger brother, Frank, worked at Antonio Compagno's oyster saloon and grocery—indeed, Frank went on to marry Antonio's daughter, Maria. All of these *usticesi* were closely aware of and perhaps cooperated with each other in their business ventures. When F. Tranchina and Company opened, Terry Tranchina shared a house at 177 St. Mary Street with Manuel Delerno, Astredo's business partner.[25]

In 1884, when Felix Tranchina died, Terry and Joseph purchased the Excelsior Restaurant from Astredo and Delerno. By all appearances, the business thrived through the 1880s, and at the end of the decade, Frank bought out Joseph and became a partner. Joseph found that New Orleans's topography meant that he could make just as much money and maybe more in oyster shells as in the bivalve itself. Not only is there no bedrock beneath what passes for terra firma in Orleans Parish, there is also no gravel larger than an outsized grain of sand. Therefore, well into the twentieth century, oyster shells represented the cheapest, most readily available resource for paving the city's notoriously muddy roads, and the Astredo, Tranchina, and Compagno families produced several tons of shells every few weeks. They were hardly alone. The 1876 New Orleans city directory listed 195 oyster saloons. Oysters were so ubiquitous that a person walking the fifteen miles between the St. Bernard Parish line in the Lower Ninth Ward all the way upriver to Jefferson Parish would never be more than a few blocks away from a dozen raw on the half shell. Joseph Tranchina was not the only dealer of oyster shells, but he handled such a volume that in 1892 he petitioned the city for fifty feet of frontage on the river to pile them. These mountains of shells added up to quite a bit of money.[26]

While the Tranchina brothers continued growing their operation on Magazine Street, Astredo and Delerno sought out new opportunities in even grander establishments. In the final decades of the nineteenth century, Ocean Springs, Mississippi, became a retreat for middle- and upper-class New Orleanians seeking to escape the summer heat of the city, and John Astredo took over the operation of a resort hotel, Oak Cottage, on June 1, 1877. There, promised the

New Orleans Daily Picayune, patrons would find "all the comforts of a home, with a table beautifully supplied from the best the market affords" by "the great caterer, John Astredo." The stretch of Gulf Coast just beyond the Mississippi state line held other charms for New Orleanians, particularly as moral improvement societies strengthened in the city toward the end of the century. When the Louisiana legislature made prizefighting a felony in 1882, the promoters of a bout between bare-knuckle brawlers John L. Sullivan and Paddy Ryan reached an agreement with the Louisville and Nashville Railroad to run excursion trains for the day to Mississippi City, where the event would take place. Though Hurricane Katrina's storm surge destroyed much of the antebellum architectural wealth along the Mississippi Gulf Coast and Mississippi City has now been subsumed into greater Gulfport, a landscape dotted with casinos, golf courses, and outlet malls, on a February morning in 1882, Barnes's Hotel hosted an eleven-minute bout during which Sullivan beat Ryan senseless, thrilling the five thousand onlookers who gathered among the live oaks in the hotel's yard. Despite its remote location, the fight not only cemented Sullivan's legend but also decided the fate of hundreds of thousands of dollars in wagers. Conveniently connected by rail, Mississippi's Gulf Coast served as a social extension of New Orleans and made it an attractive location for Captain Astredo, whose ventures increasingly trended toward the sporting life.[27]

The next year, Astredo and Delerno branched out to another resort area much closer to home when they opened a hotel and restaurant at New Lake End, an area that soon became known as West End. This was the site where spade-wielding Germans and Irishmen finally reached Lake Pontchartrain in 1838, completing the quest to dig the New Basin Canal, an engineering feat that connected the lakeshore with downtown's bustling American sector some three miles away—but not before taking the lives of numerous laborers. Land-reclamation projects in the first half of the twentieth century and postwar development have rendered this area almost unrecognizable from the way it appeared in the late nineteenth century, but an 1885 map produced for the World's Industrial and Cotton Centennial Exposition shows that the canal projected into the lake, hemmed in by jetties on each side, with the Southern Yacht Club and West End Lighthouse commanding the two tips, much as they do today. Along this projection's western edge ran a revetment and platforms where hotels and pavilions stood elevated on piers, capturing cooling lake breezes that attracted the "can't get-aways" who were unable to leave New Orleans during the hot summer months in this age before air-conditioning.

Although originally conceived as a commercial waterway, the canal's terminus at West End was almost from its inception a site of leisure, and by 1880 this was its primary use. One of the first resort establishments there, the Lake House, welcomed guests from 1838 until disgruntled kitchen employees burned it to the ground in 1870. Samuel Clemens visited West End at this time while writing *Life on the Mississippi* and observed the "inviting modern-style pleasure resorts" there, "with broad verandas all around, and the waves of the wide and blue Lake Pontchartrain lapping the thresholds." Theodore Bruning built a restaurant and saloon here in 1859, and it operated continuously in various locations until 2005, when Hurricane Katrina ended its long run. Popular activities at West End included swimming, sportfishing, rowing, and yachting on the water as well as eating, drinking, and after 1885 dancing under electric lights.[28]

Along the revetment, on piers over "fifteen feet of water," Astredo built "a magnificent restaurant and bar" where diners could feast on the sort of seafood that had made the Excelsior Restaurant a success. "Man wants but little here below, but wants it nicely cooked and served so when his palate craves for all the good things on earth he should call at John Astredo at the West End and he will get just what he wants," promised the proprietors. "Commodore Astredo's restaurant at the West End will be open all winter and as usual the smiling welcome of Manuel Delerno will be a solace to the hungry," reminded another ad. "Call on John and Manuel and have your appetite appeased." Indeed, Twain might well have been describing Astredo's when he wrote of eating at a table set on a "ground-veranda over the water," where he enjoyed pompano, a fish he declared "as delicious as the less criminal forms of sin."[29]

Getting to West End from the city was simple enough. Travelers could reach by taking a boat down the canal or, like Twain, by riding in a carriage along the shell road that paralleled "the canal on one hand, and a dense wood on the other." Most people, however, boarded the open-air cars of the New Orleans City and Lake Railroad on the neutral ground of Canal Street between Baronne and Carondelet. In 1880, the railroad signed a twenty-five-year lease on most of the area at West End and then went about increasing the location's profile as a resort destination. In addition to an outdoor music pavilion, the railroad built an ornate hotel across the road from the Astredo House where guests could "take strolls in the open air under the electric lights." Over the ensuing decade, the company sublet these premises and various lots to different restaurateurs, including caterer E. F. Denechaud, who in 1907 opened Poydras Street's Hotel Denechaud, a building we know today as Le Pavillon Hotel.[30]

In 1895, the New Orleans Railroad replaced the old hotel and pavilion with new ones and used that opportunity to bring in Astredo's friend, Terry Tranchina, who leased out the West End Hotel for five thousand dollars a year. The move was a significant step up from the Excelsior Restaurant for Tranchina, though his experience on Magazine Street prepared him to create the sorts of seafood dishes West End diners expected. Recognizing the need for a professional dining room manager, Tranchina partnered with yet another *usticese*, Joseph Vincent Olivieri, who had spent more than a decade as a waiter and later manager of Leon's Restaurant, a large establishment across the street from the St. Charles Hotel. Like most West End structures, Tranchina and Olivieri's hotel sat perched on piers overlooking the lake. A 1900 photograph shows an airy two-story frame structure with a proud cupola. In the shade of the building's wide-colonnaded veranda, seated diners enjoy lunch at tables draped with white cloths. Although the photo was clearly taken in winter, it is easy to imagine a banquet served on a warm July evening later that year for the retiring chair of the New Orleans Railroad. Guests enjoyed Manhattan cocktails while the hotel's serving staff brought out a feast worthy of the French-language menus found at Antoine's, including *crevettes marinière*, soft-shell crabs (known at the time, as they sometimes are today, as busters), *filet d'boeuf perigeux*, and *farcis*, all paired with an assortment of alcoholic beverages ranging from Sauternes and Roederer Champagne to sherry. "This prettily decorated banquet board had been spread upon one of the wide galleries which overlooks the lake," noted a reporter, "and the cool breezes and moonlight joined the sweet music of the concert band in making the spot ideal for such an occasion." Music played into the night, as diners spooned tutti-frutti ice cream out of cantaloupe halves, drank café mocha, and smoked cigars. The offerings attested to the fact that the Tranchinas had long since graduated from serving only oyster saloon fare.[31]

The 1898 visit of comedic actor Roland Reed reveals the degree to which saloonkeepers and restaurateurs such as John Astredo and Terry Tranchina belonged to the world of Gilded Age showbiz as well as their social and political identities as white southerners. Reed was born into the theater in Philadelphia but had deep ties to and affection for New Orleans, where he found fame at David Bidwell's Academy of Music on St. Charles Avenue in the early 1870s. "He is one of us," recalled the *Daily Picayune*'s entertainment writer in 1898, because he had come during the trying years of Reconstruction "to make people laugh." In one of his most celebrated roles, Reed starred in Fred Marsden's *Cheek* playing Dick Smythe, a newspaperman who tries to get prominent people to pay him for mentioning them in his column. (Lost on us today, the humor in *Cheek* would have resonated with turn-of-the-century audiences accustomed to the incessant positioning of names in society columns.) Every time he came to New Orleans, Reed would bring a bouquet to Bidwell's tomb and visit "Captain John Astredo, who was a warm friend of the young actor in his early days, and is still in the thirty-third degree of his affections." As younger men, Bidwell and Astredo had run competing oyster saloons.[32]

One gray January afternoon, Reed decided to meet up with some friends at Astredo's Restaurant at West End and perhaps "catch one of the big garfish" rumored to swim in the lake. Finding the place deserted save a monkey who gamely munched on a banana at the door to McGouldrick's Saloon, and with two hours to kill before his friends showed up for lunch, Reed persuaded "a new boy guarding a row of bottles" to let him into Astredo's and left his hat and coat outside on the boardwalk with a note reading, "The day has been filled with disappointments. I expect those who come for me will look in the lake for my remains." Reed then "bribed the new boy" to lock the door to Astredo's, and Reed's compatriots had to pry it open. Reunited, the group "adjourned to the West End Hotel, opposite, where Tranchina had a smile of welcome, where a smile came sparkling and gurgling from a Roederer bottle, where a smile played over the dignified face of the waiter." Reed would visit West End on his next tour, noted the paper, "but it will not be on a dull gray day, and [he] will not take his gar hooks with him."[33]

After thriving in the 1890s, West End steadily declined in the first decade of the twentieth century, with most of the names that had once made it famous leaving for elsewhere by the start of the First World War. One of the first to depart was Captain John Astredo. In 1900, when he was in his early sixties, Astredo decided to concentrate his business interests at his Mississippi City hotel and live most of the year at his nearby summer house, which was "surrounded by a clump of oaks" and "pleasantly cool." He sold the Astredo House to Olivieri in what turned out to be a bad move for both men. The following year, on one of the region's signature thick, hazy midsummer afternoons, a bolt of lightning—literally out of the blue—struck Astredo's summer house, instantly killing Astredo and the traveling salesman to whom he had been talking. Two years later, on a breezy April night in 1903, a fire broke out at a soda stand next to the old Astredo House, now run by Olivieri. By morning, the three-story building had been reduced to cinders, as had several other buildings and a sizable portion of the fleet moored at the Southern Yacht Club's marina.[34]

Terry Tranchina stayed at West End for the remainder of the prewar period, but efforts to stabilize the marshy shoreline and improve its appeal as a public park could not reverse the area's decline as a destination for the city's pleasure seekers. As the resort's biggest leaseholder, Tranchina encouraged the city to repair the wharf and the increasingly shabby rides and other amusements located on it. In 1910, the city filled in the revetment, creating gardens, but the work required the temporary closure of the West End Hotel, forcing Tranchina to operate a café on the shell road not far from the site of Astredo's old place. Though he opened champagne for a celebration marking the 1912 opening of the "New West End" seawall and park, the caterer had already cast his net elsewhere, making plans for a new operation at the revitalized Spanish Fort, a longtime West End competitor located at the mouth of Bayou St. John. Tranchina operated establishments at both locations for a few years, but on the eve of World War I, he concentrated all his efforts at Spanish Fort.[35]

West End's heyday provides a fascinating glimpse into the leisure activities of turn-of-the-century New Orleanians and adds to our understanding of what it meant to be a Sicilian immigrant in the Crescent City at the time. At the same time that John Astredo, Terry Tranchina, and J. V. Olivieri and the other members of the *usticese* restaurateur class were taking their leisure at the Southern Yacht Club, then as now an organization with considerable social cachet, oceangoing steamers were arriving at the Nicholls Street Wharf with holds crammed with Sicily lemons and penniless Mediterranean peasants. In 1888, while these immigrants were streaming into the French Quarter, Astredo was racing his schooner, *Frolic*, against other yachts on the lake. In 1899, Tranchina and Olivieri sponsored a cup awarded in the races that year, and the following year, after the men had ended their business partnership, they donated cups individually. For the first decade of the twentieth century, the Tranchina Cup, awarded to open-class sloops, was an important Southern Yacht Club trophy.[36]

These Sicilian restaurateurs, many of whom belonged to the Uptown *usticese* colony, also began to appear regularly in the society columns of New Orleans's daily papers. On August 9, 1901, the *New Orleans Times-Picayune* reported, a birthday party took place at the corner of Washington and Coliseum Streets, an address known to devotees of fine dining around the world today as Commander's Palace. The guest list for the elegant society debut of Emile Commander's daughter, May, could have been the register from a ship bearing immigrants from the island of Ustica in the late 1860s, with Bertuccis,

Tranchinas, Disimones, and Mancusos, among others. Three years later, an article covering a St. Joseph's Day gala at the French Quarter home of Anthony Patorno Jr. at 915 Royal Street, featured a "flash photo" of costumed "Italian Colony Beauties." Once again, familiar family names from the *usticese* migration appear alongside those of other important Sicilian clans. Patorno's father, a major liquor importer and distributor, had bought the house after a 1900 fire there necessitated a complete renovation of what had originally been an elegant 1850s brick townhouse. The setting itself was in some measure a symbol of the economic and social maturity of New Orleans's Sicilian elite as the twentieth century began. Tourists from around the world today know Patorno's whimsical Queen Anne–style mansion as the Cornstalk Hotel, though the hotel itself makes no mention of its intersection with this era in the city's past despite the fact that the building's design and much of its décor date from the Sicilian period. As one observer noted at the time, it was "an exact replica, in façade, of one of those castellar structures in Italian cities."[37]

The Commander family's journey from Ustica's rocky shores to the society pages of New Orleans's newspapers resembled the path taken by the members of the Tranchina clan, though if measured by culinary place-names, the Commanders' legacy has proved much more enduring. Patriarch Pietro Camarda was among the earliest migrants to come to New Orleans from Ustica, arriving in this country in 1852, though he seems to have returned to Italian soil during the American Civil War. Eldest son Emile was born in New Orleans in 1857, while a second son, Anthony, was born in Sicily in December 1861, as was a daughter, Amie, the following year. A third son, Charles, was born in New Orleans in 1867. The Camardas/Commanders originally settled in the heart of the *usticese* community along Dryades Streets, but Peter and his sons spent much of the next two decades working the grocery and saloon trade on the South Rampart and South Basin Street corridors.[38]

After years of hustling in the grocery and saloon business, Emile Commander opened the doors to his Palace Saloon and Restaurant at the corner of Washington and Coliseum in 1893—substantially later than popular lore in New Orleans would have it. Most of the confusion about the year of the restaurant's genesis originated in 1906, when Commander succumbed to tuberculosis at a Welsh sanitarium. His *Times-Picayune* obituary claimed that he had operated the place for "twenty years." What led the author of a 2011 *Times-Picayune* article to place the restaurant's opening in 1880 remains unclear, but the mistake probably had something to do with Beebe's midcentury writings.

In reality, "twenty years" before his death, Emile was still living with his father and two brothers in the rear of 190 South Rampart Street, and as late as 1889, he was driving a delivery wagon for Wreckerling Brewing. Emile moved to the Garden District in 1890 to open a saloon of sorts at 188 Washington Avenue (old numbering), diagonally across the street from Commander's current location. Preparations for the first iteration of what became the restaurant as we know it began in the fall of 1892, when Emile secured a permit to erect a one-story building fronting Coliseum, possibly to enlarge or improve the structure at the corner of Washington Avenue, which already featured the now-familiar turrets. A large illustrated Christmas display ad that appeared in the *New Orleans Item* a few weeks later announced that "Emile Commander Will Be Prepared to Receive His Friends at His Magnificent New Saloon and Restaurant . . . about January 15," though he does not seem to have received his liquor permit until sometime shortly thereafter. Not surprisingly, oysters featured prominently on the menu. For a dime, diners could choose between a dozen "Bayou Cook" oysters on the half shell and a "small sized" oyster loaf, which could be enjoyed with "choice wines, liquors, [and] imported cigars." Commander's Palace Saloon and Restaurant soon built a loyal following.[39]

The Commander brothers were a tight-knit trio and relied on each other's experience in the restaurant and saloon business in their own ventures. Anthony had worked as a bartender for Thomas Handy, the onetime owner of the Sazerac Bar. By 1893, Anthony had opened the Bon Ton Café and Saloon at 36 (308) Magazine Street. He had also become one of Plaquemines Parish's leading citrus growers, and as late as 1929 he persisted in believing that Louisiana stood on the verge of becoming the nation's most profitable orange-producing state. Charles J. Commander worked as a waiter at the Acme Restaurant in 1889, operated groceries and saloons on Rampart Street, and briefly attempted to establish the American Broom Factory on the same premises as his grocery in 1894. None of these enterprises matched the success of his older brothers until New Year's Day 1904, the moment that C. J. Commander made his mark on New Orleans dining history.[40]

The creation story of the Delmonico on St. Charles Avenue contains every bit as much mythologizing as Commander's Palace and perhaps more, because a significant chunk of the legend was in all likelihood the willful fabrication of the restaurant's founder, C. J. Commander. Though remarkably brief, his tenure at the establishment was enough to invent a legend. The LaFranca family, not Commander, took over the Delmonico in 1911 and ran it for most of the twentieth century. Anthony LaFranca died of cancer in the 1940s, and his widow and daughters continued the business until 1997, when celebrity chef Emeril Lagasse purchased the restaurant, which today bears the name Emeril's Delmonico. At the time of the sale to Lagasse, a reporter dutifully reiterated much of the "history" of the restaurant created by Commander, who supposedly "had worked at the famed New York Delmonico's, [and] opened an independent New Orleans Branch in 1895 with the blessings of the New York family."[41]

The marketed Delmonico narrative contains numerous improbabilities. The building at 1300 St. Charles Avenue had been an ice cream parlor, complete with a marble-topped counter and soda fountain, until it was offered at auction in August 1903, almost a decade after C. J. Commander supposedly bought the building and converted it into a restaurant and bar. It is also unclear when C. J. would have had time to work at Delmonico's in New York, given the numerous other New Orleans enterprises in which he was involved. It is, however, highly unlikely that the establishment in New York gave any sort of "blessings" for the use of its name. Until the advent of domestic trademark laws in 1905, the year after Commander opened his establishment, the New Yorkers would have been powerless to do anything about his infringement. In fact, in turn-of-the-century America, the name *Delmonico* had been appropriated and applied to everything from ice cream flavors to restaurants in most major cities. The name had already been borrowed a decade and a half earlier in New Orleans for the Hotel Delmonico on Poydras Street (where the parking deck for One Shell Square now stands) and for the short-lived New Delmonico restaurant, which opened on Canal Street in 1887. Longevity, however, certainly sets apart the establishment on St. Charles and Erato Streets, which is the only Delmonico restaurant that operated continuously throughout the twentieth century. (Since the 1960s, even the one in New York has had a variety of locations and owners and has intermittently closed.) The New Orleans Delmonico eventually lived up to C. J. Commander's hype and to the grandeur of its namesake. Yet it owes its longevity entirely to the LaFranca family, whose decades of service and devotion to their customers secured its reputation for excellence.[42]

One of the great challenges facing anyone writing about the history of New Orleans is to crawl out from under the weight of the city's cultural mythology and try, however imperfectly, to accurately re-create the past. As with all historical writing, the narrative hinges on the author's vantage point. There is probably no single cultural phenomenon in the city better remembered, celebrated, marketed, repackaged, and even fabricated than the notion of "Creole New Orleans." The phenomenon is so omnipresent—on restaurant menus and tomatoes and haunted history tours—that the meaning of *Creole*, in the sense in which it has traditionally been identified with New Orleans, grows more vague every day. This tendency has also led us to correlate our ideas of nineteenth-century New Orleans cuisine with something along the lines of the menu at Antoine's or at the numerous other places that by 1890 had begun to market themselves as self-consciously Creole.

But if we imagine New Orleans as complex and as composed of multiple cultural paradigms—much in the way that the tens of thousands of immigrants and migrants saw the city in the nineteenth century—alternative narratives emerge. Visitors to New Orleans also thought of Astredo's and Tranchina's, resorts and popular tourist destinations that were in many ways about as un-Creole as one could get. They wanted to see comedy productions and vaudeville acts, listen to popular band music, enjoy amusement rides, and promenade under the technological phenomenon of electric lights. New Orleans was where the Gilded Age met the Gulf Coast. Diners, locals and tourists alike, wanted and even expected pompano, soft-shell crabs, turtle soup, and above all, oysters. The first restaurants that catered to the tastes of New Orleanians boasted of the freshness and quality of the local seafood and wild game found on their menus. This sort of feasting, which remains an important part of the New Orleans way of life, was contingent, then as now, on the bounty of the semiaquatic southern Louisiana landscape. There is no greater argument for environmental determinism than a panoptic illustration of what New Orleanians ate in the nineteenth century.

The restaurant emerged in America precisely as merchants from Palermo, Messina, and Ustica began arriving in significant numbers to New Orleans. Schooled in the business of food commodities, they began preparing and serving meals, occupations that have always required skill and perseverance. These immigrants succeeded in part because of their connection with the water. Astredo, Tranchina, and other nautical men were never far from the docks where fishermen supplied the growing restaurant operations. The houses that these entrepreneurs built were not Creole restaurants, nor were they Italian or "Creole Italian," a cuisine that did not emerge until the first decade of the twentieth century and did not receive that name until the mid-1970s. Some of these restaurants, like the great hotels of the West End, have not only disappeared from the landscape but vanished so long ago that they have been erased from popular memory. Others have lived on, becoming some of the city's most famous restaurants but having long since lost any connection with their ethnic past. Despite the enormous contributions made by the city's Sicilian immigrants more than a century ago, not until the early twentieth century did a culinary tradition become associated with them.

CHAPTER 3

Blood and Macaroni

*Becoming American in the
Sicilian French Quarter*

At the downriver end of the popularly named Moon Walk waterfront promenade, directly across from the French Market and Old U.S. Mint, clad in green aluminum panels, sits the low, long form of the Governor Nicholls Street Wharf, the last commercial port facility remaining along the French Quarter's historic waterfront. In the months following Katrina the wharf offered shelter to members of the National Guard as they sweated through early morning physical training exercises. In 2008, it became the object of intense controversy when New Orleans Cold Storage, a company that had been in business in the city since 1886, proposed relocating its operations there. Vocal opponents from the adjacent Faubourg Marigny claimed that the facility "would degrade the area's historic character," while the executive director of the French Market Corporation worried that the development might "prove a nuisance" to patrons "looking for a relaxing shopping experience" among the market's tchotchke stalls. New Orleans Cold Storage found a less controversial—and more logistically compatible—site, the Henry Clay Avenue wharf not far from Audubon Park, where most of the port's activity has been concentrated since the advent of automation, and relocated there in 2012. While a cold storage facility hardly conflicted with the "historic character" of the French Quarter/Marigny riverfront—a place that as recently as 1960 remained the bailiwick of rusting cargo ships and tough longshoremen—it most definitely ran counter to the modern tourist economy of the Quarter and quality-of-life demands of the Marigny's gentrifying bohemians and transient Airbnb devotees. In another generation, few people will remember a waterfront alive with the sounds of stevedores rolling cotton and unloading bananas.[1]

The Governor Nicholls Street Wharf deserves a place in the city's memory, for it is where the American chapter began for generations of immigrants, including the roughly forty-five thousand Italians who came through the Port of New Orleans before 1910. The Moon Walk is home to a monument to these immigrants funded and built by Italian American businessmen during the 1980s after they realized that the city's role as a major immigrant port had gone largely overlooked. Standing by this statue, one might gaze over the water and imagine a steamer deftly nudged by tugboats, their powerful propellers churning through the turbid brown water as the side of the foreign vessel gently kisses the wharf's edge. The substantial distance between the French Quarter and Port Eads some seventy miles below the city meant that people living here had sufficient advance notice of a ship's arrival that they might crowd along the levee at the appointed hour. Where the Moon Walk now stands, shipping line employees and the biggest, toughest policemen would stretch a double line of ropes "to prevent invasion of the space alongside the vessel by the hundreds of Italians awaiting the arrival of their compatriots." At moments like this, chaos ruled on deck, with one observer noting "the confusion and din and the shrill voices of the women rising high above the deep tones of the men who crowded and squeezed to the ship's side as they called and bawled out greetings to frantic and joyous relatives and friends that were packed and massed like sardines in a box along the line of ropes." He continued, "Such yells and gesticulations, as mutual recognitions flashed across from ship to shore and shore to ship are only of the domain of actuality when an Italian immigrants' contingent touches at our wharves."[2]

After the gangplank was lowered, the passengers surged toward the shed on the wharf where U.S. Customs inspectors examined baggage for contraband. According to a 1901 account, "The feminine contingent wore shawls of deep blue or red or flaming yellow, and skirts and bodices of pronounced hue, and as they trotted down the gang plank at double quick," they looked "like a distracted and wildly-excited flock of variegated tropical birds." By the end of this particular day, the 759 passengers of the *California* had "dispersed helter-skelter to the four points of the compass," melting into the French Quarter with family and friends. "With the first twinkling of the harbor electric lights," noted the *New Orleans Daily Picayune*, "the tasks of the United States inspectors and of policemen were concluded." And so ended what for most of the new arrivals would be the most memorable day of their lives.[3]

While thousands newcomers from Sicily arrived in New Orleans in circumstances that mirrored those of the steerage-class passengers aboard the *California*, the broader portrait was much more complex. By 1900, the Sicilian enclave in New Orleans had long since evolved into a socially and economically diverse community. Migration to the city in the nineteenth century had favored the merchants and tradesmen of Messina and Palermo over *contadini* from the poorer agricultural Sicilian hinterland, and within the French Quarter this urban class had grown remarkably wealthy and socially influential. More important, they had grown American in outlook if not in language and culture. These elites may not have viewed the immigrants who began pouring into New Orleans at the end of the century with as much alarm as their middle-American Protestant counterparts, but they surely recognized that the sudden arrival of so many of their countrymen had just as much potential for risk as for reward.

Despite the fact that this flood of Sicilian peasants was not the first time huge immigrant waves hit New Orleans, the city was shockingly unprepared to handle these new arrivals. The rapid pace and slipshod nature of Custom House inspections gave New Orleanians pause, and their fears were not completely unfounded. The hunger for Italian labor in the fields of Louisiana, Arkansas, Mississippi, and Texas certainly influenced this laxity, but so, too, did the complete absence of any sort of immigrant-processing facility like the one found at Ellis Island. As early as 1896, observers described the situation as "an injury to the section," but not until the summer of 1906 did construction begin on the modest facility at the foot of Elysian Fields Avenue. Until then, doctors from the Marine Hospital rode a tugboat into the river, within sight of the French Quarter, and climbed up the side of each ship to conduct health inspections. In November 1902, for instance, a handful of doctors took just four hours to examine the 1,345 immigrants aboard the *Manila*. Custom House examinations of luggage often took even less time. With no land-based facility, more thorough inspections were impractical and unrealistic. For fugitives or those suffering from concealable ailments that might have otherwise ensnared them at Ellis Island, New Orleans represented a much more forgiving port of entry.[4]

Dr. Allan McLoughlin, in charge of the U.S. Marine Hospital and Public Health Service at the New York Immigration Bureau, took a philosophical stance toward native fears about the habits of the thousands of Sicilian immigrants pouring into the nation's cities. In a revealing interview with *Popular Science*, he observed that "the crimes charged to the Italians are usually crimes of violence, actuated by revenge for real or fancied wrongs. These are outgrowths of the custom of taking the law in their own hands in a country where the poor had little or no redress from the law. But in the aggregate of crime the Italian, by reason of his sobriety, presents a better record in this country than many of the races commonly classed as desirable." McLoughlin was essentially right, yet his words did little to allay the fears of white Protestant Americans who saw in this ethnic group the seed of a dangerous criminal class. To a degree, their fears are with us still, perpetuated by a variety of forces, both real and imagined, transmitted across the decades through media outlets ranging from televised coverage of the House Un-American Activities Committee hearings in the 1950s to the popular HBO series *The Sopranos* half a century later. That Sicilian Americans are often as complicit as outsiders in cultivating the mystique of the mafioso only increases the breadth of this cultural phenomenon's reach.[5]

At the same time, an alternative narrative that also originated in the nineteenth century chronicles the Sicilian immigrant's sustained successful embrace of American-style capitalism. Building on their dominance of the fruit trade and finding in bananas a more profitable substitute for the Sicily lemon, Sicilian American entrepreneurs embraced new industries, making business decisions a century ago that established the foundations of commercial empires that most Americans would recognize today. This entrepreneurial impulse could not be reconciled with cultural violence and vendetta, traditions carried to America in the ancestral baggage of the old country, without bloodshed.

The debate over the presence and extent of Black Hand or Mafia culture in Sicilian New Orleans has attracted a disproportionate amount of attention from historians and journalists over the past forty years, leaving New Orleanians of Sicilian descent sensitive about the conspicuous role of this focus in renderings of their history. Before agreeing to an oral history interview, one of my subjects looked at me dubiously and asked, "You're not doing one of those 'Who killa da chief?' things, are you?" That taunt was directed at several generations of Sicilian kids and supposedly originated in the electrically charged atmosphere surrounding the 1891 trial of the men accused of murdering New Orleans police chief David Hennessey. Some authors speculate that the Mafia originated in New Orleans as early as the Reconstruction era, while others argue that despite the presence of a few criminal figures with ties to the Sicilian Mafia in the late nineteenth century, organized crime as we know it did not truly materialize in New Orleans until the late 1920s. A distinction exists between what we understand as a syndicated Mafia and gangland or factional violence. Turn-of-the-century New Orleans might not have had the former, but it definitely had its share of the latter, often amplified in news coverage fed to an audience hungering for true-crime narratives.

Indeed, Sicilian New Orleans could be incredibly violent in the first two decades of the twentieth century. The media's fascination with Black Hand and Mafia activity died down in the immediate years after the Hennessey lynching but reemerged more keenly than ever around 1900 with an outbreak of grisly extended violence between Sicilian-born rivals. The bloodshed often resulted from personal feuds over property claims or a share of the macaroni market as well as from the low-rent style of kidnapping and extortion that was common in Sicilian enclaves at that time. Kinship ties and the tradition of vendetta tended to perpetuate these feuds, often yielding multiple related attacks and homicides. Yet to label this activity the product of an organized Mafia or Black Hand society, as sensationalized by the newspapers of the era, credits such crimes with greater powers of systemic planning than they deserve. An organized crime syndicate eventually emerged in New Orleans under Sylvestro Carollo and later Carlos Marcello, although even this view may overstate the extent of the organization: although hearsay is abundant, more tangible evidence is scant. Organized or semiorganized crime operated for decades with the willing cooperation of people from a broad spectrum of ethnic backgrounds. In contrast, the crimes attributed to the Black Hand in the first decade of the twentieth century had no greater foe than the Sicilian businessmen who had begun to achieve the American Dream, although they, too, resorted to violence to protect their mercantile empires.[6]

The Jefferson Parish suburb of Kenner is today literally indistinguishable from the rest of the sprawling residential and light commercial development that stretches between the Orleans Parish line and the protection levee that divides the metro area from the waterlogged western half of Lake Pontchartrain. This geographic border is most evident today when driving eastbound on Interstate 10 or flying into Armstrong International at night, when the edges of the lake and Bonnet Carré Spillway are neatly delineated from the pitch-black darkness by a cordon of lightbulbs. The New Orleans, Jackson, and Great Northern Railroad cut through this sugar-planting country in 1854, but not until the 1890s did Sicilian immigrants—both those who had recently arrived and those who had migrated away from the cane fields—begin to settle in large numbers the area known as Kennerville. Not only were their truck farms a mere day's wagon ride down River Road from the vendor stalls in the public markets of New Orleans, but when the Illinois Central took over the rail line, fast-growing Chicago entered the commercial orbit of those who tilled Kenner's fertile acres. At the peak of production, "over sixty refrigerated carloads of locally grown produce" headed north on the Illinois Central every month, an arrangement that tied the modest farms of Kenner to the wholesale produce tycoons living in the French Quarter. The same was also true of any number of Italian enclaves along the great rail line, including the strawberry fields of Tangipahoa Parish. In the first three decades of the twentieth century, the parishes surrounding New Orleans functioned the same way that Southern California and large swaths of Florida do today, supplying the rest of the nation with fruits and vegetables. But like West End's hotels and restaurants, these enterprises have both vanished from the landscape and disappeared from our historical consciousness.[7]

A notorious 1907 incident revealed the close linkages between the Sicilians who worked in the produce fields in the outlying parishes and in the Italian Colony in the French Quarter. The inexpensive regularity of the Illinois Central had enabled workers to commute between the city and country to find employment as seasonal laborers at harvest time. Difficult work, it attracted many of the people who filled the transient lower social strata in New Orleans. On a July Saturday night, a group of conspirators drawn from this peripatetic class used the promise of candy to lure young Walter Lamana, the son of prosperous undertaker Peter Lamana, into a wagon and carried him away from the city. They took the boy to a truck farm in St. Rose, where they locked him in an outhouse and sent a clumsily worded demand to his father for a six-thousand-dollar ransom. Meanwhile, the boy's cries soon proved so obnoxious that his captors strangled him. A Hahnville jury later concluded that a barely seventeen-year-old boy, Leonardo Gebbia, masterminded the affair with the help of his sister, Nicolina; his brother, Frank; and their parents.

The way in which the crime unfolded revealed the intense locality and social proximity of the Italian Colony as well as the growing tension between recently arrived Sicilian immigrants and the established merchant class of New Orleans. The Gebbia family, who lived at 613 St. Philip Street, right across the street from the Lamanas at 624 St. Philip, certainly played an active role in the conspiracy, probably serving as the city liaison for the St. Charles Parish criminals who planned and executed the crime. Newspapers throughout the region publicized the ransom demand, with tabloid journalists suggesting that the conspiracy was the work of the Black Hand. Indeed, the kidnappers themselves fueled the rumor of Black Hand involvement, possibly hoping that the prospect of such a mythological foe would frighten the elder Lamana into meeting their demands.

They had not bargained that the undertaker would turn to the police, who quickly cracked the flimsy extortion scheme. After a surprisingly short interrogation, a frightened Leonardo Gebbia confessed in full to his part in the crime, while another conspirator led officers to the boy's decapitated body, which for some days had bobbed half submerged under a tree root in the swamp. The members of the kidnapping conspiracy, including the individual who may have strangled the child, went to trial first and received life imprisonment, much to the dismay of a crowd of observers who had gathered to see a sterner form of justice meted out. Several other members of the gang remained fugitives, while young Leonardo Gebbia, the final conspirator tried and sentenced, hanged for the deed.[8]

Lamana's killers and others who committed crimes against their countrymen labored under the increasingly inaccurate notion that Sicilians, having come from a country where they could not trust the law, would continue to deal with such brigandage without the aid of the police. The criminals were only partly correct in their thinking: the merchants of New Orleans were willing to use both legal and extralegal means to protect their own. The Lamana kidnapping galvanized support among wealthier Sicilians for the creation of the Italian Vigilance Committee, which aided state and local authorities' pursuit of the kidnappers and ultimately proved essential in their capture and punishment. The committee even took the unusual step of hiring a special prosecuting attorney, Chandler C. Luzenberg, whose selection carried great symbolism since he had prosecuted the Italians accused of murdering David Hennessey nearly two decades earlier.

The committee represented the aspirations of those Sicilians who had come to New Orleans before 1890 and prospered under the American system. Its chair was J. Lawrence Federico, who operated a macaroni factory with his brother in the French Quarter at 1000 Chartres Street. (The factory he built on this site in 1920 is today home to Irene's Restaurant.) Another "leading spirit" of the committee was a forty-six-year-old Partanna native, Vincent Taormina, an importer and commission merchant who became a U.S. citizen in 1892. A third key player, Charles Patorno, was a judge with close political ties to the Democratic Ring, a political alliance in the fashion of late-nineteenth-century urban bossism and associated with ethnic groups and labor unions. Yet despite vowing to work closely with law enforcement, the vigilance committee also operated within the traditional confines of Sicilian secrecy when doing so suited the group's purposes, and it received a significant amount of sympathy from the press when it engaged in extralegal intimidation or acted in "self-defense." Indeed, one article suggested that the committee would soon seek a charter under the suggestive name White Hand League, a nod to the city's tradition of elite reformer vigilantism. The Lamana case marked a turning point for Sicilian New Orleans, motivating immigrant elites to crush the sort of petty banditry that had always hampered economic progress in the old country—and crush it they would, one way or another.[9]

These prosperous macaroni makers, importers, and produce wholesalers made their feelings toward extortionists and petty criminals even more clear in the aftermath of a bloody episode at the Beauregard-Keyes House, now one of the more popular French Quarter historic sites. Located on Chartres Street across from the old Ursuline convent, the grand mansion was built for a wealthy auctioneer in 1826 when the neighborhood still retained some of its cachet as a desirable location for the Creole elite. In 1866, the elegant house passed into the hands of Dominique Lanata, a wealthy commercial merchant and native of Genoa who intended to use it as rental property. His first tenant and house's most famous occupant, Confederate general Pierre Gustave Toutant Beauregard, had recently returned to his home state after the war. Recently widowed for the second time, the Little Creole needed spacious quarters for his children and extended family, and Lanata's property was available at an attractive price. Beauregard's sons later recalled this era with little affection, pointing out that it occurred during a time of yellow fever, "and much distress was all around them." The French Quarter had already begun to decline before the Civil War, with wealthier families moving further up the Esplanade Ridge or to the Garden District. Lanata's house was an elegant and airy home with an increasingly undesirable address. The general stayed in the mansion only briefly, as his recovering fortunes enabled him to acquire more stately accommodations in Uptown by 1868. Yet his ties to the city's Italian community lasted much longer. In 1873 he served as the president of the Immigrant and Homestead Association, which later encouraged the migration of Sicilian peasants.[10]

In 1904, Lanata sold the landmark to Corrado Giacona, the scion of a wealthy wine-importing family. A photograph of the mansion from this time reveals just how much the elements had deteriorated its splendor. The wood grain of the porch's Doric columns has been laid bare by rain and sun, paint is peeling across the facade, and the large chunks of stucco broken away from the foundation bring to mind Clarence Laughlin and Robert Tebbs's black-and-white photographs of abandoned southern plantation homes that have since burned to ash. Hand-painted lettering on the front of the house reads "C. GIACONA & CO. WHOLESALE LIQUOR DEALERS." Tour guides today still exclaim in amazement that the Giacona family sought to have the building demolished in the 1920s to build a macaroni factory. True or not, the allegation reveals the persistence of the powerful memory that the Sicilian era in the French Quarter constituted a time of architectural crisis.[11]

The wine merchant's father, Pietro, emigrated from Sicily with his wife, Maria, and eldest daughter in 1875, though the rest of their children, including Corrado, did not arrive until 1893. Pietro Giacona also made money by pressing wine from raisins in the basement of his New Orleans home, "selling principally to his countrymen, especially those living in the country." A 1907 ad run by Corrado Giacona warning "all parties" against claiming a lost negotiable warehouse receipt for 300 boxes of raisins held at the New Orleans Cold Storage warehouse gives some indication of the volume imported. Oenophiles may still buy "raisin wine" (*vini passiti*) produced in Sicily, though most vintages pressed on the island today fall into the classification of dessert wine or liqueur. The far more popular dry red Amarone della Valpolicella results from a similar process in which grapes age to a near-raisin state that intensifies the tannins yielded from the fruit's skin and deepens the flavor of the resulting wine. Pressing semidried grapes necessarily yields less juice per ton, resulting in a more expensive product. Yet *vini passiti*, also known as straw wine because straw mats are traditionally used in the drying process, also has very desirable cellaring properties, and the varietals produced in Sicily would have done well in the similar though wetter climate of New Orleans. Thus, cultural expectations, forgiving shelf life, and environmental conditions made *vini passiti* a logical choice for Giacona and Company to market to rural Sicilian farmworkers on this side of the Atlantic.[12]

About 9:30 on one mid-June evening, just one year after the Lamana kidnapping, four men came calling at the home of Corrado and Pietro Giacona. The men were not unknown to the Giaconas: one of them, Ciro Cusimano (no relation to importer and strawberry grower Jacob Cusimano), worked as a laborer and lived nearby in the French Quarter. Two of the others, Giovanni and Nunzio Barreca, were from New Sarpy and Sellers, Louisiana, farming communities near present-day Norco and not far from the St. Rose community where the Lamana kidnappers lived. Both had purchased raisin wine from Giacona. The fourth man, Francisco Vitalli, had been in the United States for just six months and worked driving a wagon hauling oyster shells. The Giaconas invited the visitors through the iron doors that led into the basement of the home and spent some time discussing wine and other business. The Barrecas apparently owed Giacona a considerable amount of money for wine but had just ordered another shipment. Now they seemed to be making more demands, suggesting that they were not men with whom it was wise to trifle. Like Walter Lamana's kidnappers, the men from the rural parishes believed that making their victim believe in the terror of a supposed Black Hand would prove an advantage. They soon discovered the magnitude of their error.

The four men suggested that Pietro Giacona feed them a late-night supper, perhaps because refusing his guests ran against the Italian sense of hospitality or because he believed that he had no choice in the matter—or because he had already settled on a plan of action. The dining room of the Beauregard-Keyes House is in the rear of the building, with a series of narrow French doors that lead out to a wide gallery and a double set of stairs that descend into the courtyard. The extortionists consumed large quantities of their host's wine and became increasingly loud: tenants living in the old dependency buildings that surrounded the courtyard could hear Pietro through the warm night air beseeching the men to tamp down their outbursts and coarse language. Occasionally peering over their windowsills, these witnesses saw the six men sitting in their undershirts under the yellow glow of the dining room light and passed a sleepless evening aware that something out of the ordinary was under way. A little before 2:30 in the morning, Ciro Cusimano and Giovanni Barreca began demanding money from the older Giacona, who protested that he had no cash on hand. When the men refused Pietro's offer to write a check, he excused himself from the table and returned not with cash but with his hands wrapped around a new Winchester repeating rifle. Ciro Cusimano was probably the first to die, shot through the chest with Giacona's first "steel jacketed" bullet. The Barreca cousins made a break for the doors leading onto the gallery, but they were too late, with Giovanni meeting death on the gallery and Nunzio cut down as he descended the back steps, his body tumbling to the courtyard below. In the commotion, Corrado Giacona retrieved a semiautomatic pistol and joined his father in blazing away at the men. He later recalled, "I was like a crazy man. My father was standing in the door. I pushed close to him and began to shoot. Some of the men fell, and I continued to shoot at them on the floor. I don't know whether I emptied the pistol or not." Only Vitalli, who had been shot through a lung while fleeing through the courtyard, made it out alive. He burst through the door of one of the tenants' rooms and climbed over a wall. When the police caught up with him, he was "lying beneath a shed, with a [dead] spring chicken pressed to his wound" in an unconvincing effort to pretend that he hadn't been shot.

When Detective D'Antoni and Captain Capo—themselves Italian—arrived fifteen minutes later, they found bullet holes in walls and floors, spent shell casings, three dead bodies, and Vitalli's blood spoor tracing his route of escape. Pietro and Corrado Giacona were unhurt. Taking them as well as a third man who lived in the household, Pietro Bellone, into custody, the policemen surely knew that they had a complicated case on their hands. Trying to get some neighborhood intelligence the next day, the *New Orleans Daily Picayune* heard nothing but positive feedback from "the good Italians of the city" who "were jubilant and lauded the deadly work of Pietro Giacono [*sic*] to the skies." Once again raising the specter of organized crime in the Sicilian community, the paper noted that "extreme satisfaction at the probable extinction of the curse of the Black Hand was apparent to all who spoke for the better class of Italians of this city."[13]

The members of the Italian Vigilance Committee swung into action almost immediately to their fellow merchant. Meeting in the banquet hall of the brand-new Hotel Denechaud (today Le Pavillon on Poydras Street) they agreed to the necessity of "concerted action on the part of the Italian citizens and the police department," but subsequent conversations about the appropriateness of presenting Pietro and Corrado Giacona with medals for gunning down Cusimano and the Barrecas surely undermined their claimed devotion to objective justice. So, too, did the fact that neither the Giaconas nor the badly wounded Vitalli would initially admit to having been present in the courtyard despite the trail of blood leading directly from the mansion and where the police had apprehended Vitalli. As in the Lamana kidnapping, the committee turned to Luzenberg, hiring him to act as the Giaconas' defense counsel. The Associated Press picked up the story of the shooting, leading to sensational headlines such as "Rich Italian Slays Blackmailing Guests" and "Death to Black Hand" in newspapers from Pensacola to Los Angeles. The country as a whole shared in the keen media fascination with immigrant criminality, seeming to revel in the gory details of how these supposed Black Hand extortionists met their deaths.[14]

Almost all of the testimony from the trial benefited the Giaconas, who were denied bail and consequently lingered for about a month in the "boarding" section of the prison, where they could receive an unlimited number of guests. Pietro appeared in court each day neatly dressed and wearing a medallion reportedly given to him by the queen of Italy. (Family lore held that his wife had worked in the royal household.) If witnesses testified to the upstanding nature of the defendants, the dead men and their families endured intense scrutiny from a press interested in proving that they belonged to the dreaded Black Hand. Furthering the suggestion that such crimes formed part of a coordinated conspiracy, the *New Orleans Times-Picayune* noted that the Barrecas had been questioned regarding the Lamana kidnapping. While visiting the morgue to examine the bodies, the judge handling the Giacona case noticed that Giovanni and Nunzio Barreca and Ciro Cusimano all had unusual marks on their feet. Although the coroner had dismissed the scars—all of which were "identical in size" and ran "on each side of the beginning of the heel, nearly under the instep"—as the product of bad shoes, the judge questioned some Italians, "and several of them expressed the opinion that the scars were marks of identification made in an Italian prison." The revelation seemed to confirm what many Americans already believed: the poorly regulated flood of immigrants from Southern Europe contained a criminal element that endangered the nation's peace and tranquility.[15]

The Giaconas won acquittal on all charges on grounds of self-defense and returned to their wine business, but their troubles continued. They began carrying handguns at all times and installed a heavy wrought iron brace on the mansion's front doors that "would baffle the most active jimmy-worker" (and that remains in use today). Such precautions were not the result of paranoia. On a September evening in 1910, an open wagon covered with a canvas tarp deliberately made its way down Chartres Street and slowed to a crawl in front of the Giacona compound. Two men burst out from under the tarp and joined the driver in firing pistols and shotguns at the rocking chairs on the house's gallery, acting out what might be the first documented drive-by shooting in New Orleans history. Their work seemingly done, the driver cracked the whip and the wagon took off through the streets of the French Quarter. A witness ran after the wagon and saw it disappear up Esplanade Avenue and turn onto Claiborne heading toward the Seventh Ward. Near St. Anthony Street, the wagon's left rear wheel fell off, "and the men jumped out of the conveyance and disappeared," bringing to an end the badly executed attack: in the dark, the gunmen could not tell that the rocking chairs were empty.[16]

Clues in the case soon led police detectives back to the Kennerville farm where John Barreca, the son of one of the men who had died at the Giacona home in 1908, and his cousin, Antonio, grew vegetables. They and a third man, Verusa, had supposedly bought a wagon from an acquaintance living in another marginal part of the metropolitan area, the Lower Ninth Ward. The three men were tried, but the jury refused to convict them, though it is not clear whether their acquittal resulted from insufficient evidence or from jurors' belief that the criminals would probably receive justice through unofficial channels. What is crystal clear, however, is the mainstream media's tacit acceptance of the methods employed by those unknown parties who dealt with Tony Barreca and his friends in the months after the botched attack on the Giacona house.[17]

The first to die was J. Di Christina, who divided his time between Donaldsonville and New Orleans and whom many of the city's merchants believed was a key leader in the violent extortion rackets that had plagued Sicilians over the previous few years. The trial of his killer, Peter Pepitone, revealed that Di Christina was really Paolo Marchesi and that he was a fugitive from a Sicilian jail. Pepitone's attorney, Captain Albert David Henriques, pled with the judge for leniency even though the defendant had admitted to gunning down Marchesi "in broad daylight as he was entering his saloon and grocery store at the corner of Liberty and Calliope." Marchesi had rented a building from Pepitone directly across Calliope Street from Pepitone's store but had refused to pay his rent and twice beat up the older Pepitone when asked for payment. Did Pepitone get the green light from others in the tightly knit Sicilian community to take action? We will never know for sure what motivated the soft-spoken shopkeeper to walk across Calliope Street on the morning of April 13, 1910, with two loaded shotguns, but the coincidences of time, place, and person are compelling. If the first blast from Pepitone's single-barreled model didn't kill Marchesi, then the buckshot from a sawed-off double surely did. The judge sentenced the old man to twenty years in Angola Penitentiary for manslaughter.[18]

On the same April morning that Pepitone killed Marchesi, an unknown assailant gunned down Tony Barreca as he worked the fields of his New Sarpy farm in St. Charles Parish. Barreca had been released only a month earlier after his acquittal in the botched shooting. Barreca's son reported seeing a man with a red kerchief over his face emerge from the trees in the early morning fog and open fire with a "Winchester rifle of heavy bore." Three shots sent the son as well as Barreca's plow mule running in a panic away from the scene. A grisly spectacle awaited those who returned later for the body. Tony Barreca's head had been split open with an axe, and his brains had been removed and placed on a sheet of paper by his head. No one was ever charged in the murder, which took place not far from where police had found Walter Lamana's body several years earlier; police suspected that the Barrecas had been involved in that crime.[19]

Another associate of Barreca and Marchesi, George Di Martini, died two months later. Blond, freckled, and very tall—looking "anything but Italian," as the *Times-Picayune* noted—Di Martini stood out among the dark-eyed inhabitants of the Sicilian French Quarter. Perhaps for this reason, witnesses noticed him standing with two other men on the streetcar tracks at the intersection of Bourbon and St. Ann Streets just before noon. Without provocation, one of his companions pulled a revolver and shot Di Martini just below the arm at a range so close that it left powder burns on his clothing. Wounded, Di Martini fled into a nearby bar, but his assailants followed, shooting him several more times before departing. One of the men apprehended was a United Fruit employee, Vincent Moreci, whom police carried to Charity Hospital in hopes that the dying Di Martini might be able to identify the perpetrator. When Di Martini shook his head *no* to indicate that Moreci was not the shooter, the police let him go although several witnesses placed him in the street with Di Martini. Some months earlier, Moreci himself had been wounded in an attack in which a bullet grazed his forehead. He was also a friend of the Giacona family and a professional associate of many other prosperous French Quarter merchants. Yet in keeping with popular perceptions, the *Picayune* headline declared that Di Martini had been "killed in [a] real Mafia way."[20]

Henriques, who had represented the poorer Pepitone, also served as defense attorney for the middle-class Moreci. Henriques was born in the Caribbean but moved to antebellum New Orleans as a young man, and he, like many of the city's other elite young men, joined the Confederate army in April 1861, just weeks after he was admitted to the bar. As part of Colonel Charles Dreux's battalion, Henriques served under luminaries such as Charles Fenner and fought throughout the war, though not as an officer. Like John Astredo, Henriques did not gain the title *Captain* until Reconstruction, when he organized a company of White Leaguers during the Battle of Liberty Place, a hallowed event in the pantheon of elite white New Orleans families. His defense of those accused of gunning down the criminal element among the Sicilian community revealed the close economic and perspectival ties that had developed between the leaders of the Sicilian French Quarter and the city's older elite white power structure. The difference between perceiving such violence as organized crime or as retributive justice seems to have hinged greatly on an observer's proximity to power.[21]

The local press lauded the means by which the Sicilian elite had stamped out the city's "Black Hand" element. "As to the last member of this gang," noted one journalist, "he has left the country and returned to Italy. He will hardly venture back here again, unless he should succeed in enlisting another band of cutthroats and murderers, in which event they will soon be heard of and Black Hand stories again become frequent." The Italian Vigilance Committee hardly erased Sicilian criminality, but the Giacona affair seems to have placed some boundaries around it by the start of the First World War, creating a terrain on which the city's wealthy Italian merchant class might operate unmolested, though poorer Sicilians might still feel the sting of petty criminals. Prohibition, of course, eventually changed the entire relationship between Sicilians and the criminal landscape.[22]

Though Corrado Giacona is commonly considered "the first boss of the New Orleans crime family," that claim is complete nonsense. Nevertheless, it will doubtlessly live on through the workings of a cottage industry of online Mafia groupies whose undocumented claims feed the obsessions of a willingly cooperative audience. Giacona and the other members of the Italian Vigilance Committee indeed took collective and violent action to protect their mutual commercial interests in the French Quarter between 1890 and 1910. Most of these men had immigrated to America in the nineteenth century and understood the dangers of anti-Italian nativism, especially in the wake of the lynching that followed the acquittal of the alleged Hennessey assassins. Yet these men were also "progressive" businessmen who had found in New Orleans the path to wealth and position, and they were not about to allow a collection of recently arrived criminals to undermine their growing acceptance as the captains of the city's emerging economic sectors. The hiring of Luzenberg, a scion of the city's white elite, and of Henriques could not have sent a clearer message to the political class about the Vigilance Committee's willingness to be associated with mainstream America. The Sicilian tycoons identified more closely with the Hennessy lynch mob and the White League than with those countrymen who stood accused of dastardly crimes. In this regard, these founding families of the city's Italian food industry took part in a long tradition of extralegal vigilantism practiced by the oldest and most respected names in the city. This spirit harmonized surprisingly well with the ancient Sicilian custom of vendetta.

As Sicilian immigrants became more culturally and economically Americanized in the 1910s, they in turn began to Italianize the American diet. No single food was more responsible for this than dried durum wheat pasta, better known to most Americans of the era simply as *macaroni*. Its journey to the American dinner table unfolded hand in glove with the rise of urban Sicilian prosperity and demographic growth. Any child who has joyously belted out the first verse of "Yankee Doodle" should realize that Americans have been aware of pasta since before the nation's birth, yet a century and a half passed before the noodles went mainstream. According to Italian food expert John Dickie, European travelers taking the "grand tour" in the late seventeenth and early eighteenth centuries witnessed the poor *lazzari* of Naples gobbling up steaming handfuls of *maccheroni* bought from the city's street vendors. (These noodles were also the inspiration for a macaroni wig and the word's subsequent journey into the lyrics of "Yankee Doodle.") The Neapolitan screw press, a machine that forces the dough down a tube and extrudes it through a metal plate with holes in it, had by the 1730s transformed durum wheat pasta into one of the Western world's first cheap mass-produced foods. By the end of the eighteenth century, its manufacture had spread beyond Italy. As Dickie notes, "The best guide to late eighteenth-century pasta manufacturing techniques was published by Parisian baker and pasta maker Paul-Jacques Malouin in 1767." Captivated by tales of this machine, Thomas Jefferson in 1789 became the first American to import a macaroni press.[23]

The first pasta made in New Orleans was not manufactured by a Sicilian but instead by a Spaniard, Francisco Sambola, who had immigrated from Catalonia as a teenager in 1816. An 1832 city directory shows him manufacturing "vermicelli" on a stretch of St. Claude Avenue in the neighborhood of Tremé today called Henriette Delille Street. Sambola prospered and ultimately acquired a three-story brick building on Levee Street (today Decatur) near the corner of Ursulines so that he could expand his operation. Here he branched out into making chocolate, an activity that in July 1849 led an early morning fire that fully consumed the building. The blaze moved so rapidly that Sambola had only enough time to flee with his important papers, but he was luckier than Charles, a twenty-two-year-old slave who burned to death in the blaze. Sambola rebuilt his macaroni factory, only to lose it to another fire thirty-three years later. The timing was unfortunate: the local market for pasta was about to explode.[24]

In 1882, the year of Sambola's second factory fire, fewer than three thousand people classified as Italian lived in Louisiana, and the regional demand for pasta was easily met through local production and imports arriving on the same ships that brought Sicily lemons. By 1910, however, almost forty-five thousand Italian nationals and their children called the Pelican State home. The growth of this population spurred the creation of a thriving local pasta industry that introduced the Crescent City to the possibilities of a staple ingredient that would one day become as ubiquitous on local menus as shrimp and oysters.

Significant American production of macaroni by Italian immigrants took root first in New York City, which by 1900 had surpassed New Orleans and soon far eclipsed all other American destinations in its popularity among Sicilian émigrés. In 1894, a reporter described a four-story brick macaroni factory on New York's West Side that (erroneously) claimed to make all the pasta consumed in America. This "odd and interesting place" featured all the latest forms of mechanized macaroni pressing, looking "as if they might have figured conspicuously in a medieval torture exhibition." Even before the turn of the century, pasta had become popular in larger northern cities as a side dish, introduced to the American table at restaurants featuring table d'hôte dinners. "Our grandfathers never ate spaghetti, vermicelli, macaroni and dishes of that sort," noted the reporter with a degree of ignorance, but macaroni began to grow in popularity in the 1880s as Americans began sampling the broader array of ethnic foods brought by the immigrants pouring into the nation's urban core.[25]

While macaroni was manufactured in New Orleans as early as the 1830s, the city's dailies probably did not notice Sicilian involvement in its production until it was already well under way. In 1894, Custom House inspectors arrested an Italian, Gaetano Rizzuto, for trying to smuggle two macaroni machines into the city. Five years later, the president of New York's A. F. Ghiglione Macaroni Company complimented the emergent "home industry" of pasta makers in New Orleans for meeting the growing demand in the southern region.

The macaroni magnate attributed the shift toward domestic production to the Dingley Tariff Act of 1897, which raised the duties on imported pasta as much as 45 percent. "Before that bill went into effect," he observed, "imported macaroni in New Orleans amounted to 50,000 and 60,000 boxes a year." By 1899, that amount had dropped to no more than 20,000 boxes. Months before the passage of the tariff bill, the executive had gone to Naples and "contracted for the entire output of fifteen or twenty factories of that famous macaroni-making city," but the Dingley Tariff "knocked our scheme higher than a kite," and he rushed back to Naples to cancel his orders before they ruined the company. The incident not only exemplified the ripple effects of a transportation revolution that had upended old economic patterns but also marked the beginning of an opportunity for Sicilian immigrants, who recognized macaroni's potential in America.[26]

The Dingley Tariff certainly coincided with a boom in new macaroni-making operations in New Orleans, transforming the French Quarter into the hub of this nascent industry. In 1901, the Quarter was home to seven of the city's eight macaroni factories, six of which were owned and operated by Sicilians. In addition, there is no way to know how many small-scale operators produced macaroni in back rooms of stores or at home. Yet the pasta or *paste* business was definitely heading toward industrialization. In 1903, Salvatore Messina, who had lived "in the neighborhood of the French Market" for thirty-five years, hired a prominent engineer, Robert Palestine, to build a macaroni factory equipped with the latest technology. With electric fans to hasten the drying process, Messina and Palestine hoped that such forward thinking would ensure New Orleans's role as "the macaroni center of the United States."[27]

The early fortunes of Giacomo Cusimano illustrate the interconnections among the business of food, kinship networks, and the transatlantic perspective of Sicilian immigrants who grasped the potential of the comparatively great economic freedom New Orleans offered. The twenty-year-old Cusimano had been married for only a fortnight when he left Palermo for New Orleans in 1882, leaving behind his sixteen-year-old bride. Almost immediately Americanizing his name to Jacob, Cusimano spent the next six years apprenticing in the produce business of his kinsman, Angelo Cusimano. Once joined by his wife and growing family, Cusimano founded a wholesale fruit business and expanded into imports, "dealing chiefly in lemons from Italy." Yet to have truly arrived in the commercial world in the turn-of-the-century Sicilian French

Quarter, one needed to be in the macaroni business. In 1897, despite some opposition from neighbors, Cusimano persuaded the city to permit him to convert an 1840 Greek revival structure at 625 St. Philip Street into a *paste* factory (later the home of Ruffino's Italian Restaurant and Bakery). At the height of production, the machinery whirring away inside the old antebellum structure consumed fifty sacks of flour a day.

Cusimano's financial ascent epitomized the way in which the Sicilian conception of the American Dream unfolded in New Orleans. In a move that surely makes preservationists today cringe, the entrepreneur decided that it made the most business sense to replace his retrofitted Creole townhouse with a purpose-built facility for manufacturing macaroni products. The site he selected for this enterprise was the corner of Chartres and Barracks in the French Quarter, which as late as 1902 contained only the gardens for the once-proud Forstall House. The construction of a three-story brick pasta factory certainly intensified the industrial feel of the French Quarter's Esplanade side, but to onlookers from diverse quarters, the din of construction reverberated with the sound of optimism. At the cornerstone-laying ceremony, Sam Guarini, the editor of *L'Italo-Americano*, climbed atop a platform decorated with American and Italian flags and spoke in Italian "of what the building of the factory meant to New Orleans; of how it showed a spirit of progressiveness." When the speeches were done, Cusimano invited members of the crowd to an adjacent building for a luncheon where "there was a profusion of all sorts of delicacies, and wine flowed freely." So lubricated, "the guests formed into a procession," noted the *New Orleans Daily Picayune*, "and, placing Mr. Cusimano at the head, marched to his residence, where a reception was held last evening."[28]

When Cusimano's factory opened for production later that summer, the newspaper labeled its proprietor "a progressive young Italo-American" and proclaimed the facility the largest of its kind in the United States. Its daily output of ten thousand pounds of pasta tripled that of the old facility on St. Philip Street, and it produced a variety of shapes that astounded the reporter: "Here the strings which become sticks are cut and prepared in all sizes, from the thickness of a pin to the large tubes which are considered so delicious by some." The factory proudly featured electric power and freight elevators and employed thirty men. Noted the *Picayune*, "At present, the manufacturers of Italian paste in New York and other northern cities control most of the output, but with this new factory New Orleans can practically control the southern business." As plant manager, Cusimano hired Leon Tujague, the brother of the city comptroller and not even an Italian.[29]

To many, the factory was indeed the oft-touted embodiment of "progress." Cusimano was indeed a "progressive" immigrant who became an American citizen less than a year later. He also mastered the national ethos of capitalism, transforming a corner of a run-down neighborhood into a productive enterprise and providing jobs. His energy brought to New Orleans and the South a tangible manifestation of the sort of industrial growth of which it had long dreamed and boasted but had often failed to produce. Cusimano's Americanism was not in question.

The seeds of Jacob Cusimano's overt patriotism may have been planted when Angelo Cusimano had a brush with an escaped convict from Sicily, Giuseppe Esposito. In 1876, Esposito was among a group of bandits who kidnapped an English mining agent in the rough country south of Palermo, and the following year, they were captured by Sicilian police. These highwaymen often operated with the cooperation of local officials, so it was probably not a complete surprise when Esposito disappeared from custody while awaiting trial. It is even possible that his connections with the Palermo and Monreale Mafias had facilitated the escape. After fleeing to New York, Esposito made his way to New Orleans, where he assumed an alias and met produce importers Angelo Cusimano and Giuseppe Grande.

Recently arrived immigrants commonly purchased wholesale produce from their countrymen on the levee, oftentimes on credit, and then peddled it in the interior or on the city's streets. Cusimano and Esposito developed such an arrangement, with Cusimano extending particularly generous terms, perhaps because he was bullied into doing so. In 1881, however, a young detective, David Hennessey, caused quite a stir in the French Quarter's Italian Colony when he arrested Esposito—Cusimano and Grande were not the only businessmen who had associated with the fugitive. While in jail awaiting deportation, Esposito, with the aid of a New Orleans woman whom he had married, sued the two importers, claiming that they had wrongly seized his property, including his fishing lugger, the *Leone*. Cusimano and Grande thus were not sad to see Esposito sail back to Sicily in chains, and the Orleans Parish Civil District Court dismissed his suit the following year. They also must not have feared reprisal from any lingering underworld figures lurking about New Orleans when they sold the *Leone* to satisfy Esposito's debts. Journalist Thomas Hunt and other authors have seen in the Esposito affair a greater Mafia conspiracy in New Orleans, an accusation that certainly found currency in the sensationalized newspaper reports of the time. Yet both Angelo and Jacob Cusimano ultimately proved that greater and more enduring fortune lay in legitimate business ventures forged in the American mainstream, a historical narrative of greater substance if not drama.[30]

It is doubtful, however, that Jacob Cusimano could have anticipated his most visible legacy in the twenty-first century. In 1912, he invested heavily in real estate near the Italian enclave of Independence, in Louisiana's Tangipahoa Parish. With the turn-of-the-century introduction of the Klondyke variety of strawberry, cultivation of the crop in this region took off, and Cusimano decided to get in on the action. For a time, his Crescent Marketing Association, which distributed berries in the Upper Midwest, was the nation's fourth-largest supplier of the fruit. The label that appeared on crates of Patriot brand strawberries produced for J. Cusimano and Company depicts a bugler dressed in World War I–era olive drab uniform alongside a pile of deep red strawberries with lush green stems set on a deeply saturated blue background. This and other labels were the creation of a German-born lithographer, Ben Walle, who was known for printing elaborate invitations to Mardi Gras balls and whose designs helped sell Louisiana produce to a national market. A classic example of early twentieth-century graphic arts, they have found new life with online vendors who sell the nostalgic images printed on a wide range of products, among them coffee mugs, wall clocks, throw pillows, ties, and infant onesies.[31]

According to family lore, Jacob Cusimano also played a pivotal role in ensuring the future of an Italian food products empire. Giuseppe Uddo came to New Orleans in 1907 with his wife, Eleanora Taormina, to work with his in-laws in the grocery importing business. Unfortunately for Uddo, they stepped ashore at the Governor Nicholls Street Wharf just as the national credit market collapsed in what historians now call the Panic of 1907. The fledgling partnership between Uddo and the Taorminas struggled for just over two years, but on Christmas Eve of 1909, the operation fell into bankruptcy. Walking home dejectedly through the streets of the French Quarter that night, Uddo ran into Jacob Cusimano, who quickly spotted the concern on his friend's face. The prosperous merchant expressed a willingness to extend merchandise on credit for Uddo to sell, work that was familiar to the young immigrant; indeed, Uddo's sales had so impressed Eleanora's father back in Sicily that he had promised his daughter in marriage, much to her dismay. Now, having changed his name to Joe, Uddo ventured out to the rough and rural enclave of Kennerville in a two-wheeled cart pulled by a horse named Sal. Some of the merchandise was of the scratch-and-dent variety, and the Uddos would polish the cans with brick dust and reattach the labels before selling the goods. The couple made the most of the lifeline offered by Cusimano, and in the coming decades, the Uddos and the Taorminas reaped enormous dividends from their thrift and business acumen.[32]

The story of the Uddo dynasty's early days also reveals the tension between those newly arrived immigrants who sought freedom from the oppressive Sicilian ways and those who hoped to perpetuate those ways in America. As a girl in the 1930s, Rose Uddo Testa frequently accompanied her mother on visits to Corrado Giacona's sister, Rosina, a devout spinster living in a house on the edge of the French Quarter. Signorina Rosina frequently told her guests how her father killed men who sought to harm the family. When Giuseppe Uddo finally began turning a profit from his travels in Jefferson Parish, he attracted the attention of a band of extortionists, but his connections to the Giaconas ultimately protected him and allowed Uddo Brothers to continue selling canned goods and macaroni in the fields of Kennerville.[33]

In the winter of 1912, Will Branan published a colorful and insightful account that depicts how Protestant America viewed the growing macaroni business in New Orleans. A native of Georgia, Branan graduated from Alabama Polytechnic Institute at Auburn and spent time writing features for the *Atlanta Constitution* before moving on to comparatively exotic New Orleans to do the same for the *Daily Picayune*. A skilled writer with a humorous light touch, Branan carried his readers through the French Quarter "Spaghetti District." "Sitting in a Decatur Street Italian restaurant," opened Branan, "and gazing [in] open-mouthed awe at a marvelous prestidigital exhibition in which a plate of spaghetti disappeared from view in front of a swarthy Neapolitan, I was seized with a frantic desire for some of the stuff myself." When Branan asked for "a plate of that spaghetti," the waiter retorted, "He ess not spaghetti—ees capollinia noche." According to Branan, the "obliging waiter" then spent half an hour explaining "the difference between spaghetti, spaghettina and all of the other members of the macaroni family, big, little, and indifferent." Although Branan's playful (and to modern sensibilities chauvinistic) comments reflect the banter of a features writer in his element, his description of the range of pasta shapes and names was not far off the mark. "In fact, there is something futile about the very idea of a directory of pasta shapes," notes Dickie. "Probably no mathematical limit can be placed on the variety of threads, tubes, grains, ribbons, twists, shells, bows, nests, ears, curls, and hoops into which dough can be molded, rolled, squeezed, and cut. So it will surprise no one to learn that Italy has no unified system for cataloguing them." It is little wonder that native-born Americans still found pasta puzzling in the 1910s.[34]

For Branan, spaghetti was the most reliable barometer for measuring the rise of Italian culture in New Orleans:

It is affirmed, and not denied, that it is a physical impossibility for an Italian to go to bed without eating his plate of spaghetti. I do not know how true that is, but I do know that somebody makes away with an awful lot of spaghetti, and the other members of the macaroni family, in New Orleans. There are nearly a dozen macaroni factories on the downtown side of Canal Street, and only two on the uptown side. What does that signify, you ask? It demonstrates more conclusively than a ton of maps that the French quarter is being rapidly Italianized and that the process has already been completed in that portion of it which extends from Canal to Esplanade Avenue, and from Bourbon to the river. Go anywhere in this "spaghetti district," as in my attempt at facetiousness I called it, and it is not English or French that is heard on the lips of the children—it is Italian.

Branan also found virtue and even pride in the local production of pasta products. Italian manufacturers claimed that their product would always be superior to noodles made by Americans because of the special "farini" flour found in Italy. Yet, as Branan noted sardonically, "the local manufacturers claim that a good deal of the American wheat exported to Europe comes back to this country as macaroni, and that the greatest difference between the local product and its imported cousin consists in the ink that is used on the labels and the price that is paid by the consumer." At five cents a pound, a domestically produced package of pasta cost roughly half as much as its imported counterpart. The tariff on imported pasta as well as shipping charges greatly increased its cost. Branan closed his feature with observations on Sicilians' value to the city: "The financial success of an Italian may be traced by definite stages. Perhaps he was a penniless immigrant. He starts his business career as a peddler. The he acquires a fruit-stand; next a small grocery and bar; a larger barroom; then he branches out into whatever business or industry appeals to him." Conspicuously missing from the column are mentions of criminality or social defects.

Those New Orleanians who did not wish to travel to the working-class

Italian restaurants of the French Quarter to try pasta could always make it at home. Women's columns increasingly carried recipes to guide homemakers in the preparation of the unfamiliar food. "It is to be regretted that macaroni does not enter more largely into the dietary of the working classes of America," noted the author of the *Daily Picayune*'s "Woman's World and Work" column in 1912, "not less because of its cheapness and the ease with which it may be prepared than because of its nourishing qualities." A casserole that featured boiled noodles baked in layers of butter, cheese, and cream appeared regularly on the paper's luncheon menu by the turn of the twentieth century. The instructions were a far cry from today's familiar spaghetti and meatballs, however. Few modern cooks would disagree with the assertion that pasta "should always be plunged into plenty of boiling water to which there has been added a little salt," but they might weep with anguish at the idea of leaving it in the pot "from thirty to forty minutes, or until the macaroni is tender, when the tubes should have become double their original size." While pasta had been made in New Orleans for almost a hundred years, not until the manufacturing boom led by Sicilian immigrants in the first decade of the twentieth century did a wide audience learn to appreciate this delicious, nutritious, convenient, and inexpensive food.[35]

There was no greater sign that pasta had finally arrived as a staple of the American diet than when the former manager of Jacob Cusimano's macaroni factory, Leon Tujague, along with his brother, Albert, and Louis Robichaux, chartered the Southern Macaroni Company in 1914. The new enterprise differed from the many pasta factories that had sprouted over the previous fifteen years in the French Quarter in that none of the principals were of Sicilian descent. Later incorporated as National Food Products, Southern marketed its product as "Luxury Brand Macaroni." By 1922, the company's lines included the most popular shapes of pasta, including spaghetti, vermicelli, elbows, and egg noodles. In what was perhaps an allusion to the notoriously dirty French Quarter of the 1920s, an ad proclaimed that Luxury Macaroni came "from a factory where cleanliness reigns supreme." National Food Products operated at 1000 Fulton Street (now the site of a multistory parking deck serving the Ernest Morial Convention Center) until 1971, when production shifted to a plant in suburban Harahan. Borden Foods bought the company a decade later, when the food industry as a whole went into a period of consolidation, and shut down the Harahan facility, moving production to a larger facility in St. Louis. Today, Luxury Pasta is part of the ConAgra empire, though the packaging that greets shoppers all over the country still proudly proclaims it "A Louisiana Classic since 1914."[36]

Many of the buildings that once housed macaroni factories remain standing in the French Quarter, though all have long since been converted to other uses. Tourists are often surprised to learn that the quaint historic district was once a semi-industrial area thickly populated by Sicilian immigrants. When asked if she knew if the white marble cornerstone of Jacob Cusimano's pasta factory was visible, the desk clerk at Le Richelieu Hotel confessed that she had no idea that the building had once been a macaroni factory. More conspicuous on Jackson Square is Muriel's Restaurant, the site of the Taormina Brothers' former pasta factory and imported goods business. This lot on St. Ann sandwiched between the Presbytère and the Lower Pontalba buildings has been occupied continuously since the first decade of the city's founding. A mapping of its use over the decades reveals the distinct phases in the French Quarter's demographic life cycle. What began as a modest cottage in the 1720s soon evolved into an opulent residence whose occupants included the Marignys, the Jourdans, and the Poydrases. After the Civil War, the building declined along with the rest of the neighborhood. A photo dating from the 1880s, when Sicilian citrus importers had begun to grow rich yet paradoxically the French Quarter was well on its way to becoming a Sicilian slum, depicts the once proud mansion as a "Branch of the Absinthe House." In the 1890s, citrus importer Pietro Lipari purchased the site and demolished the Spanish Colonial structure that had stood there since the late eighteenth century and replaced it with the two-story brick commercial building that we find there today. He sold the property to the Taorminas in 1916.[37]

Father Andrew Taormina, the pastor of St. Francis Xavier Catholic Church in Old Metairie, described working in the factory in the 1950s while he studied in the seminary. Using processes that differed little in spirit from those developed in Naples during the eighteenth century, the Taormina employees extruded strings of spaghetti and draped them over wooden broom handles to dry. Women would then package the spaghetti under the Little King brand, readying it for delivery in a truck that made monthly runs to outlying destinations such as Morgan City, Independence, and Gulfport. Until 1969, when Andrew Taormina's father and grandfather retired and the factory closed, customers could still walk into the corner doors and buy imported olives and other goods alongside the pasta made on site for as little as thirteen cents a pound. The changes that doomed the factory included not only technological developments but also the decline of the neighborhood in and surrounding the quarter, which made delivering groceries both dangerous and unprofitable.[38]

Between 1900 and 1914, New Orleans witnessed the maturation of three powerful cultural mythologies associated with its Sicilian immigrant population. The first—and perhaps most enduring because of its perpetuation in popular culture—was the creation of the Black Hand legend and the powerful image of secretive Sicilian criminality. The second legend, conversely, was that of the industrious and prosperous Italian immigrant, a model citizen in the making who became an asset to the economic and social life of New Orleans. The third was the national emergence of Italian Americans as an identifiable ethnicity, made tangible for most people through foodways, especially the rapid integration of dry pasta into the American diet. With the start of the First World War in the late summer of 1914, immigration from Italy slowed to almost imperceptible levels. By the time immigration resumed after the war, fundamentally different realities governed the transatlantic movement of people between Sicily and New Orleans. By 1920, the importation of the Sicily lemon had almost totally stopped, while the sugarcane fields, once requiring so much human toil, sat mostly fallow. Further, the onset of Prohibition in January 1920 changed entirely the dynamics of the profitable business of liquor. But perhaps most important, the children of the immigrant generation were finding their own ways to become American.

Advertisement for
Louis Prima's novelty hit,
"No Squeeza da Banana,"
Billboard, May 12, 1945.

Sicilian agricultural workers harvesting lemons in the Conca d'Oro region near Palermo, 1906.
(Underwood, *Picking Lemons in a Grove on the Conca d'Oro [Golden Shell], Outside Palermo,
Sicily*, stereograph, 1906, Prints and Photographs Division, Library of Congress,
http://www.loc.gov/pictures/item/2003670813/)

Tenant housing that previously sheltered Sicilian cane workers at the Laurel Valley Plantation outside Thibodaux, Louisiana, 2010. (Photo by author)

Anne Parker, granddaughter of Vincenzo Brocato and Anne Bananto Brocato, holds an account book from Brocato's Store, 2010. Located outside Raceland, Louisiana, the store operated from 1905 to 2000. (Photo by author)

The interior of the grocery half of Brocato's Store, Raceland, Louisiana, 2010. The doorway behind the cash register led to the adjacent barroom. (Photo by author)

Advertisements for Anthony Astredo's oyster saloon and Terzula and Angella's oyster saloon, *New Orleans Daily Picayune*, April 15, 1853. Oyster saloons were such a ubiquitous feature of mid-nineteenth-century dining that newspapers offered restaurateurs the option of placing an oyster cartouche next to their ads.

Advertisement for John Astredo's Excelsior Restaurant, near the Magazine Market, *New Orleans Daily Picayune*, May 27, 1876. Josh Astredo rebuilt his family's reputation for oysters after his brother's departure in 1862, opening the Excelsior in 1874. "The Proprietor gives notice to his numerous customers and the public in general, that having completed arrangements with a number of fishermen, he is in daily receipt of fine SOFT SHELL CRABS and other FINE FISH, which he will offer during the entire season at the greatly reduced price of $1.25 Per Dozen, thus placing those luxuries within the reach of all. Come, one and all, and see for yourselves."

Sicilian Upper French Quarter
BOURBON CORRIDOR
circa 1900–1955

RAMPART
BURGUNDY
DAUPHINE
BOURBON
ROYAL
CHARTRES

Jackson Square

Site of
French
Opera
House
(1919)

©2014 Justin Nystrom

1. 16 Royal (old number): Anthony Astredo's Oyster Saloon, 1852–62. Located in the Old Post Office Building, Astredo's was one of the most popular oyster saloons in antebellum New Orleans. The first two blocks of Royal were sort of the Bourbon Street of the antebellum era, with the Gem and Sazerac saloons located in the first block. Anthony Astredo moved to San Francisco during the Civil War, but his brother, John, became a major restaurateur and hotel operator at West End and on the Mississippi Gulf Coast. Today, the site features the parking deck for the Wyndham New Orleans French Quarter.

2. 201 Royal (27, 29, 31): A. M. & J. Solari, Groceries, Wines, and Liquors, 1870s–1965. Started at Royal and St. Louis in 1864, moved to this site in the 1870s. Renovated in the 1920s; bulldozed in the 1960s. Today the site of Mr. B's Bistro. For several generations, Solari's *was the* place to buy fine groceries and did a national mail-order business.

3. 214 Royal: Hotel Monteleone, 1886–present. Expanded several times, the Monteleone is one of the few holdovers from a time when Italian immigrants played a prominent role in the commercial life of Upper Royal.

4. 800 Bourbon: Panzeca family grocery, 1918–33; La Lune nightclub, 1933–59. Johnny Panzeca became a major New Orleans East landowner and founded the Krewe of Virgilians (1935–64) after he was excluded from elite Carnival Society. La Lune was a Latin-themed club featuring Mexican food. In late 1960, the space became Pete Fountain's French Quarter Inn, and today it is the site of Oz, a gay dance club.

5 & 6. 809 St. Louis and 501–507 Bourbon: Anthony "Antoine" Masera's Oyster Saloon and Restaurant, 1871–1944. Masera immigrated from Sicily in 1868 and started an oyster saloon that evolved into a more full-fledged restaurant, emblematic of the ascent of the Sicilian restaurateur. He bought 809 St. Louis at auction in 1885. The club featured jazz until the city shut it down at the behest of the U.S. Navy in 1918. By 1923, the establishment had expanded to 501–507 Bourbon and was known as Masera's Restaurant and the World Famous Nut Club Bar, and it continued under that name through the 1930s despite several conspicuous run-ins with Prohibition agents. In 1944, Joseph and Ola Segreto took over management of the restaurant, and in 1947 it became Diamond Jim Moran's first restaurant. In later years, 501–507 housed Stormy's Casino Royale, home of Evangeline the Oyster Girl; in 1964, it became Al Hirt's club. It is now home to Big Easy Daiquiris. In the early 1960s, 809 St. Louis became a separate venue, the Eight-O-Nine Club.

7. 441 Bourbon: Leon Prima's 500 Club, 1947–58. Prima and partner Joe Segreto operated the club, which featured performances by Louis Prima and the Cat Girl. Next door at 437 Bourbon was the Latin Quarter club, whose owner and hostess stood trial in 1950 for killing a patron with a knockout drink.

8. 426 Bourbon: The Dream Room, 1956–64; Your Father's Moustache, 1964–75. Owned by Frank Amato, Sam Anselmo, and Walter Noto, the Dream Room was most famous for its front man, Dixieland great Sharkey Bonano. Under new ownership, Your Father's Moustache was a traditional Dixieland jazz club promising music in the style of Preservation Hall. A 1978 faux historic renovation changed the entire facade of the building.

9. 231 Bourbon: Sloppy Joe's Haven, 1949–50. After leaving the 500 Club, Joe Segreto opened Sloppy Joe's and brought in clarinetist Irving Fazola and burlesque star Evelyn West, whose "obscene" performance with Esky, the G-String Thief briefly resulted in the suspension of the club's liquor license.

10. 229 Bourbon: Turci's Restaurant, 1924–34; Shim-Sham Club, 1935–38. Turci's relocated to this building as well as 231 Bourbon from 827 Decatur Street. While at this location, Ettore Turci received a nine-month prison sentence for violating the Volstead Act. In 1934, the Turcis sold the building and moved down the street to 223 Bourbon. The new owners, Louis and Leon Prima, opened the Shim-Sham club in 1935. The structures now at the site were built in 1989.

11. 223 Bourbon: Joe Toro's Restaurant, 1922–34; Turci's Restaurant, 1934–44; Tosca's, 1944–?. Toro's was known for its spaghetti and ravioli as well as its frequent run-ins with Prohibition agents. When Turci's moved to Poydras Street, it was replaced by the short-lived Tosca's, which was managed by Joe Segreto until he left to take over Masera's at 809 St. Louis. Today, the building is part of the Hustler Club.

12. 739 Iberville: Felix Oyster House, 1938–present. From 1938 to about 1946, Felix Rando's Oyster Bar operated across the street at 736 Iberville, which was demolished in 1950 to make room for a Woolworth's; it, in turn, was demolished in 2002, when the current structure was built. Felix Oyster House moved to 739 Iberville shortly after World War II and is noteworthy for its oysters as well as for hosting Sam Saia's sports book operation in the 1940s and 1950s.

13. 724 Iberville: Acme Oyster House, 1912–present. Originally at 117 Royal Street, the Acme Oyster House was bought by Algiers grocer Felipe Sierra in 1913. After numerous Prohibition violations, the restaurant was ordered permanently closed—but not until two weeks after a fire destroyed the building. Acme moved to its current location in 1924 and was purchased by John Ciolino in 1936. Gambling remained an important part of Acme's business model through the 1940s and 1950s, when the restaurant not surprisingly advertised in the sports pages. Its current owners have operated it since 1985.

14. 725 Iberville: La Louisiane, 1881–present. Operated by Diamond Jim Moran from 1954 to 1958 and by his sons through the 1960s. The building was the site of a rare Brennan's failure, Anything Goes, during the 1970s. Joe and Sammy Marcello took over the enterprise in 1978, and today it is an event facility.

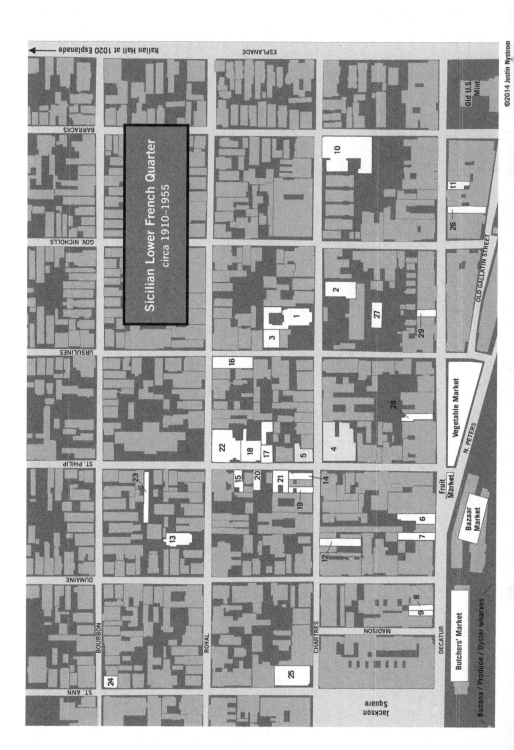

Sicilian Lower French Quarter
circa 1910–1955

Italian Hall at 1020 Esplanade

ESPLANADE

BARRACKS

GOV. NICHOLLS

URSULINES

ST. PHILIP

DUMAINE

ST. ANN

BOURBON

ROYAL

CHARTRES

DECATUR

MADISON

Jackson Square

Old U.S. Mint

OLD GALLATIN STREET

N. PETERS

Vegetable Market

Fruit Market

Bazaar Market

Butchers' Market

Banana / Produce / Oyster wharves

©2014 Justin Nystrom

1. 113 Chartres: Giacona and Sons, 1904–26. Liquors and wines. Scene of deadly 1908 shootout and resulting drive-by shooting in 1910. Now known as the Beauregard-Keyes House. Today, the Giacona family runs Giacona Container in Jefferson Parish, inventor of the Mardi Gras cup, among many other things.

2. 112 Chartres: St. Mary's Italian Church, built in 1846. The diocese changed the name to Our Lady of Victory in 1976 but received so many complaints that it eventually changed the name back.

3. 617 Ursulines: Angelo Brocato's Gelateria and Bakery, 1920–81. Tile work executed in 1924. Business opened in 1905 near intersection of Ursulines and Decatur and then moved to 623 Ursulines (next door to this location) in the 1910s.

4. 1000 Chartres: Federico Brothers Macaroni Manufacturing, 1920–50s. Nineteenth-century structures on the site were demolished. Lawrence Federico was a prominent figure in the Italian community and president of the Vigilance League. Currently houses Irene's Restaurant, with storage for the Louisiana State Museum upstairs. Symbolic of the sort of destruction that alerted early preservationists to the French Quarter's peril in the 1920s.

5. 1001 Chartres: Residence of the Evola and Loguidice families, 1947–56. Owned by Owen Brennan, 1946–47. Converted to the Chateau Hotel in 1962.

6. 923 Decatur: Central Grocery, 1906–present. Originally located in the 1000 block of Royal; moved to current location in 1919.

7. 915 Decatur: Progress Grocery, 1924–2001. Run by the Perrone family, which today operates a major food importing and wholesale business in Jefferson Parish.

8. 831 Decatur: Salvatore Segreto's Saloon and Restaurant, ca. 1908 or 1909–1940s. Segreto survived a 1916 assassination attempt on the sidewalk in front of the bar. His son, Joseph, ran several nightclubs, including Sloppy Joe's Haven at 231 Bourbon, which opened in 1949. Joseph's son, Salvatore "Joe" Segreto, became a noted restaurateur whose final establishment was Eleven79 at 1179 Annunciation.

9. 827 Decatur: Turci's Restaurant, 1917–23. Relocated to 223 Bourbon Street in 1924 and Poydras Street in 1945. Ettore Turci was friends with Enrico Caruso, who ate at the restaurant (and at Tujague's next door).

10. 1230 Chartres: Jacob Cusimano's macaroni factory, 1902–ca. 1964. Converted to the Le Richelieu Hotel.

11. 1222 Decatur: Home to Salvatore, Joseph, Frank, and Gaetano Uddo, 1900s–1910s. The brothers were half of the Uddo-Taormina corporation, which became Progresso Foods.

12. 916 Chartres: Home to Giuseppe Uddo and Eleanora Taormina Uddo, 1900s–1930s. The Taorminas played a key role in the formation of Progresso Foods. As legend has it, the family got its start from Jacob Cusimano in 1907.

13. 915 Royal: Cornstalk Hotel. Purchased and rebuilt in 1900 by Patorno family after fire heavily damaged the original mid-nineteenth-century structure. The house was built to look like an Italian castello. Scene of Italian society gatherings.

14. 943 Chartres: Owned by James Evola and

15. 630 St. Philip: Ruffino Bakery, 1916–25, and Ruffino family residence.

16. 626–630 Ursulines: Gaiety Theater (Garlic Theater). Owned by Frank Ruffino, 1927–? Rebuilt in 1937 after a fire. Torn down in 1970.

17. 619–621 St. Philip: First macaroni manufacturing location of Jacob Cusimano, 1898–1904. The perpetrators of Walter Lamana's 1907 kidnapping lived at 619; gangster Sylvestro "Silver Dollar Sam" Carolla lived at 621 in 1920.

18. 625–631 St. Philip: Ruffino's Bakery, 1924–1940s; Ruffino's Restaurant, 1950s–1970s.

19. 935 Chartres: Philip Glorioso's pastry shop, 1910s–20s. A feud with Glorioso about ricotta cheese inspired Angelo Brocato to make cannoli.

20. 624 St. Philip: Purchased in 1903 by Peter Lamana, undertaker to the Italian community and father of Walter Lamana, who was kidnapped in 1907. Beginning in 1825, Peter Lamana's son-in-law, Jack Panno, lived there with his wife, Stella Lamana Panno, and their family. The Lamana-Panno-Fallo funeral home operated for many years on Rampart Street in what is today the New Orleans Mission.

21. 612 St. Philip: Jacob Cusimano and Giuseppe Impastato's macaroni factory, 1910–21.

22. 1000 Royal: Owned by Evola/Ruffino families, 1919–present.

23. 724 St. Philip: B. Montalbano's "Angel of Peace" Delicatessen, 1917–56. Biaggio Montalbano's son, Martin, developed

24. 800 Bourbon: Panzeca family grocery, 1918–33; La Lune nightclub, 1933–59. Johnny Panzeca became a major New Orleans East landowner and founded the Krewe of Virgilians (1935–64) when he was excluded from elite Carnival society. La Lune was a Latin-themed club featuring Mexican food. In late 1960, the space became Pete Fountain's French Quarter Inn, and today it is the site of Oz, a gay dance club.

25. 801 Chartres: Taormina pasta factory and wholesale grocery imports, built in 1890s and owned by the Taormina family, 1916–present. This site has been occupied nearly continuously since the city's founding. The current building replaced one that was constructed at the turn of the nineteenth century and was owned by Italian citrus importers.

26. 1210 Decatur: F. Lombardo Bakery, 1910–40. Had a walk-up window at which people would buy Italian bread to take to Angelo Brocato's gelateria around the corner.

27. St. Mary's Italian School, ?–1960s. Educated several generations of Italian kids.

28. 1019 Decatur: Restaurant known as the Union Restaurant, LaNasa's Union, and LaNasa's Spaghetti, 1902–22; LaNasa Bakery, 1922–?

29. 1119 Decatur: Messina Restaurant, before 1908–1916; Original Italian Spaghetti House, 1916–? Messina's catered a 1908 spaghetti dinner at the St. Louis Exchange Hotel.

the olive salad recipe for the muffuletta sandwiches sold today at the Napoleon House.

Nick Evola, 1939–2009. Site of the Starlet Lounge, a haven for cross-dressing that was raided by police in 1954. Symbolic of the rise of the gay French Quarter.

The building at 2015 Magazine Street where John Astredo and later the Tranchina brothers operated the Excelsior Restaurant from 1874 to 1912. In 1920, the cavernous space was converted into a silent movie theater, and although the building now houses a rug dealer, the interior still appears much as it did in the early twentieth century. (Photo by author)

Tranchina and Olivieri's West End Restaurant, 1900. Built long before the advent of air-conditioning, the West End resorts sat atop piers over Lake Pontchartrain where the shore met the New Basin Canal. The same cooling breeze that made visitors comfortable also periodically led to catastrophic fires. (Detroit Publishing Company, *West End Pavilions, New Orleans*, glass plate negative, 1900, Library of Congress Prints and Photographs Division, http://www.loc.gov/pictures/item/2016800691/)

The view from Tranchina and Olivieri's balcony, 1901. The turn-of-the century West End resort landscape included smoke from a steam launch in the canal. (Detroit Publishing Co., *West End, New Orleans, La.*, glass plate negative, 1901, Library of Congress Prints and Photographs Division, http://www.loc.gov/pictures/item/2016799388/)

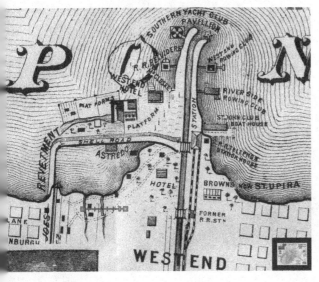

Detail from an 1885 Cotton Centennial Exposition map depicting West End. Significant changes subsequently were made to the shoreline, including the creation of West End Park in 1914. (*The World's Industrial and Cotton Centennial Exposition* [New Orleans: Southern Lithograph, 1885], David Rumsey Map Collection, David Rumsey Map Center, Stanford University)

1113 Chartres, home of C. Giacona and Company Wines and Liquors, 1906.
This building is now known as the Beauregard-Keyes House. (Morgan Whitney, *1113 Chartres*, glass plate negative, April 1906, N-1051. Southeastern Architectural Archive, Special Collections Division, Tulane University Libraries)

Jacob Cusimano's pasta factory, 1964. Built at 1230 Chartres Street in 1902, the factory was subsequently converted into the Le Richelieu Hotel. (Dan S. Leyrer, *726 St. Peter St*, N-1455D, March 11, 1964, Historic New Orleans Collection)

Aerial view of Spanish Fort, 1922. The large building in the center of the shell parking lot is Tranchina's Restaurant. The road and streetcar access to Spanish Fort cut through the forest in what is today suburban Lakeview. An ambitious land-reclamation project in the 1930s completely altered the lakefront's geography. (Charles L. Franck, *Aerial View of Spanish Fort and Bayou Saint John*, photograph, 1922, Franck-Bertacci Photographers Collection, Historic New Orleans Collection)

Advertisement for Beverly Gardens, D. J. Tranchina's short-lived restaurant and casino on Metairie Road, *New Orleans Times-Picayune*, January 1, 1926.

The seven LaNasa brothers of Decatur Street, early 1900s. (Courtesy of Colin Hulin)

Turnetto #5 (SAM)   NINO #3 (tony)   MATTEO OLDEST   Guiseppe (JOE) 2ND SON   JOHN 7th DOMINIC (JOHNNY)   Michaele (MIKE) 6th   Sebastiani (SEBASTI

Johnny Panzeca (*left*) in the Bourbon Street grocery operated by his parents, Giorgio and Angelina Panzeca (*center*). The man on the right may be George Parker, the Panzecas' porter. Johnny Panzeca later transformed this location into La Lune, a Latin-themed nightclub. (Courtesy of Vincent Mariano)

730 South Rampart Street, the site of Anthony Loscasio and Victor Lemane's saloon, 2012. This street was once lined by similar buildings that housed stores and workingmen's bars. Both Loscasio and Lemane were arrested in 1915 and again in 1917 for violating the segregationist provisions of the Gay-Shattuck Law. Developers razed this building in 2015 to make way for a retail and condominium complex in the bustling South Market District. Allowing its removal, the City Planning Commission made the particularly Orwellian observation that although the building "is significant as it relates to the development of Jazz and the urban history of South Rampart Street, it is undermined by its position as the last remaining historic building on the square, an artifact devoid of the context necessary to impart meaning" (Preliminary Staff Report, Design Review 150/14, New Orleans City Planning Commission, December 9, 2014). (Photo by author)

Sicilian work gangs unload bananas on the riverfront, 1900. (Detroit Publishing Co., *[Unloading Bananas, New Orleans, Louisiana]*, glass plate negative, 1900, Library of Congress Prints and Photographs Division, http://www .loc.gov/pictures/item/ det1994013503/PP/)

The French Market, 1936. Works Progress Administration funding in 1934 gave the market the appearance familiar to most people today. Long cucuzza squash hang from the rafters. (Carl Mydans, *Marketplace at New Orleans, Scene of . . .* , nitrate negative, June 1936, Library of Congress Prints and Photographs Division, https://www.loc.gov /item/fsa1997001873/PP/)

Biaggio Montalbano's "Angel of Peace" Delicatessen, 724 St. Philip Street, 1956, and the same building, 2011. This structure did not conform to the Vieux Carré Commission's design motif and received significant alterations to return it to its 1830s appearance. (Robert Drew, *718–720, 724, 726– 728 St. Philip*, photograph, 1956, N-231, Historic New Orleans Collection; photo by author)

Central Grocery's signature olive salad, a key ingredient in the muffuletta sandwich. In the 1970s, the muffuletta shifted from a side business to a crucial component of the store's financial survival. (Photo by author)

Salvatore Vitale, one of the two men questioned in a 1943 murder case that forged much of the mythology about Mosca's in Waggaman, *New Orleans Times-Picayune*, November 23, 1943.

Salvatore Segreto (*seated*) and Carlos Marcello outside Segreto's saloon at 833 Decatur Street, 1930s. Segreto survived an assassination attempt at this location in 1916. (Courtesy of Sophia Segreto)

An early Elmwood Plantation menu reflected the elegance to which owners Joe Marcello and Nick Mosca aspired. (Louisiana Menu and Restaurant Collection. Howard-Tilton Memorial Library, Louisiana Research Collection)

(*left to right*) Joe C. Marcello, Joe Segreto, Sammy Davis Jr., and Nathaniel Burton at Broussard's, 1977. (Courtesy of Sophia Segreto)

Salvatore "Joe" Segreto in the kitchen of his final restaurant, Eleven79, 2014. (Photo by author)

CHAPTER 4

Booze, Red Gravy, and Jazz

The Birth of the New Orleans
Italian Restaurant

Three days before Mardi Gras of 1908, a large group of mortgage bankers and their wives attended a banquet under the dome of the French Quarter's old St. Louis Exchange Hotel. The once-proud design of Jacques Nicholas Bussière de Pouilly had decayed considerably since the day it first received guests in 1838, but it remained a tangible reminder of antebellum New Orleans, when the notorious slave auctions held in the filtered light of the grand rotunda's oculus were a must-see for knowledgeable tourists. Now, forty years after emancipation, the proud doyenne sat in the midst of a Sicilian slum. Nevertheless, the hotel's cracking plaster and peeling paint did little to dampen the spirits of the main street financiers who gathered under its historic roof. "The old rotunda dining-room at the old St. Louis, with its frescoed panels, representing history and art and statesmanship, may have had banquets that cost more . . . but it could hardly ever have had a more enthusiastic and noisy and jolly gathering than the crowd which filled every inch of the room." So popular was the event that some attendees had to settle for tables that spilled out into the lobby.[1]

The program, planned by local elites and hosted by Mayor Martin Behrman and literary light Alcée Fortier, among others, was conventional by the standards of the day, with obsequious tributes to the Confederacy and patriotic musical numbers, but the meal served for dinner was anything but traditional. "The spaghetti supper," observed the *New Orleans Daily Picayune*, "was served in the most approved style of the Messina Restaurant, with Italian waiters and all the attachments." Despite the popularity of that Decatur Street restaurant, pasta was a daring catering choice in 1908, bewildering many non-Italian diners only beginning their acquaintance with red sauce. "Such a supper is a matter of education, and not all those present were educated to eat it," the reporter noted. Whether the result of poor planning or a deep desire for irony, the entertainment included a federal judge who offered "an Italian impersonation," even as Messina's staff cleared plates and refilled coffee cups.[2]

Yet even as they listened to Judge Charbonnet's tone-deaf attempt at humor, some of those in attendance may have realized that they were witnesses to the social and economic transformation wrought by the immigrant class. The antebellum jewels of French Creole New Orleans, the St. Louis Hotel and the French Opera House on nearby Bourbon Street, would both be gone in just over a decade—the hotel demolished by a salvage crew in 1916 and the opera house destroyed by fire three years later. By that time, Sicilian immigrants had emerged as the ascendant population in the old Creole stronghold. Mediterranean immigrants and their children had already made their mark in such industries as shipping, importing, and wholesaling to restaurants and hotels. The mortgage bankers present at the banquet were probably more aware of their city's shifting demography than was the average New Orleanian. The food on the plates symbolized the Sicilians' seat at the city's table. The dinner also signaled that in the French Quarter, especially along Decatur Street, a distinct form of dining had started to take root: it would eventually become known as Creole Italian.[3]

The start of the First World War in 1914 marked a turning point in the relationship between New Orleans and its Sicilian community. Submarine warfare sent the costs and dangers of transatlantic shipping skyrocketing, decimating the trade in Mediterranean goods such as citrus, olives, olive oil, wine, and macaroni. The war only exacerbated the rising tide of protectionism and other economic pressures on imports, creating a vacuum that enabled the blossoming of the U.S. citrus and pasta industries. This phenomenon also fostered development of California wine and to a lesser degree olives, both of which soon became dominated by Italians. The conflict also shut off the flow of immigrants from Sicily to America at a time when many surely would have made the trip had such a passage remained possible. Never again would entire shiploads of Sicilian immigrants crowd the chaotic docks along the French Market. The war also coincided with the social maturation of New Orleans's Sicilian immigrant community. Many of the destitute laborers who had sailed to Louisiana beginning in the late 1880s were now American citizens and the parents of adult American-born children. By the time that the Guns of August heralded the advent of generational slaughter and human catastrophe in Europe, most observers had become aware of New Orleans's vibrant, numerous, and increasingly affluent Sicilian community.

One tangible marker of cultural change appeared on the menus of those restaurants opened by Sicilian immigrants and their children in the heart of the French Quarter's "Italian Colony." Unlike the oyster saloon trade of the nineteenth century, which concentrated on meeting local expectations for fresh seafood, these new houses made their name on emergent Italian American dishes like spaghetti and ravioli. Not only had enough of a local ethnic community finally emerged to make spaghetti houses financially viable, but a broad spectrum of Americans had come to accept and appreciate pasta as a valuable contribution to the national diet. Despite lingering prejudice against Italians, food may have helped these immigrants find a new level of broad acceptance in the American heartland. In 1920, however, this newfound embrace would collide with the Volstead Act, which ushered in a period that forever altered the image of Italians in America. The positive imagery of food and culture intermixed with the perception of clannish criminality forged in the first three decades of the twentieth century fostered a curiously enduring duality of cultural perception, one not entirely rejected by Italian Americans themselves.

Prohibition meant that restaurateurs across America had to continue to accommodate changing customer tastes in food while finding a way to satisfy guests' continuing demand for a product that was now illegal—and to avoid running afoul of efforts to enforce the law, which were unpredictable and even capricious. Remaining profitable was a difficult enough task for restaurateurs even without the uncertainty of alcohol sales. The emergence of criminal syndicates in the 1920s and their increasing control over the importation and distribution of booze also required restaurateurs to engage in a certain level of complicity with illegal schemes. The experience of Sicilian immigrants in New Orleans mirrored that of different ethnic groups in other cities, particularly that of the Jewish immigrant community in New York. New Orleans's Sicilians were deeply invested in the restaurant and food-service industry, an economic space that could scarcely thrive without booze. At the same time, they had built their place in the city on the basis of importing, manufacturing, wholesaling, and retailing all manner of goods, including wine and liquor. Flouting the Volstead Act was a natural fit. Moreover, few people at the time understood just where enforcement against alcohol would lead. Both the city's restaurant culture and the reputation of Sicilians in New Orleans were destined to emerge from Prohibition irrevocably transformed.[4]

The rise in popularity of Italian food in New Orleans and the legal battlefield of Prohibition legislation converged inside the spaghetti houses that evolved into nightclubs during the late 1910s and early 1920s. The mortgage bankers' 1908 banquet at the St. Louis Hotel occurred at the beginning of the national embrace of Americanized Italian pasta dishes. A decade later, ravioli and spaghetti restaurants had become popular, even stylish destinations for banquets, luncheon meetings, and holiday dinners. By the 1920s these establishments were no longer the earthy lunch houses of Decatur Street frequented by sailors and Sicilian immigrants but had become white tablecloth restaurants with tuxedoed waiters, fine china, and silver-plate service. They also offered live music, dancing, and illegal booze. Just like their counterparts at Spanish Fort and West End, the Sicilian restaurants of the French Quarter presented jazz music just as that genre was making inroads among American mainstream listeners. Booze, red gravy, and jazz helped transform Bourbon Street and its intersecting thoroughfares from a seedy semi-industrial and residential strip into the (still somewhat seedy) nightclub district that experienced a golden age in the 1940s and 1950s.

The rocky relationship between Sicilians and the enforcement of liquor laws was at least a generation in the making by the time of Prohibition's arrival in January 1920. Indeed, the battle between morality crusaders and the city's liquor vendors had begun in the nineteenth century with the enactment of the state's first Sunday "blue law," which went into effect at the stroke of midnight on December 31, 1886. The act not only made it illegal for bars to serve on the Sabbath but prohibited a wide range of activities that also encompassed "making groceries" and delivering milk. Many saloon operators believed that the law would go largely unenforced, and they were generally right, although the police department conducted episodic sweeps designed more to mollify those who wanted a dry town than actually to render it so. Yet barkeeps also underestimated the staying power of the Sunday Rest League, a group of concerned Baptists whose missionary zeal moved them to antagonize the city's countless drinking establishments. While the law was a minority issue in New Orleans, its presence on the books served as an ominous sign of the hinterland's growing political power relative to that of the metropolis and signaled the advent of a rural-urban divide on morality legislation that remains with Louisiana to this day.[5]

West End's restaurants and bars felt the grip of the Sunday Law during a flurry of enforcement activity in early September 1896. A few months earlier, the city attorney had opined that the Prohibition law did not apply to West End, leaving "the gourmands and bon viviants [*sic*]" who frequented the resort feeling safe from prosecution. This sense of invulnerability evaporated when the Sunday Rest League found compliant police officers willing to make arrests and test the city attorney's authority. Charged with violating the Sunday Law, Terry Tranchina, John Astredo, Theodore Bruning, John McGouldrick (who kept a monkey at the entrance to his bar), and a variety of other proprietors appeared in the Carrollton Recorder's Court on a Monday morning. That none of them brought legal representation undoubtedly reflected their lack of concern, and in a comic twist, they decided to cross-examine the witnesses for the Sunday Rest League themselves. The *New Orleans Daily Picayune* reveled in re-creating McGouldrick's Irish dialect as he asked a witness, "Wad ye say that ye'd swear th' sloof ye saw was beer in them glasses?" The witness could not swear that it was beer, prompting McGouldrick to follow up with, "Thin how d'ye know it wasn't ginger ale? Ginger ale looks like beer, an' ye can't swear it wasn't." A spectator then shouted out, "Bully for you McGouldrick! You'd make a good lawyer." When a witness disagreed with Astredo about whether the men serving alcohol were waiters, the restaurateur exclaimed with annoyance, "What is a man to do in such a country with such laws as this?" It was a valid question.[6]

West End's saloon and resort operators continued fighting the Sunday Law for the next decade, with mixed results. The question of whether it applied to the semiaquatic businesses dragged on for several years, with the Sunday Rest League prevailing in the end. The law did not fully impact Tranchina because his restaurant retained the right to sell wine with meals. No one was allowed to vend beer or liquor on Sunday, one of the busiest days of the week and an important part of beverage sales at West End. More troubling for the smaller operators were the enterprising competitors who hastily threw up bars and gambling houses just on the other side of the protection levee in Jefferson Parish (today's Bucktown), which sat within shouting distance of the West End boardwalk and where enforcement of the Sunday Law was more selectively lax. For his part, Tranchina cultivated a closer relationship with the police officers detailed to enforce sobriety, an approach that brought dividends at a hearing following a September 1901 arrest, when none of the policemen could recall seeing any Sunday Law violations at his restaurant. Such tactics had their limit, but Tranchina seems also to have had some insight into the force's raid calendar. When a swarm of plainclothesmen arrived on a Sunday in 1904, all they could procure was the allowed champagne. "So far as the general public knows," mocked the newspaper, "the Sunday Law has been strictly observed by Mr. Tranchina of the West End Hotel." The empty-handed police were left to enjoy the evening's vaudeville show. These cat-and-mouse games, which were replicated in another context a generation later, were surely another factor in the resort's decline in the first decade of the twentieth century.[7]

The battle over liquor in New Orleans took a more serious turn in 1909, when a new, broader Prohibition law went into effect. The Gay-Shattuck Law (Act 176 of 1908) had been the product of a state legislative session punctuated by enormous victories for morality crusaders who had tapped into the nation's xenophobic zeitgeist. In June, the Louisiana Senate narrowly passed the Locke Anti-Racing Bill, which outlawed pari-mutuel betting on horses. On the greater issue of alcohol, realistic reformers acknowledged that a bill proposing outright Prohibition faced grim prospects but found solace in an alternative proposed by S. O. Shattuck of Lake Charles that required applicants for state liquor licenses to navigate a labyrinth of restrictions that enforced Prohibition through mechanisms of harassment and bureaucracy. The measure had the added benefit of raising revenue in the midst of a budget crisis; strict Prohibition, in contrast, would only cost the state money. Ostensibly a liquor license law, Gay-Shattuck not only tripled the amount that average saloonkeepers paid for the right to sell booze but also banned a host of other activities. Foremost, it was a segregation law, part of an emerging trend across the rest of the Jim Crow South in which municipalities required that businesses take out occupancy licenses based on the race of their intended clientele. Blacks and whites could—and did—still work side by side in bars, but they could not drink together as customers. The law also made it illegal for women to work in or be served in barrooms, a provision intended to clamp down on "loose women" that hurt family-run corner bars and banned anyone under age twenty-one from purchasing alcohol or working in saloons. Gambling of any kind now became illegal, a ban that included the various mechanical gaming devices popular at the time, as was keeping musical instruments for the purpose of performance. Gay-Shattuck might not entirely outlaw drinking but certainly promised to make it less fun. However, the law applied only to bars and groceries, not to restaurants.[8]

New Orleans was also in the midst of two profound demographic transformations in 1909. More pronounced was the massive influx of immigrants from Sicily, which had begun in the 1880s and was now in full swing, but a close second was the steady migration of African Americans from the rural areas of Louisiana and Mississippi that had begun during the Civil War and continued well into the 1950s. These newcomers labored together along the city's busy waterfront and lived in similar neighborhoods, drank in corner bars, gambled, and every now and then ran into trouble with the law. The specter of Sicilian and black criminality certainly resonated with many New Orleanians in the first decade of the twentieth century, and the shootings at the Beauregard-Keyes House involving the Giaconas remained at the forefront of people's minds. So, too, did Robert Charles, an African American drifter from Mississippi who had a series of run-ins with the law before he gunned down twenty-four people from a Central City house in 1900, an incident that provoked a riot. Racial integration was definitely not an issue at fancier establishments like Commander's, Delmonico's, or the West End Hotel, but they felt the law's impact all the same.[9]

Almost from the outset, the city's law enforcement apparatus resisted upholding the Gay-Shattuck Law. Graft had for decades been so intrinsic to the police department that gambling operations and other forms of vice commonly operated with official complicity. Almost comically, the first set of defendants prosecuted by district attorney St. Clair Adams included the Boston Club; the Pickwick Club; the Chess, Checkers, and Whist Club; and the Hotel Grunewald, all of which allegedly operated within three hundred feet of churches. When asked to explain his decision, Adams declared that he "thought it would be better to commence the work on the 'big fellows'" who could afford a defense rather than to hassle the "little fellows." The president of the Pickwick club said that the charges "amused him greatly" and that he "showed [the citation] to a number of his friends, saying 'Just look with what I am charged.'" New Orleans's elites certainly did not uniformly back the law. At the Louisiana Bar Association's May 1909 meeting in Alexandria, association president William Parkerson, who in 1891 had led the mob that lynched the Hennessey defendants at the Orleans Parish Jail, shocked his North Louisiana associates with a speech calling the Locke and Gay-Shattuck laws the result of "religious madness" and "such an interference with personal liberty that blondes will soon be forbidden to marry brunettes." The alcohol issue divided the old-time elites and proponents of social reform from the Baptist-led morality crusaders of the Progressive era.[10]

Arrest records from 1909 through 1919 offer some insight into how the Gay-

Shattuck legislation affected Sicilian bar owners. A total of 188 bar owners with Italian names were arrested for Gay-Shattuck infractions during this period, with more than 60 percent charged with "selling liquor to whites and negroes" despite holding licenses that only permitted sales to one race or the other. Two-thirds of the 191 people arrested on this charge were Italian. Thus, even though Gay-Shattuck was a liquor-licensing law, most of those arrested for violating it were Italians who had run afoul of the law's segregationist aspects.[11]

Plotting the locations of these arrests on a map reveals that enforcement efforts seem to have focused on the working-class neighborhood bars that Sicilian immigrants often operated and to have generally avoided the sorts of upscale establishments run by Tranchina and others. Many of the arrests took place in the Italian Colony of the French Quarter and neighboring Marigny as well as in the working-class areas of the Seventh and Eighth Wards and the Central City. The edges of town along Carrollton Avenue between the Illinois Central Railroad tracks (now the Earhart Expressway) and Canal Street saw many arrests, as did the Basin, Liberty, Rampart, and Perdido Street neighborhood where young Louis Armstrong played his first gigs. All of these areas constituted blue-collar neighborhoods where Italians and blacks lived—and drank—side by side. Conspicuously absent, however, are racial arrests in the red-light district of Storyville, where officials focused on prostitution in the context of alcohol; even there arrests were episodic. Also absent are arrests at the resorts of West End and Spanish Fort as well as the wealthier portions of Uptown's streetcar suburbs. People of a certain class either did not violate the law or, like Tranchina, figured out ways to avoid prosecution. Perhaps the members of the Sunday Rest League felt that attempting to enforce Prohibition against such establishments was not worth the risk. One League member who went into a West End roadhouse was "set upon and beaten" by its owner, James Thom. The criminal court dropped both liquor and assault charges against Thom, agreeing that the concerned citizens had overstepped their authority.[12]

In contrast to the stories that followed splashy headlines in the newspapers, the criminal court records depict Italian operators of neighborhood bars who lacked the political connections necessary to avoid harassment. Among them was Joe Impastato, who held a license to serve African Americans and was arrested in 1914 for selling beer to white customers at what we know today as the Napoleon House. Anthony Loscasio and his partner, Victor Lemane, paid a fine for doing just the opposite at their bar and grocery at 730 South Rampart, a building more recently known as the Who Dat Shack that remained standing until 2016, when it was demolished to make way for a faceless upscale condominium building. A flurry of January–February 1913 arrests included one at Fortune Salvaggio's barroom at 200 North Clark Street in Mid-City. Pullman porter Robert Grant had come from Chattanooga to New Orleans to help handle the extra trains bringing tourists to Mardi Gras. He sought to take a break from his work at the New Orleans and North East Rail Yard by having a beer at Salvaggio's tavern. After Grant drained his glass, he and Salvaggio found themselves arrested by a plainclothes police officer. A frightened Grant promised that if the judge let him go, he would immediately leave town.[13]

Terry Tranchina's 1913 relocation of his main restaurant operation from West End to Spanish Fort marked the beginning of the old lakefront resort's last hurrah, a period that bridged the prewar ragtime era and the Jazz Age and ended with the birth of what became Bourbon Street. Located at the intersection of Bayou St. John and Lake Pontchartrain, Spanish Fort was geographically important even before Europeans settled the area. That the banks of the bayou featured a mostly dry portage between the lake and the river factored heavily in French selection of the site for what is today the Vieux Carré. Like Milneburg to its east and West End to its west, Spanish Fort functioned as a resort area through much of the nineteenth century, offering an escape for city dwellers who could afford the six-cent train fare from the intersection of Canal and Basin Streets. Spanish Fort fell into decline during the 1890s heyday of West End, where the ongoing drainage work and city ownership added incentive for the New Orleans Railway and Light Company to invest in a thorough renovation, including amusement rides, music pavilions, and a large new restaurant. Tranchina's West End operation had enjoyed a loyal following with an influential clientele, and arranging for him to lease the redeveloped West End restaurant bolstered the chances of success. At a banquet marking the May 1 opening, guests marveled at the new rides and the "thousands of electric lights" that would illuminate the route patrons followed to vaudeville acts, silent films, and "Tosso's Military Band."[14]

Felix Tranchina took over the operation after his father's 1917 death, bringing change to the restaurant. At the time, orchestral jazz was gaining in popularity among the sorts of white audiences that spent summer evenings dancing at Spanish Fort. Unlike the wilder, more improvisational forms of jazz emerging in the same era at Milneburg's run-down and racially diverse joints, Tranchina's featured modern music that appealed to middle-class tastes, a style embodied by the Creole orchestra of Armand J. Piron, who is probably best known today for coauthoring a jazz standard, "I Wish I Could Shimmy Like My Sister Kate," which was composed during the band's tenure at Spanish Fort and may have first been performed before a live audience there. Piron was both a contemporary of Jelly Roll Morton and the temperamental opposite of the outspoken self-proclaimed inventor of jazz. Quiet and dignified, Piron took his band out of New Orleans only once—a brief 1924 trip to New York during which Oscar "Papa" Celestin's band subbed at Tranchina's. Piron was also early to recognize the importance of records and opened his own recording studio in 1915. As a consequence, Piron's Orchestra recorded more sides than any other black band from the early period of jazz. Bruce Raeburn, curator at Tulane's Hogan Jazz Archive, has observed that white audiences liked Piron's playing style because it was "excellent dance music." The Piron Orchestra played for more than a decade at Tranchina's, and a 1922 photograph shows band members wearing tuxedos and smiling pleasantly for the camera. At the edge of the frame stands a xylophone, which band member Peter Bocage described as Felix Tranchina's idea: "Mr. Tranchina liked it and he say he was going to buy one—that thing cost $300-some dollars, too."[15]

The fragments that remain visible today make it difficult to imagine Spanish Fort as it was in the 1920s. The masonry ruin of the early national period fort rests along the rim of Bayou St. John, along with a few curious stone structures left over from the turn-of-the-century amusement park. Standing on these ramparts facing the lake, with the bayou to the right, one must imagine a roller coaster towering over what is today a pleasant subdivision of mid-century ranch homes. Heading toward Pontchartrain were a series of open-air pavilions, a water slide, the Over the Rhine beer garden, cup-and-saucer rides, and eventually Tranchina's Restaurant, overlooking the westerly bank of the bayou's entrance from the lake. Few photographs remain of this Spanish-style stucco building, its archways shaded by awnings and protected by screen doors that let in the lake breezes, but it appears on the margins of panoramic photographs of company outings taken to commemorate a relaxing time away from the office, with men wearing straw boaters and women in patterned day dresses. In the evenings, Tranchina's changed from a place of family leisure to one of elite entertainment. "Mostly awful rich people come out to that place; it was an exclusive joint, you know—all high-class," remembered Bocage. Among the visitors whom Bocage recalled were Nelson Whitney of the Whitney Bank, and "Sam the Banana Man" Zemurray, the president of Cuyamel Fruit and subsequently the head of United Fruit Company and the builder of the St. Charles Avenue mansion that is today the residence of Tulane University's president. Crowds moved across Tranchina's dance floor to the sounds of Piron's Orchestra until the early morning hours, when trains and automobiles returned them to the city and home.[16]

Like his father, Felix Tranchina had to find a way to operate a business that depended on the free flow of alcohol, but he did so under much more difficult circumstances. The younger Tranchina's ability to buy the cooperation of the local police force remained undiminished in the early 1920s, as did his counterparts in New Orleans and other urban centers where Prohibition remained a widely unpopular experiment. Liquor enforcement in New Orleans was particularly ineffective during the first several years of the Volstead Act's reign, but as the 1920s wore on, conflict between federal and local officials bore the signs of strain. In the summer of 1924, two particularly uncooperative New Orleans Police Department patrolmen tried to prevent Prohibition agents from carrying out a raid at Tranchina's Restaurant. Finding the screen doors locked, the agents entered through a window. Rather than meekly submitting to the raid, however, the guests, encouraged by the New Orleans police, rushed the agents and took back the liquor. The feds arrested the cops for interference; the policemen, in turn, arrested the agents for disturbing the peace. Matters turned more serious the following summer when a dozen dry agents raided Tranchina's in the wee hours of a Sunday morning. "A shower of bottles skidded across the dance pavilion" as the federals entered and guests ran every which way. When one patron clubbed a Prohibition agent with a bottle, the lawman fired three shots into the ceiling, unleashing a general panic in the restaurant. Tranchina was not arrested, and the federal government would hardly make New Orleans a dry town during Prohibition, but this raid was one of several that heralded the arrival of a more violent and costly period of liquor enforcement. Tranchina's operated at Spanish Fort into the 1930s but declined as the amusements fell into disrepair and the surrounding New Deal–era land-reclamation project diminished the resort's charm.[17]

As remarkable as Felix and Terry Tranchina's operations at West End and Spanish Fort had been, they were not the only restaurants in New Orleans by that name to earn renown for music, alcohol, and the sporting life in the early twentieth century. Located at the corner of Carondelet and Howard Avenue, just off Lee Circle, what was once Dominick J. Tranchina's Restaurant is now the site of a gas station. Dominick Tranchina's father, Joseph

(Felix's brother), had begun a restaurant at this location in the late nineteenth century, and his son transformed it into a fancier, racier place. "For weeks the well-known establishment has been in the hands of carpenters and decorators," noted a late August 1907 newspaper article, "and when it is opened again to-day the patrons will find a complete reconstruction. Mr. Tranchina has spared no expense in fitting up his place of business, and as a result he has secured a restaurant and café which is second to none in the city in point of comfort and completeness." One early employee, Anthony "Jack" LaFranca, soon married Dominick Tranchina's niece, Marie Masset, and subsequently took over the operation of C. J. Commander's Delmonico on St. Charles Avenue.[18]

Although the Tranchina cousins' establishments shared a devotion to serving good food and drink and offering top entertainment to their guests, Dominick Tranchina's relationship with the difficult business of gambling defined his career. Advertisements in the months leading up to the First World War described the house near Lee Circle as the "Restaurant You Want to Know," offering "high class entertainment for ladies and gentlemen: good music, good singers." During the 1916–17 winter races at the fairgrounds, the proprietor sponsored the "D. J. Tranchina's Restaurant Handicap" to attract stylish vacationers. A large display ad announcing the trophy featured a line illustration of three women dressed in modern attire seated around a linen-draped table and chatting as well as a photograph of a racehorse, Leochares, and a chart showing the line for the six races in the handicap. The 1916 repeal of the Locke law had reinstated pari-mutuel betting, ending eight years of financial devastation of the area's racetracks. "Come in and have a good dinner after the races," invited Tranchina. "This is a favorite rendezvous for New Orleans' winter visitors. They like it here because they get good things to eat, well served, and there is music and dancing besides. The Bohemian spirit prevails—everyone is a 'good fellow' here." Only months after the racing season, however, Dominick Tranchina found a key element of "the Bohemian spirit" threatened by a new city ordinance shuttering houses labeled *cabarets* under the auspices of the U.S. Navy and the war effort. This ordinance is generally known for bringing about the beginning of the end of Storyville, but clubs in the French Quarter and other parts of the city also felt its pinch (although it did not apply to West End and Spanish Fort). Arguing that the city council had no constitutional authority to prevent him from staging performances when so many of his competitors were allowed to do so, Tranchina fought the measure all the way to the Louisiana Supreme Court but lost.[19]

Having bid farewell to New Orleans proper, Dominick Tranchina opened the doors to the Beverly Gardens, a nightclub located along the Metairie Road inside Jefferson Parish, in February 1925. The club promiscuously violated the Volstead Act, but the relocation to a more forgiving municipality resulted primarily from more lax attitudes toward the state's gambling laws. At the very least, it meant that Tranchina would have to pay off a smaller circle of government officials to operate unmolested. Like his cousin, Felix, who greeted guests on the margins of town at Spanish Fort, Tranchina's Beverly Gardens promised its middle- and upper-class clients a night of escape and fun. Unlike Spanish Fort, however, Beverly Gardens was accessible only by automobile, though just a "12 minute ride" would take a man to what was an ideal place to "bring the girl friend." As one visitor observed, "The gambling equipment is of the finest, most highly decorated variety." Patrons would have no trouble finding the night spot, as "a half dozen roads" led there, and the entrance was marked with "a large electric sign" and "crowded with expensive cars each evening."[20]

Tranchina remained connected to the pari-mutuel industry, with a large New Year's Day 1926 advertisement encouraging patrons to "invest your winnings and forget your losses in a jingling good time." The music of Piron's Orchestra drove the dancing feet of the Beverly Gardens' guests on "the brilliantly polished dance floor"—the band "just makes your feet Charleston and you can't keep still," promised one ad. "Was plenty of money in those days," remembered Bocage. "We used to make as high as twenty, thirty dollars apiece, just collections. And we was getting sixty-some dollars a week salary, you know? Oh, them guys, money was like water with them." According to Bocage, the proprietors kept a one-hundred-thousand-dollar bankroll in the club. But after a Prohibition sweep of habitual violators that included Lafranca's Delmonico restaurant, Beverly Gardens faced the prospect of a padlock order from a federal judge in 1925. Both establishments continued to operate, but Tranchina faced even greater challenges from his partners, a problem that dogged the rest of his career in the nightclub business. Tranchina lost his lease to the Beverly Gardens in 1926, as the owner of the building clearly sought to replace him with another manager.[21]

Tranchina simultaneously operated the nearby Victory Inn, another of the fabled Metairie Road gambling houses, though less opulent than Beverly Gardens. Piron's band played at the Victory, but it was not always a peaceful scene of good times. "They had that great killing scrape there," remembered Bocage. "They was gamblers—all friends, but they wound up murdering one another. . . . Some was from St. Louis, and some was from Detroit." That "scrape" was the April 1927 murder of Ted Werner, one of the Victory Inn's owners. According to sensational testimony, Werner's bodyguard, Joseph Bernstein, put a .45 caliber bullet in his boss's head as he slept in the upstairs front bedroom of his home on 860 Broadway Street. The bloodlust apparently stemmed from a dispute over sixty thousand dollars in jewels the two had stolen from a wealthy woman's New York Ritz-Carleton apartment. The sporting life forced Tranchina to partner with some rough characters. After the Victory Inn closed in August 1927, Tranchina set out with a new venture.[22]

Perhaps inspired by the murderous affair the previous spring or a mostly ineffectual Town of Metairie ordinance that sought to clean up what was increasingly becoming a destination for housing subdivisions, Tranchina and his business associates ordered all of their gaming equipment loaded onto trucks and transported to a large new club located on Jefferson Highway. Rumor suggested that this new gambling palace cost an astonishing two hundred thousand dollars to build, a sum that may have contributed to the casino's ongoing financial trouble. It probably did not help matters that in a fit of rage aimed at political enemies, Governor Huey Long ordered the National Guard to raid the gambling houses in Jefferson and St. Bernard Parishes, among them Tranchina's nightclub. A "hula girl" keeping company with the governor called a contact at Tranchina's and tipped off the club of the pending calamity, a move that allowed employees to spirit out much of the cash before the National Guard arrived. The raids, conducted as illegally as the gambling that they intended to punish, did little to diminish sporting activity in Jefferson Parish, but Tranchina's club on Jefferson Highway proved short-lived. By 1930 it had been sold to St. Agnes Parish to be used as a church, while tract homes began to sprout from the soil of the surrounding acres. Dominick Tranchina briefly operated a restaurant on Canal Street in the 1930s, but it was nothing like the hopping establishments of years past, and by the time of his death in 1937, much of the gambling activity had long since moved to the Southport Lounge, just over the Jefferson Parish line on River Road, and the Suburban Gardens nightclub, establishments owned by powerful men who soon left their own mark on the city's dining and entertainment.[23]

As the lakefront's glory days wound down and much of the gambling and jazz-driven nightlife moved to the far more compliant confines of Jefferson Parish, modest spaghetti houses and saloons began to appear along

Decatur Street and other key avenues of the French Quarter's Italian Colony. In a relatively short time, these workingman's lunch houses evolved into some of the city's earliest nightclubs, renovating, expanding, and taking firm root on Bourbon Street and its cross streets as the 1920s dawned. Sicilian-style pasta had likely been served in small saloons and boardinghouses in the Quarter since at least the last decade of the nineteenth century, but such unprepossessing businesses did not advertise in newspapers or merit listings in city directories, so it is impossible to determine their exact origins. Their existence only became noteworthy when something went awry, as it did for John Amato when his Star of Naples spaghetti restaurant on Customhouse Street caught fire in 1899. The term *ravioli* first appeared in the *New Orleans Times-Picayune* in 1896, when a group of Italian ladies made the dumplings for a fund-raising picnic; Ravioli au Parmesan, presented as an elevated dish, appeared on Antoine's published menu as early as 1901. When Salvatore Messina's spaghetti house served dinner to the mortgage bankers at the St. Louis Hotel in 1908, his modest restaurant was among the small but growing number of Italian-style cafés along Decatur Street that were maturing into destinations for the culinarily curious. By 1920, they had captured the imagination of the broader dining public, signaling an important shift in the way that non-Italians perceived what would ultimately become a central element of New Orleans and American cuisine.[24]

One of earliest Italian restaurants to emerge was the Union Restaurant, also known as "the famous spaghetti restaurant of LaNasa," located at 1019 Decatur Street. Anyone who lived or worked on the lower end of Decatur Street in the early twentieth century would likely have come into contact with some member of the LaNasa family. Like so many of his countrymen in the 1870s, Antonio LaNasa began sailing his eponymous bark between New Orleans and Mediterranean ports, carrying fruit, wine, and other produce. By 1900, other members of the clan, including seven of Antonio's brothers, had become major property owners in the Lower Quarter, where they operated a large boardinghouse, saloon, wholesale produce business, and hardware store in addition to their restaurant. LaNasa's Union Restaurant probably evolved from a saloon in the very late 1890s: by 1902, the Union advertised that its "spagetti [sic] and macaroni" were the best in the city. "Strangers to the city are Cordially invited to give us a call." Situated across the street from the bustling French Market, where sailors and merchants of all kinds mingled, LaNasa's surely entertained its share of newcomers.[25]

The menu at what was eventually dubbed the LaNasa Italian Restaurant steadily grew more elaborate. A large display advertisement from 1916 suggested that its proprietors aspired to be in the same league as the city's other fine eateries, mirroring their elaborate multicourse French-language table d'hôte menus but in Italian. The meal began with anchovies and olives, followed by an Ostrica a la Chef (oyster) soup, and the classical French Filet Sole a la Orly, but rounded out with a decidedly Italian entrée, Cottoletti di Dendo con Piselli (veal cutlet), "Spaghetti a la Nasa," and "Cauliflower a Caruso." The meal continued with another veal dish (this one named for the Duke of Genoa), biscotti and cheeses, coffee, and Chianti. A later ad promised local foods such as pompano and oysters alongside Chicken Cacciatore. For its Thanksgiving dinner, LaNasa advertised *brosciollone* (*bruciolone*), a now-classic New Orleans Sicilian dish consisting of a veal pocket filled with stuffing and hard-boiled egg. The fusion of gulf bounty and Italian tradition might cause modern diners to classify the restaurant as Creole Italian. La Nasa's also began to offer live music and to attract a late-night crowd: like Dominick Tranchina's on Lee Circle, the Decatur Street establishment was among the cabarets targeted by the city and U.S. Navy in 1918. Perhaps because of the difficulties of Prohibition, the LaNasa brothers exited the club business altogether by 1922, converting the restaurant into a bakery that by the 1940s had expanded its operation to a large factory on St. Claude Avenue.[26]

Just as John Astredo's nineteenth-century oyster saloon business gradually transformed into his popular lakeside and Gulf Coast resort fine-dining restaurants, the oyster saloons of other Sicilian immigrants, like Figallo's at 722 Iberville Street, evolved into spaghetti houses in the young twentieth century. Gaetano Figallo came to New Orleans in the 1860s and, like so many other immigrants from the Mediterranean, entered the oyster saloon business. By the turn of the twentieth century, his house served the sort of fare that diners had long since come to expect in New Orleans—"oysters, fish, meat, and game . . . the best the market affords." After Gaetano's death, his widow and son, Emile, continued to run Figallo's as a Tranchina's-style seafood restaurant until 1914, when they sold a controlling interest in the restaurant and nearly forty years' worth of name recognition to Anthony Guiffria. The next year, under Guiffria's management, Figallo's began to advertise "The Real Italian Dish: Ravioli a la Genovese." More changes soon followed. Guiffria took out an advertisement announcing that Figallo's would now be serving "Italian Dinners," markedly de-emphasizing its oyster saloon past. Revealing just how popular Italian food had become in World War I–era America, Guiffria explained, "These dinners are famous throughout the United States and will be introduced for the first time here tomorrow." The next year, he opened the Rose Room at Figallo's, taking out an illustrated display ad that portrayed the newly renovated Iberville Street restaurant as an elegant café featuring tuxedoed waiters and stylish patrons. "With the Biggest, Brightest, Best Jazz Orchestra New Orleans has ever known," boasted the ad, "this is the favored rendezvous for Society to dine and dance in an atmosphere of Refinement." Regardless of whether his band was indeed the biggest, brightest, or best (another ad claimed that Figallo's was the only Italian restaurant in the city), Guiffria positioned Figallo's as one of the Italian hot spots beginning to take their place in the city's nightlife.[27]

In 1920, Figallo's success on Iberville Street allowed it to move into more spacious quarters at 229–231 Bourbon Street, with Guiffria purchasing the building. The French Quarter's spaghetti restaurants had attracted notice from the growing number of tourists who came to New Orleans in search of nightlife, and Guiffria publicized his fancy new dining room in an advertising section of the *New Orleans States*, aiming phony news copy and photographs of the interior and exterior directly at out-of-town visitors. "Figallo's Ravioli Can't Be Duplicated," boasted one faux news story. Declared the ad copy, "The Figallo Restaurant reminds one of the old-time cafés of New Orleans, which were famous throughout the country and in parts of Europe." The combination of Italian specialties and local seafood favorites such as fish and soft-shell crabs continued the established fusion of ethnic dishes and Louisiana ingredients.[28]

Italian food had somehow become hip, much in the same the way that people outside the culture "discovered" Vietnamese food in the Gulf South during the early 2000s. Restaurants dominated an advertising section run by the *States* during the 1916 horse-racing season that also featured illustrations of "points of interest to visitors in quaint historic New Orleans"—the French Market, the Peristyle at City Park, and the (soon to be demolished) Slave Block at the Hotel Royal. In addition to touting Antoine's, Tujague's, and the Old Absinthe House, the section featured three ads for relatively new Italian houses. A photograph of Frank Manale headed copy that beckoned tourists to his "quaint little place in the Garden District." Just three years into its existence, what we know today as Pascal's Manale served "oysters any style" alongside "spaghetti Italian style." Just to the right of Manale's ad ran another for Messina's Restaurant at 1119 Decatur Street, which had been taken over earlier in the decade by Peter Latino. Messina's continued to operate as an oyster saloon and could accommodate "Ladies, Parties, Banquets, Etc." while still boasting of its role as the "Original Headquarters for the Famous Italian Spaghetti." Next to Messina's ad ran a post for Joseph Toro's Savoy Café and Restaurant, located at the corner of Bourbon and Iberville Streets. Like Figallo, Messina, and Manale, Toro promised "Real Italian Dishes," including spaghetti and ravioli. When Toro moved just two doors down from Figallo's at 223 Bourbon, he, like Guiffria, decided to run newsy advertisements in the *States'* Industrial and Commercial section. A photograph depicted Toro's courtyard, where a "monster umbrella" of "cheerful red stripes" created a "delightfully cool place to eat" even on a "sultry Sunday in July." According to the "story," Toro's fare was as much local as Italian, including turtle soup, "slices of the tenderloin of a large fresh trout," and "chicken sauté with mushrooms" (probably a chicken cacciatore dish).[29]

Perhaps the most famous institution of this kind was Turci's, which opened its doors in 1917 in the 800 block of Decatur Street near the corner of Madison, right next door to Madame Bégué's Exchange, which had become famous for its brunch. The restaurant was the progeny of traveling opera singers Ettore Turci and his wife, Teresa Barteli Turci, who had come to the United States in 1909 and had for the last several years been performing at Fabacher's Rathskeller on St. Charles Avenue. Early advertisements referred to the restaurant as "the cozy place to eat Italian dishes" such as ravioli or antipasto and where "other good things" could be had. Though they were not Sicilian— Ettore Turci was born in the northern Italian city of Bologna, while Teresa was Neapolitan—their cooking proved enormously popular with New Orleanians, whether of Italian heritage or not.[30]

Ettore Turci's association with legendary opera singer Enrico Caruso probably did as much to cement the restaurant's reputation as the food did. The world's best-known tenor, Caruso arrived in New Orleans in late June 1920 aboard the *Cartago*, a United Fruit Company steamer bound from Havana. Turci and Caruso had known each other in Italy before the latter had become famous, but not until he and his entourage ate at Turci's did their relationship grow. On a hot Sunday afternoon, the "sizzling of butter and the aroma of garlic" yielded dishes that reminded Caruso of home, and according to Teresa Turci, the singer "came here that Sunday just as if he had been here a hundred times before and I remember how he joked with me and pretended to find fault with my cooking, to tease me. When he left I felt as though we had been friends for years instead of only a few hours." Caruso invited his new friends to visit him at his country estate, the Villa di Bellosguardo, near Florence, but the following summer, as Ettore Turci was en route to Italy for their reunion, he received word that Caruso was dead.[31]

In the summer of 1924, Turci's moved to 229 Bourbon Street, a much larger and more elaborate establishment dubbed Turci's Italian Gardens. The space was leased from Anthony Guiffria, who had decided to close Figallo's restaurant and concentrate on his growing real estate business. The enforcement of Prohibition may have influenced Guiffria's decision—Figallo's Restaurant had a scrape with the law that Guiffria and his partner, Anthony Figallo, narrowly escaped. In a ruling that would have doubtlessly mystified a drier town, a Prohibition commissioner ordered the $1,000 in alcohol returned because perjury had been employed to secure a seizure warrant. In the early 1920s, both violating the Volstead Act and eating Italian food had become so mainstream in New Orleans that the Women's Auxiliary of the City League, a good-government group, hosted a spaghetti dinner at Turci's Italian Gardens not long after it opened.[32]

For New Year's Eve 1924, Turci's took out a large display ad in the newspaper that reflected the sort of dinner cabaret that it had become. Calling itself "the place that is different" and a "cosmopolitan café," Turci's offered diners and dancers "unequalled and delicious Italian menus" in the "unusual setting of the Italian Gardens," which offered "the natural accompaniment to such dishes." A correspondent for the *New Orleans Daily Picayune*'s "Letters to Elizabeth" buying and advice column—a thinly veiled advertising feature—described Turci's "fancy" dining room: "One enters the Garden through a tiled corridor and innumerable little gates of lattice and green vines into a realm of joy, light and beauty. Flowers and lights all over the place and in the center a Christmas tree brilliant with color. Attractive tables, attentive servitors and Monsieur and Madame Turci to see that all is 'just so.'" Suggesting the presence of alcohol, she closed her note with "we danced until closing time."[33]

Like many other proprietors of New Orleans eateries, the Turcis' run-ins with the law over Prohibition became more frequent and costly beginning in 1926. In early February, Ettore Turci posted a one-thousand-dollar bond that, in conjunction with forbearance from a federal judge, prevented the Italian Gardens from receiving what amounted to a death sentence for a restaurant: an order requiring the padlocking of the premises for a year. In light of Turci's pleas that he had spent "$21,000 in alterations and improvements" and had a ten-year lease and of the fact that only three of the government's sixteen witnesses turned up for the hearing, the judge eventually gave Turci a suspended sentence of a year and a three-hundred-dollar fine. "Turci's place would be closed under a padlock order and he would forfeit a $1000 bond if dry officers prove liquor is sold in the restaurant again," observed the *Picayune*. Ettore Turci's luck ran out in May 1931, however, when his waiters sold wine and liquor to undercover agents. Judge Wayne Borah sentenced the restaurant owner to nine months in prison but spared Teresa Turci by giving her only five years of probation, following the custom of not sentencing both spouses to prison at the same time.[34]

When Turci's lease at 229 Bourbon finally ran out in 1934, the new tenants were none other than Leon and Louis Prima, who opened the short-lived but eternally famous Shim-Sham Club. The change symbolized things to come after the fall of Prohibition. No longer was it necessary to go to Suburban Gardens in Jefferson Parish to enjoy drinking and dancing, although it remained a haven for gambling; instead, both locals and tourists could enjoy the vibrant music scene on the French Quarter's Bourbon Street. The *Picayune* touted Deco's arrival, announcing the imminent opening of the Prima brothers' new club after "elaborate redecoration in modernistic style is practically complete." Turci's moved just up the street to 223 Bourbon (later the site of Toro's), remaining as popular as ever with those seeking Italian food, including traveling opera stars. On one occasion, a Metropolitan Opera tenor, Beniamino Gigli, walked several blocks from the Louisville and Nashville station at the foot of Canal Street to Turci's to catch some dinner before his train left for Dallas. The maître d' brought Gigli through the kitchen to a private room at the back of the restaurant. When Ettore Turci arrived at the table, "Gigli asked him something in Italian and then gave instructions to his secretary. The secretary went out and returned with a brown paper bundle. The paper was creased, apparently from repeated wrapping and unwrapping." It was the opera star's special pasta—the key, he claimed, to his prescribed diet. "So saying, he opened a carton of the special preparation, grabbed a handful of it and handed it to the restaurant manager. 'Cook it eight minutes,' he instructed." Turci's remained on Bourbon Street until 1945, when it moved to 914 Poydras Street, the location familiar to most of those who still remember the restaurant. Even today, people still talk about Turci's red sauce.[35]

Nowhere was the transformation from turn-of-the-century oyster saloon to 1930s nightclub more fully realized than at Anthony "Antoine"

Masera's place at the corner of Bourbon and St. Louis Streets. Masera came to New Orleans from Genoa in 1868 and three years later married Louisa Persigo, about whom we know little except that she had been born in Louisiana to Italian parents. Like so many members of this early generation, young Masera worked at a physically demanding job—in his case, dealing wood and coal—before opening an oyster saloon sometime in the 1880s at 809 St. Louis Street, a building that for the ensuing century and a half has housed a series of clubs and restaurants reflecting the Bourbon Street of the day. (Today it is home to a daiquiri shop.) By the first decade of the twentieth century, Masera's could be found in city directories under "lunch houses" and "restaurants" as well as "oyster saloons," and it must have thrived on this busy corner if its commercial endurance serves as any indication. Masera's family grew alongside his restaurant: by 1910, he had eight adult children, including three sons who eventually transformed the business.[36]

Masera's made the transition from oyster saloon to cabaret sometime before 1918, when the same law that ensnared Dominick Tranchina's on Lee Circle and the LaNasa restaurant on Decatur Street shut down Masera's ability to pair live music with alcohol. "The snare drum rolled forth its last note. The sliding trombone gave vent to its last moan. The pianist touched the last key, and the voice of the singer was silenced," declared the *New Orleans Times-Picayune*, "for the lid had descended on cabarets and for the duration of the war it will remain clamped down." Fans of jazz today would surely ache at the chance to hear the music being played in these houses in 1917, but before the 1920s, many self-described respectable white New Orleanians considered the hotter forms of jazz at best low culture. The taint was about more than just music: In defining *cabaret*, the police superintendent described "an establishment where there is music, singing, and dancing, and which is frequented by men and women of questionable character." The official predicted that Masera's, located on the edge of the French Quarter's Tango Belt, where prostitution thrived, and other such houses would "be lost without the wild wails of the jazz bands." Far from lost, Masera's was an extraordinary survivor, exploiting a loophole in the law that allowed cabarets to survive by marketing themselves more fully as restaurants. An ad encouraging diners to enjoy Thanksgiving 1918 at Masera's promised "Delicious Italian and French Dishes."[37]

Antoine Masera did not live to see the transformation of his restaurant into a modern nightclub, but his death in 1919 also spared him the drama of the Prohibition era, a busy time for his sons. The first raid conducted by dry officers, in February 1922, netted comparatively little booze—sixty-six bottles of beer, seven bottles of wine, and four dozen one-ounce bottles of liquor—yet there is little doubt that the Masera brothers were in the business of bootleg alcohol in a significant way. When federal authorities seized Louis Masera's cabin cruiser, the *Loiterer III*, just off Bayou La Batre on the Alabama coast in the summer of 1923, its owner claimed to know nothing about the twelve thousand dollars' worth of booze on board, declaring, "I loaned the yacht to a party of friends for a few days to fish along the Gulf Coast." A more determined raid conducted six months later at the restaurant revealed elaborate plans to evade detection. At first, agents failed to find any alcohol, but their search ultimately led to the discovery of a trapdoor leading to an adjacent building, and "passing through this they found themselves in Gaspar Locolomo's pressing shop at 507 Bourbon Street, which abuts the rear of the restaurant. More than 300 bottles of whisky, wine, gin, benedictine and other liquor were seized," noted the *Times-Picayune*. Laundryman Locolomo took the fall for the Maseras and claimed the liquor as his own. Two weeks later, police seized a seven-passenger car worth ten thousand dollars as it drove away from the wharves at Orange Street in the Irish Channel. Inside were sixteen sacks of Champagne and four cases of whiskey. The car belonged to Louis Masera's older brother, Joseph. There is little doubt that booze supplied a substantial chunk of the family's income during the 1920s, much if not all of it falling by necessity off the books; like Turci's, however, Masera's remained popular for its food as well. An ad from the late 1920s and early 1930s shows a fashionable couple seated as a tuxedoed waiter takes their order—perhaps Masera's "famous . . . chicken and spaghetti."[38]

With the end of Prohibition, Masera's expanded into 805 St. Louis and 507 Bourbon (where the restaurant had once hid its alcohol) and became "Masera's Restaurant and the Nut Club," promising "The Last Word in Night-Club Entertainment." With the end of the cat-and-mouse games of alcohol enforcement, drinking at Masera's and elsewhere came out into the open with a vengeance. The Nut Club featured live music, dancing, and "Your Favorite Drink as You Like It"—around the clock. A 1935 ad for G&W London Gin paid Walter Winchell to opine on New Orleans's night spots, including Masera's. Of the Nut Club he offered, "stepper outers and dropper inners will like this one—your friends are that way about the food—and why not—there's soft lights and sweet laughter with a hot-cha-cha—not to mention Charles Fisher and his orchidaceous orchestra." Despite Joseph Masera's 1935 run-in with the law for selling smuggled liquor and a sensational episode the same year in which a twenty-three-year-old woman stabbed to death a wealthy young man from a prominent Mississippi family while he was seated in the bar's dining room, the Nut Club remained a popular destination for the rest of the 1930s, often mentioned in the same breath as the Primas' Shim-Sham and the Roosevelt Hotel's Blue Room.[39]

Just three blocks down from Masera's, at 800 Bourbon Street, stood one of the most prominent Sicilian-owned restaurants of the 1930s and 1940s, the fancy La Lune. Yet La Lune was also something of an anomaly in that it was a Mexican- rather than Italian-themed nightclub. John Panzeca's parents had opened a grocery store at the location in 1918, after coming to New Orleans from Sicily by way of St. James Parish. Before long, however, their youngest son began using the prime location in the French Quarter as an operational base for his Prohibition-era alcohol business. A picture from about 1930 shows the tidy store well stocked with an assortment of canned and dry goods as well as a conspicuous display of Anheuser-Busch "Extra Dry" ginger ale. In the center of the photo stand George and Angelina Panzeca, the store's proprietors, clad in modest shopkeepers' garb. Behind the bar on Angelina's right stands a well-dressed African American man in a fedora, while on the opposite side, partially concealed, stands a dapper John Panzeca wearing a three-piece suit. Neither of the younger men appears attired to fill a grocery order. John Panzeca was arrested several times beginning in 1928 for possessing large amounts of liquor; on one occasion in early 1929, his "negro porter, George Parker" (possibly the man in the photo) was also arrested. In both instances, Panzeca posted a $1,000 bond. More seriously, in 1931, dry agents found "an elaborate rectifying plant and more than 350 bottles of whisky and gin" next door to La Lune at 808 Bourbon Street. Yet despite these troubles, Panzeca, like hundreds of other saloon operators, obtained a liquor license in April 1933, as Prohibition came to an end. He soon began running a want ad for "Two Mexican young men, able to sing Mexican folk songs and play guitar."[40]

Panzeca's transformation of 800 Bourbon Street from old-fashioned grocery and saloon to modern nightclub spoke to his canny navigation of and profit from the risky Prohibition years. He renovated a building from the 1880s or so into a studied imitation of the sort of older "French Quarter–style" structures that visitors to New Orleans wanted to see. By the mid-1930s, the club also hosted the eclectic stage shows, targeted at an increasingly tourist crowd, that poured the foundation for Bourbon Street's golden age in the following decades. When Panzeca's regular piano player departed in 1937, an observer noted tongue-in-cheek that "everyone has been missing the blond, horn-rim-spectacled esthete who used to improvise soul-stirring runs and variations to 'Liebestraum,' 'Orchids in the Moonlight,' or 'Smoke Gets in Your Eyes.' Sentimental sippers in La Lune's patio would drip long, salty tears into their West Indian Daiquiris; young couples would moon vacantly at each other. That pianist seemed so perfectly to fit his regalia of dark trousers and white satin peasant blouse with flowing red tie. He was equally good at jazz or Mexican folk music." When *Look* magazine ran a piece on the French Quarter, it used a photograph of La Lune's patio, "the only place of its kind used in the layout," even though the Vieux Carré Survey would later term it "inappropriate construction." In the 1940s, local radio station WWL broadcast from the dining room. One of Bourbon Street's longer-running nightclubs from the 1930s, La Lune survived until 1960, when it finally gave way to Pete Fountain's jazz club.[41]

Alcohol has always been and remains still an important part of the economy and culture of New Orleans. An early morning run in the more commercial parts of the French Quarter demonstrates that for thousands of tourists and a fair number of locals, days seem to roll by on a lazy current of booze, even well past the time when the sun has risen on tomorrow. More broadly, the social acceptability of casual drinking at hours of the day not normally countenanced in great swaths of America is a truism of living in the Crescent City. Prior to the city charter of 1896, anyone with the proper business license could sell liquor, and even enforcement of the Sunday Law of 1886 was selective. More than two decades later, the Gay-Shattuck law upped the ante in the war between the Protestant Progressive era worldview and the city's deeply ingrained tavern culture.

It was no accident that such alcohol enforcement emerged precisely at the moment when immigrants from Southeastern Europe began to fill the polyglot slums of the nation's urban spaces. Anxieties about social hygiene, race, crime, alcoholism, political corruption, and "immorality" fueled the rise of the Progressive movement, itself a sometimes contradictory coalition of religious crusaders and devotees of scientific progress. In New Orleans, these national movements targeted black and immigrant citizens. A quick review of those arrested for violating the Gay-Shattuck Law reveals that many of these literally uncountable businesses, particularly in the "back of town," on the margins of human habitation, never advertised or even appeared in the city directory.

Had they not run afoul of the law, we would not know that they ever existed. Selling liquor was one way that immigrants could further their ascent of the economic ladder. To reformers, the presence of such establishments—whether run-down bars in tough neighborhoods or stylish cabarets on the city's main thoroughfares—caused numerous other societal problems.

Non-Sicilians' understanding of "Italian" culture in New Orleans underwent a transformation in the 1920s as a consequence of the paradoxical rise of Prohibition and embrace of Italian food. Dishes such as spaghetti and ravioli burst onto the nation's culinary consciousness both in restaurants and in the home. This cuisine originated in modest surroundings, like the humble cafés that once sold inexpensive fare to seamen and produce vendors along Decatur Street. Yet Italian food had also begun to appear in some of New Orleans's nicer dining establishments that are often associated with the culture of early jazz. Spaghetti became so embedded as a marker for Italian culture in America over the next fifty years that when Sergio Leone's Italian-shot productions featuring a young Clint Eastwood became popular in the 1960s, they became known, not entirely flatteringly, as "spaghetti westerns." Also during this time, the image of Mario Puzo's *Godfather*, the Sicilian immigrant turned gangster, was modeled on the media legends surrounding such real 1920s figures as Al Capone and Charles "Lucky" Luciano. The relationship between Prohibition and the rise of the Sicilian gangster persona during the Jazz Age remains alive in the public imagination, most recently fictionalized in the popular HBO series *Boardwalk Empire*. One wonders what the popular culture image of Italians in America would be today had it not been for the enactment of the Volstead Act. Yet the connection cannot be entirely denied. Widespread participation in the business of alcohol combined with the meteoric rise in popularity of both jazz and Italian food put all the ingredients together in the form of the 1920s nightclub, an image forever redolent in the American imagination.

The relationship between Sicilians, their restaurants, and Prohibition is of course more complicated than popular culture would have us believe. John Panzeca, the owner of La Lune, had been fully immersed in the business of bootleg alcohol during the Prohibition years. Yet after alcohol became legal again, he entered into a broad range of economic and civic activities including real estate, banking, and the opera association. Philip Sciortino, Panzeca's nephew, remembered that despite Panzeca's wealth, he could never gain acceptance to such old-line Carnival krewes as Rex and Proteus, though "he got into Hermes. And we used to go his house . . . and many times we had picnics, and you would hear him tell the stories. He said, . . . 'I have the money, but I don't have the prestige of saying I belong to Rex. . . . But these fellas come to me when they can't go anywhere else when they're having a ball for their daughter to be a debutante, or when . . . they're in financial straits . . . they come to me.'" Panzeca, like the other wealthier Italians, had emerged as a sort of parallel society to the traditional, hereditary Uptown New Orleans elite. When barred from Old Money New Orleans traditions, members of this Italian class created their own, such as the lavish Krewe of Virgilians, which existed from 1935 until 1964, by which time its members received greater acceptance into the city's elite social circles. Despite earning his money as a bootlegger during Prohibition, Panzeca went on to greater, legitimate business and civic pursuits, and they were often connected to his pride in his Sicilian heritage. New Orleanians saw a vast difference between selling whisky and wine to customers and playing the role of hardened gangster. Ettore Turci's brief stint in jail did little to tarnish the reputation of the restaurant that he and his wife had built. Conversely, Masera's, which was quite invested in the business of illegal liquor, endured at the corner of Bourbon and St. Louis under other names that underscored the restaurant's connection to the city's underworld syndicate.[42]

CHAPTER 5

"Italian Heaven"

Life in the Sicilian French Quarter
before World War II

If there is a ghost of the city's Sicilian past, it surely haunts the streets of the Lower French Quarter. Even if the dying echoes of spoken Italian fell silent over fifty years ago, and in spite of the Vieux Carré Commission's obsession with erasing what does not conform to its antebellum vision, impressions of the immigrant century remain visible on the landscape if one knows where to look.

For about a century beginning in the 1860s, the part of the Quarter lying below St. Ann and fronting all of Decatur Street functioned as a landward extension of the busy waterfront, with people hauling, wholesaling, and peddling the commerce of the port. While Italian immigrants settled in every part of New Orleans, here in the Lower Quarter, an ethnic neighborhood that outsiders called the Italian Colony emerged by about 1875.[1]

Photographers working at the turn of the twentieth century have bequeathed to us a wealth of images from this time and place, and these pictures have done much to shape our vision of the French Quarter from a century ago. Dilapidated courtyards where careworn immigrant women wait for laundry to dry in the breeze. An army of men unloads stalks of bananas from the hold of a large white steel steamship into a waiting refrigerated rail car, while a man of purpose stands atop the train in a dark suit, supervising the action, and stevedores in shirtsleeves shade their eyes against the afternoon sun and stare at the camera. Five shoeless, streetwise boys sit in a mule-drawn cart at the front of the French Market, four of them looking boldly into the lens. Two other boys gaze directly at us from the margins of a fruit stand, stalks of bananas yawning from rafters in every direction. Stark and real, a heartbeat scissored out of time, these images tell a story of shabbiness and poverty—an incomplete story, written from the perspective of outsiders.[2]

It is no accident that this geography is the source of the mythologies of the Sicilian experience in New Orleans—everything from the muffuletta and Brocato's cannoli to the assassination of Chief David Hennessey. Like the photographs, the mythologies both are grounded in realism and obscure the greater picture. The French Quarter and the Sicilians who lived and worked there stood at the crossroads of a food-distribution empire. For several generations, Decatur Street and the French Market functioned as the drive wheel for the machinery that fed the city and region. While some men labored and fought on the docks for workmen's wages, others made enormous fortunes brokering cargoes bought and sold in distant markets. The French Quarter of 1900 gave birth to the familial, cultural, and financial dynasties that shaped much of the coming century in New Orleans. The Italian Colony operated beyond the reach of the camera's lens.

The citrus groves of Sicily had enabled the island's maritime and merchant class to establish a solid foothold in the trading economy of New Orleans, but diversification into other commodities that originated in Latin America and the Caribbean during the last two decades of the nineteenth century laid the foundation for greater and far more enduring fortunes. Bananas emerged as a commercial force in New Orleans by the last decade of the nineteenth century, borne by the same sort of technological revolutions in maritime transportation that made possible the great wave of Sicilian immigration to the city. While some bananas wended their way to North American ports in the age of sail, they were generally too fragile and deteriorated far too easily in the unforgiving tropical air of the Caribbean and Gulf to become a thriving produce commodity sector when subjected to the caprice of the wind. Even in the age of steam and steel, not until the advent of refrigerated holds in the late 1890s were shippers able to substantially reduce risk in this trade. Before that time, starting in the 1870s, Sicilian merchants branched out into increasing quantities of tropical goods such as coffee from Costa Rica, coconuts from Honduras, and oranges from Cuba. "There can be no doubt that New Orleans ought to be the chief market for the Western States in tropical fruit," observed a prescient local business columnist in 1872. "Not only has it a great advantage in respect of climate, but it is nearer to the sources of supply than any other port. Besides, a lower rate of freight can be obtained by river to most Western points than from New York or Baltimore." The wharves along the French Quarter's rim emerged over the next decades as the locus of this commerce.[3]

The increasingly profitable trade in bananas coincided with what has become the single-most-studied aspect of Italian American culture in the Gulf South—that is, the investigation of vigilante violence against Sicilians during the 1891 Hennessey Lynching. This literature often plumbs the question of whiteness among immigrants and the degree to which nativism drove events. Whatever the merits of this scholarship, it often fails to consider that the Sicilian community had been in New Orleans for over fifty years by the 1890s. It was economically diverse, socially stratified, and politically significant. Importers who had begun their careers handling Sicily lemons, such as Santo Oteri, J.P. Macheca, Giuseppe Grande, Angelo Cusimano, and Michael Di Gregorio diversified their trade to Caribbean routes by the 1890s. This commerce came into New Orleans along the French Quarter's levee, handled by labor gangs controlled by the Provenzano and Matranga families, both substantial dealers in all manner of produce, both imported and domestic. A feud between these two families over the handling of merchandise on the docks supplied the backdrop for Hennessey's assassination in 1890.

Whether or not the feud between the Provenzanos and Matrangas was as central to "the birth of the American Mafia," as Thomas Hunt and Martha Macheca Sheldon argue in *Deep Water*, they persuasively outline Sicilians' broader social, political, and familial relationships and how these factors shaped broader outcomes in the city. The seemingly closed nature of Sicilian immigrant society caused fear among many native-born middle-class white New Orleanians. The fact also looms that Hennessey had taken sides in the affray and was gunned down in the dark on Girod Street—in all likelihood by Italians. Abetted by sensationalistic news coverage and exploited by political leaders, the acquittal of the Sicilians accused of conspiring to murder Hennessey sparked mob violence. Among the eleven Sicilians to die in the affair was shipping magnate J. P. Macheca. Yet, inexplicably, importer and labor boss Charles Matranga escaped the same mob and walked out of the same jail very much alive, as did seven other members of Matranga's faction. This outcome seems to explode any simple explanations based in race theory save for the xenophobic rhetoric used by the mob's ringleaders. The lynching of the Sicilians stemmed from other agendas.[4]

The lynching was less an act of mob justice or race riot than one of politically and economically motivated violence. The problem lay not in the threat of the immigrant class, however much the habits of the poorer among them might offend, but rather in the fact that more affluent Sicilians now challenged the white Uptown elite's commercial and political hegemony. The fact that Sicilian immigrants and their sons dominated the important and growing trade in tropical fruit stoked the envy of those manacled to the falling fortunes of cotton and sugar. Hennessey's murder also showed that Sicilians had broken the elite white monopoly on retributive violence. White southerners had long used this tactic against people who challenged the status quo but feared the prospect of an ethnic minority doing the same. And gangland violence had plagued the Sicilian community since the arrival of the poorer rural laborers in the 1880s, peaking on the eve of the U.S. entry into World War I. From this perspective, Italians seem far less unique in the context of what had always been a violent port city.

Many native-born whites not only viewed Sicilian immigrants with suspicion in the 1890s, taunting them with "Who killa da chief?" or referring to them, jokingly or not, as *dagos*, but also bought groceries from them at the French Market or local corner store, drank and danced at Tranchina's West End Hotel, and raced sailboats with John Astredo at the Southern Yacht Club. The riot taught the Sicilians that they deserved more respect, and their elites would never again permit themselves to be so abused. Time, commerce, and broad sociological transformations were on their side. Perhaps coincidentally, Italians almost immediately appeared in exponentially greater numbers in the city's social columns, while their children attended and graduated from the most elite schools alongside the children of the participants in the Hennessey mob. It did not hurt that tropical fruit eventually propelled a small group of New Orleans Sicilians into the ranks of the nation's richest shipping magnates.

One of the giants to emerge almost overnight in the banana trade was the enterprise of Standard Fruit, the importing company of Salvatore D'Antoni and his partners, the Vaccaro brothers. Joseph, Felix, and Luca Vaccaro's father had come to Louisiana in the 1860s while working the citrus trade between New Orleans and Palermo. Agriculturalists across the circum-Caribbean had worked toward cultivating citrus locally, and the Vaccaro brothers became involved in this risky venture sometime in the 1870s on the Plaquemines Parish plantation of Reconstruction-era governor Henry Clay Warmoth. They eventually branched out into their own groves and marketed their crop on the New Orleans levee, bringing it upriver by boat and operating a thriving trading house in domestic produce on Decatur Street. However, nature upended their business model in 1899, when a massive deep freeze destroyed their groves as well as most of the rest of the local citrus industry, a threat that would always limit the size and investment appeal of Louisiana citrus.

In partnership with D'Antoni, their purchasing agent, the Vaccaro brothers bought the *Santo Oteri*, an old two-masted schooner named after its former owner, and set about buying tropical fruit off the coast of Honduras in the summer of 1899. Their first cargoes included no bananas but instead consisted of two hundred thousand coconuts and some plantains, but the profits from these first trips enabled them to charter a steamer the following season. It was a challenging time to enter the banana business. Indeed, a casual observer might correctly think that the Vaccaro operation was rather late to the tropical fruit party. The giant United Fruit had just consolidated many of the smaller operators into one big cartel, and the remainder clustered under the flag of the Bluefields Steamship Company. Indeed, a number of the independent importers sailing to New Orleans such as Macheca Brothers and Oteri had already been bought up in United's bid to corner the market when the Vaccaros and D'Antoni entered the business. What saved Standard Fruit was the rate of growth in the banana industry, both in Central American fields and among U.S. consumers. There was simply enough demand and enough unexploited acreage for a determined, modernizing new operator. The company grew rapidly, expanding operations into Honduras and eventually Nicaragua and Mexico, where it built docks, railroads, and entire towns. Generations of longshoremen on the levee opposite the French Market unloaded Standard's bananas alongside the produce of other operators and placed the goods onto waiting rail cars that distributed them all over the country. Standard remained privately held until 1964, when Castle and Cook bought a controlling interest in Standard Fruit and moved unloading operations to Gulfport, Mississippi. The direct descendants of Standard Fruit's bananas can today be found in any supermarket wearing a *Dole* sticker.[5]

Despite the heights to which the Vaccaros and some other Sicilian merchants climbed, their social distance from the lowly turn-of-the-century street peddlers could be remarkably small. Commerce, cultural commonalities, and geographical proximity all helped to bridge the gap. In 1904, six men entered the First Recorder's Court facing charges of "making a boisterous outcry" and operating their carts without a permit, an incident that revealed the close connections across the class spectrum in the Italian Colony. Although folklorists Lyle Saxon, Edward Dreyer, and Robert Tallant later extolled the cultural virtues of the songs fashioned by "street criers" who peddled their wares throughout the city, enough people found them sufficiently obnoxious that New Orleans passed a 1902 ordinance to regulate their volume. The law proved so contentious that one street vendor pressed his case all the way to the State Supreme Court, where he lost. Street peddlers, particularly those in produce, represented the bottom of the retailing food chain. They acquired their wares, often on credit, directly at the levee and generally aspired to save enough money to open a stall in the French Market or perhaps even a corner bar or grocery.[6]

The attorney for three of the men, all recently arrived Italians, was Angelo Piaggio, whose family had operated a commission warehouse on Decatur Street from a time when it was still known as Old Levee. Piaggio's father, Peter, described himself as a "seafaring man" and brought back cargoes from the Honduran bay island of Útila as early as 1869, thirty years before Salvador D'Antoni bought his first coconut. By the turn of the century, Angelo and his brother, Vincent, worked as agents for their own steamship company out of offices at 533 St. Philip, where Angelo also practiced law, within earshot of the French Market. As importers, Piaggio Brothers stood at the pinnacle of the food business, yet they remained tied to the street peddler, perhaps out of recognition that many among their class had started under similar circumstances. Indeed, peddling plays a crucial role in the collective cultural memory of Sicilian New Orleans. Unfortunately for the defendants, having powerful friends and able representation was not enough to protect them from the wrath of the law: "I am going to make an example of you people," declared the honorable James Hughes, sentencing each man to pay a fifteen-dollar fine or spend thirty days in Parish Prison. Was Hughes's ire directed at these men because they were Italian, poor, or both?[7]

At the heart of the Sicilian Quarter stood the French Market, a place no informed nineteenth-century tourist dared to miss. For correspondents who arrived by ship, as John H. B. Latrobe did in 1834, the experience was literally unavoidable because the "vegetable market" stood near the bottom of the plank that took them from the ship to the wharf. From Mark Twain in 1857 to Edward King in 1875, everyone seemed to harbor an opinion about the market's charms and failings, and these written impressions contributed, for good or ill, to the city's exotic reputation. Few opined with as much derision as Lafcadio Hearn, who described the market's slovenly appearance to a Cincinnati audience in late 1877, a time when Italians had begun to make their presence felt: "Piles of cabbages, turnips and strange vegetables adorn each side.

Monstrous cheeses smile from every corner; the walls are festooned with bananas, etc.; while fish, bread, flour, and even alligators, have each appropriate tables." Hearn heard "every language—English, French, Italian and German, varied by gombic languages of every shade; languages whose whole vocabulary embraces but a few dozen words, the major part of which are expressive, emphatic and terrific oaths."[8]

Photographs from the turn of the twentieth century show a very similar scene. Looking down Decatur Street where North Peters branches off to form a narrow pie wedge of ground at the tip of the vegetable market, one image shows the early morning sun just over the river, boiling from the lumpy, manure-strewn cobbles a warm-weather haze that clings indolently to a line of empty produce wagons and crates of the despised cabbages. Surrounded by stalks of bananas and bundles of pineapples hanging from the rafters, an Italian man in the first stall arranges oranges into tall pyramids. A few steps away, a young woman surveys a sad display of spotted bananas selling for a dime a dozen, while two nearby men survey her with significantly greater approval. Just across Decatur, where Central Grocery is now, white awnings stretch between the second-story balcony and the sidewalk in a valiant effort to repel the heat of the day. Today, all of this is gone, replaced by the decorative shrubbery in front of the Joan of Arc statue.[9]

The French Market has operated in one form or another since 1789, when it became the first in a large number of public markets that supplied fresh food for New Orleanians. The city had a total of thirty-four markets before 1911, the most of any major American metropolitan area. Some still stand today: St. Roch, for example, was originally built in 1874 along St. Claude Avenue and was completely renovated in 2014 along the rim of the contemporary city's bohemia. Most are gone—the Prytana Market is now a grassy strip between Lyons and Upperline across from the Kingpin Bar—while others have been converted to other uses. They began as places where local health authorities could inspect and presumably guarantee the safety of meats, seafood, poultry, and fresh fruits and vegetables, and for much of the nineteenth and early twentieth centuries, the city forbade private markets from operating within thirty-two hundred feet (roughly nine blocks) of public markets, all but guaranteeing them a monopoly on fresh food sales and making them neighborhood gathering places. None were as crucial as the French Market, which was always the largest and served as a distribution hub for the smaller neighborhood markets as well as for the corner groceries that dotted the city's landscape.[10]

Many New Orleanians still retain some memory of the French Market before its 1970s transformation into a strictly tourist zone, but those memories are far removed from what existed in the late nineteenth century. As far as American cities are concerned, New Orleans is old, and land uses here have changed significantly over time, sometimes more than once, particularly in the French Quarter. By the 1930s, the antebellum structures of the French Market had not only fallen into a state of disrepair but proved inadequate for distributing fresh produce around a modern city. Trucks and automobiles took the place of mules and wagons as the primary means of transportation, and the nineteenth-century footprint had simply become untenable. Meanwhile, the amount of land between the market and the levee had shrunk because of the river's encroachment. An award of $240,000 by the Works Progress Administration in 1934 set in motion a significant expansion of the produce stalls and renovation of the market into the place people remember seeing in the 1940s, 1950s, and 1960s. Whether or not anyone realized it, the renovations ultimately served less as an investment in the future and more as a temporary staving off of the inevitable decline of the public market system.[11]

Even though current memories document the twilight of the French Market's commercial relevance, the cultural processes that they describe reflect lifestyle patterns established over the course of a century. Salvatore "Tommy" Tusa, who today operates Central Grocery, remembers well the fruit market that used to operate outside the store's window: "Across the street was Sala fruit stand . . . all stacked up and decorated. What it was, was just stalls where they would pile crates of stuff to put their . . . fruit and nuts and dried fruit, but mostly produce. And each one would have their stall area. One stand was after the next. They were all in competition with each other, but [they all] had their calling, they had their draw." "If you wanted a certain amount of something," explained Maria Impastato, "they'd let you take what you wanted, you didn't have to buy a whole bushel of whatever." Her father, who operated the Napoleon House, knew most of the vendors. "He'd after work a lot of times go get a crate of whatever was in season and go deliver it to my aunt on Dumaine, bring some over here, and then bring the rest to us at home."[12]

Seafood and meat were just as important as produce in the French Market of that era. Meat has made a significant comeback at farmers' markets around the country today as consumer demand for heritage breeds and ethically raised stock grows. Two generations ago, however, "the French Market was full of butchers," observed restaurateur Joe Pacaccio. "You might have had a dozen butchers . . . all individual shops, hand-cut meat only. All the different families had a different butcher." Fridays in the pre–Vatican II Catholic city were particularly busy: "They would come with the trucks of shrimp and these big baskets, all that you wanted," noted Tusa. "That was 24/7. Come early, early in the morning, and they had two or three ice houses there, and the fishermen would come and bring their catches." John Gendusa, who spent summers delivering bread with his father, remembered that "you'd be about two blocks away from the French Market, and you could smell it before you could see it. . . . Clean as it could be, but you could smell the fish market."[13]

Either in the market itself or just adjacent to it were stands and restaurants that offered quick meals. Salvatore "Joe" Segreto, whose family roots run deep on Decatur Street, remembered many of these places from his youth. "Battistella's had a restaurant, it was very prominent seafood and breakfast place. There was a man named Lala . . . an Albanese, who had the most famous barbecue place—barbecue pork and chicken. It was unbelievably delicious—sandwiches on a seeded loaf of bread, Italian bread. . . . He sold out almost every night. That's how good it was. And . . . Roma Restaurant (1003 Decatur), was a tiny little restaurant next door to the French Market Bar that had the most delicious food and guys would come there every day for a special. Wednesday was tripe day . . . tripe special, it was so delicious I went there every Wednesday to get a big bowl of tripe." But Segreto knew that the market had been even more fascinating in his father's and grandfather's time.[14]

Most New Orleanians today associate Central Grocery and Progress Grocery (closed in 2001) with the muffuletta despite the fact that the sandwich was merely incidental to both businesses for most of their institutional lives. For most of the city's countless corner grocers, Progress and Central acted as the primary wholesalers of all manner of imported, dry, and fancy goods in the same way that the French Market operated as the hub for fresh produce, seafood, and meat. Indeed, for corner grocers—particularly those operated by Italians—Decatur Street and the French Market represented a kind of one-stop wholesale food corridor. Perhaps as a result, many New Orleans Sicilians today cite Central Grocery as an institution that represents their community's ongoing food traditions. Central is the sole survivor among the once numerous wholesale and retail grocers along Decatur Street that traded in imported goods, and returning there for a muffuletta or a pint of olive salad evokes memories of a time when Central's core business lay in gallon cans of "flag" olive oil or entire wheels of cheese, when the clatter of the French Market could be heard just outside its doors

The sign that hangs in front of Central Grocery fixes the store's founding in 1906, though the documentary record makes it difficult to confirm that date. According to the story originated by Salvatore Lupo, he opened the store in that year and operated it during its early decades with his brother-in-law, Gaetano DeMajo. Lupo immigrated to the United States in 1902 and was definitely working his way toward becoming an independent grocer in 1906. He may or may not have been the "S. LUPPO" who with two other men sold a barroom and restaurant to Augustus Macaluso in September 1903, but by 1908, Lupo was managing a grocery at 1039 Decatur for Bartholomew and Augustus Macaluso, a job at which he would have learned the grocery and importing business. The Macaluso Brothers had long been influential in the world of Italian food goods, but by 1908 their business was verging on collapse. Over the next couple of years, the Internal Revenue Service repeatedly investigated the Macalusos' firm, contributing to the emotional and physical decline of Bartholomew Macaluso and ultimately to his death in Palermo in 1911. A series of legal actions ensued, including a suit by his widow against his younger brother for fraud.[15]

Shortly before Bartholomew's death, Lupo and DeMajo partnered with another Italian, Frank Alfano, and founded Progress Grocery at 1001 Decatur, where that street intersects with St. Philip. (Not to be confused with the completely unrelated Progress Grocery operated by the Perrone family.) Alfano, whose name is all but forgotten today, was a manager of the Central Canning Company, which in the first two decades of the twentieth century canned tomatoes and tomato paste just around the corner in the Lower Pontalba buildings. Alfano also kept a saloon on North Basin, and he probably acted primarily as a silent partner in Progress Grocery, leaving day-to-day operations to the experienced grocers. In late 1918, Alfano decided to parlay his expertise in tomato paste into greater ventures and moved to San Jose, California, where he planned to start a cannery. However, he succumbed to the Spanish flu pandemic before the year was out, apparently causing Lupo and DeMajo to move a block up the street to open Central Grocery at 923 Decatur in 1919. All the contents of Progress Grocery were auctioned off in the summer of 1920.[16]

Lupo and DeMajo set about building Central into the premier wholesaler of imported goods on Decatur Street. Lupo's grandson, Tommy Tusa, has worked at Central Grocery since the early 1970s and continues to operate it today with his cousins, Frank and Larry. "We weren't as busy as we are today. We were busy, but it was different," explained Tusa. "We didn't have seating. . . . We didn't make sandwiches when the business first opened up with my grandfather—that evolved, that came later." Tusa continued, "Saturday was a big, big day. We'd have the same families come here every Saturday—the mother, the father, the kids, their aunts, their uncles. . . . It was an experience. . . . Some of them, they'd buy a wheel of cheese—I mean, that was a big deal. . . . It was maybe fifteen, twenty minutes haggling over the price. . . . They'd go check the prices next door and come back and forth, and . . . they'd buy cases of pasta— they didn't buy packs, they bought cases of pasta, olive oil. . . . Back then, it was mostly families. Saw them on a regular basis. Just like you go to the super- market once a week, they came here once a week." Betty Bellone Unsworth, whose grandfather ran a corner grocery, remembered accompanying him on pilgrimages to Central Grocery to buy salami, "that small round kind with that black anise thing in it." Her grandfather would conduct the transaction with Lupo in Italian or possibly the t'Abresche dialect spoken by ethnically Alba- nian Sicilians and then "he'd bring [the salami] back to the grocery store and cut" it. For the girl, these weekly trips were "one of the great thrills of my life."[17]

Many New Orleanians also have fond memories of Progress Grocery, lo- cated just a few doors down from Central Grocery on Decatur Street. When twenty-one-year-old Bartolomeo Perrone arrived in New Orleans in 1907 after sailing from Palermo on the *Il Piemonte*, he had ten dollars in his pocket and the name of a sponsor living on Decatur Street. After working for a time at the Southern Canning Company, he became a food salesman, and in 1924 he partnered with another Italian, Frank Aiello, and opened Progress Grocery on Decatur Street. Perrone's grandson, John Perrone Jr., remembered that "he had a lot of spunk." When a knife-wielding would-be robber came into the store, Bartolomeo "picked up a stock fish . . . a cod that was from Norway. It was air-dried and they were usually about three feet long, and it looked like a piece of driftwood. It was hard as a rock." He then threatened the intruder with the fish: "'The first thing I'm gonna do is knock that knife outta your hand,' he says. 'The next thing I'm gonna do is beat you on the head with this.'" The intruder quickly fled.[18]

John Gendusa remembered that in the back of Progress Grocery was "this big ol' barrel, and that's where [Bartolomeo Perrone would] mix his olive salad." The olive salad and many of the other products created a distinctive aroma that many patrons of these traditional Italian groceries still recall. For Joe Pacaccio, the aroma was so important that when he opened Carmine's, his restaurant in Metairie, he bought and hung nearly two hundred pounds of baccalà (dried salted cod) from the rafters so the place would acquire the same sensory quality. In addition, Pacaccio remembered the smells of "garlic, salami, cheeses—all the cheeses that you could want to eat." According to Pacaccio, every morning, Perrone would take a twelve-pound piece of Romano cheese out in the morning and "put it into a glass case that was not refrigerated on purpose. . . . You wanted it to warm up so you could cut it without it crumbling. It had so much oil and butterfat in it that we literally had a block of wood that we would use to elevate it on inside its tray so that the butterfat could drip down below the cheese and . . . not have it swimming in oil when you picked it up to make a cut from it. Well, the aroma from that cheese was incredible."[19]

Central and Progress Groceries shared several characteristics that differentiated them from most of New Orleans's typical corner stores, but their financial success probably resulted primarily from the fact that in both cases, the family's "American" generation took over the business. When Salvatore Lupo wanted to retire in the 1950s, according to Tommy Tusa, "he had no sons, and Mr. DeMajo's sons weren't interested in the business." But Lupo's daughter, Maria Lupo Tusa, was. She was determined that she would not "let this business go away," so she asked her husband, Frank Tusa, to leave his job with the Federal Land Bank and take over Central Grocery. He continued in the business until his death in 1975; their son, Tommy, subsequently stepped in to run the business.[20]

Bartolomeo Perrone's sons took a more direct path to running a traditional Italian grocery, but in some ways that route was far more unusual in the context of their generation and life experiences. John Perrone, the oldest, ran the grocery as a teenager in the 1930s while his father spent three months bedridden after a hernia operation. John's mother had already died, so he not only opened the store every morning, leaving it in the care of an employee while he was at school, and returned to work and close up in the evening but also helped take care of his siblings. In 1936, John enrolled at Loyola University, graduating on the eve of World War II. At the end of the conflict, he chose to return to New Orleans and partner with his father and brother in the grocery store in 1945. Having a college education meant that John Perrone had other options, but his decision to return to the family business perhaps offers some insight into his character or to the effect that the war had on him.[21]

By the 1920s, St. Philip Street had emerged as the gravitational center of the Sicilian French Quarter, a cultural landscape all but disappeared today save for the presence of Matassa's Grocery at the intersection of Dauphine and for Irene's Restaurant, at Chartres, nearer the river, on the ground floor of what was the Federico macaroni factory. The Italian roots run deep on St. Philip, where both Peter Lamana and his son's kidnappers lived, where Jacob Cusimano first manufactured dry pasta, and where Angelo Piaggio practiced law. Not only was the French Quarter far more densely populated than it is today, but 161 of the 171 souls who lived on St. Philip Street between Decatur and Chartres in 1920 were of Italian extraction, and 53 of them had been born in Italy. Sicilians were only slightly less dominant in the 600 block of St. Philip, where the residents included Sylvestro Carollo, known in later-day gangland lore as Silver Dollar Sam despite his stated profession as a wholesale fruit dealer. Not until one crossed over Bourbon on the way toward Rampart Street did the overwhelmingly Italian character of the Lower Quarter yield to an increasingly black and mixed-race neighborhood.[22]

Echoes remain of the food culture that thrived here in the early twentieth century, when the aroma of freshly baked bread drifted over the old cobblestone pavers. In the middle of the 600 block of St. Philip, a one-story masonry carriageway with the words "Ruffino's Bakery" stretching above the lintel offers mute testimony to the fabled muffuletta loaves that once issued forth from its ovens. Most devotees of New Orleans cuisine recognize *muffuletta* as the sandwich found on numerous city menus and identified around the world with the Central Grocery. But the name actually comes from the bread itself, a browned, airy, Sicilian-style loaf about ten inches across and topped with sesame seeds. Customers would buy the cheese and salami separately, explains former baker Nick Loguidice, "and the only bread they had was the muffuletta bread so they took it off the shelf, unwrapped it, cut it, put the stuff on it. Then they would put olive salad on it, 'cause that's what their condiments were, and wrap it back up. Well, the American people see that and said, 'Well gimme one like that.' When they took it home, the wrapper on the bread said 'muffuletta.' . . . They didn't have a sign saying that's what they sold—that's *all* they sold."[23]

Loguidice's great-grandfather, Giuseppe Ruffino, came to New Orleans in the 1890s and began baking the muffuletta on St. Philip Street for sale to his countrymen. One can imagine a street peddler, his cart clattering slowly down Chartres or Ursulines, only blocks from the bakery, crying out, "Muffuletta! Caldo de caldo!" (Hot, hot! Muffulettas!). Bread was an essential ingredient in the Sicilian immigrant's diet, and fresh bread like the loaves sold by Ruffino could be found in numerous storefronts in the Italian Colony. Lest we be too nostalgic, contemporary outsiders viewed this subculture as a problem in need of correction. One July afternoon in 1909, the city health officer made a sweep of shops in violation a recent law requiring that bread sellers protect their loaves from flies with wrappers, screens, or a glass case. A circumnavigation of Ursulines and St. Philip Streets resulted in fifteen violators, fourteen of them Italian. Thus, the sandwich's name found its genesis in a paper wrapper for each loaf that bore the name *muffuletta* and was required by largely Protestant and nativist Progressive era reformers who worried about the purity of the food and beverages sold by the immigrant merchant class.[24]

Like macaroni, the muffuletta loaf eventually found its way into the diet of a broader spectrum of New Orleanians, but the bread took longer and did so only as the vehicle for layers of capicola and provolone and a generous heaping of olive salad. The story of its baking is akin to the narrative of Sicilian New Orleans writ large, a multigenerational endeavor whose objective lies at the intersection of commercial enterprise and cultural expression. In 1913, Nocolo Evola, a musician by trade, came to New Orleans and married Stephana "Fannie" Ruffino, one of Giuseppe Ruffino's ten children, and entered the baking business with his brothers and father-in-law, who had started the enterprise in 1895. When the bakery at 625 St. Philip shut down in the 1950s and gave way to Ruffino's Restaurant, Evola moved on. He and his son-in-law continued baking the muffuletta loaf, eventually establishing United Bakery at 1325 St. Bernard Avenue. For a half a century, United Bakery was the supplier of muffuletta loaves to the city's most famous purveyors of the sandwich. The floodwaters that poured through the failed Corps of Engineers levees and filled the lower parts of the city with a stagnant murk in the days following Hurricane Katrina in 2005 not only drowned the machinery at United Bakery but also stole the will to continue from its proprietor, Sal Loguidice, Nick Evola's grandson. Today, the sandwiches at Central Grocery, the Napoleon House, and other establishments come served on muffuletta loaves baked at the Gentilly bakery of John Gendusa, whose family made its own important contribution to the culinary legacy of New Orleans when it invented the poor boy loaf for Martin Brothers in the 1920s. Though Gendusa's bread makes an admirable sandwich, old-timers often note that the United loaf was a difficult act to follow.[25]

An older generation of New Orleanians harbors even greater nostalgia for United's Italian twist bread, commonly mentioning its hard outer sesame seed crust and firm interior. As Elizabeth Williams, president of the Southern Food and Beverage Museum, remembered, United was the only bakery that "would give you that hard crust on the outside of the bread. It was really brown, and you would break it open and it would make that 'crackery' sound. The bread inside was white and fluffy." It was also versatile and was firm enough to bear up to dipping in a liquid, especially after sitting out a day. Williams recalled enjoying it with café au lait or sweet red wine. In addition, pieces broken off of the braid formed small cups that were excellent for holding toppings. According to Williams, "You would go out in the morning and get figs off of the tree," cut them in half, and then "put a hunk of Creole cream cheese [on the bread] and then on top of it figs." Maria Impastato, who operates the Napoleon House with her brother, Sal, explained, "When you say *hard*, you aren't going to break your teeth on it, but it was just . . . a great texture." Her family frequently ate it for breakfast, with the loaves still warm from the oven: her father "would stop on the way home [from the Napoleon House], and they would be baking it early in the morning, so he'd stop when he left the bar."[26]

Arthur Brocato, whose family has run Angelo Brocato's gelateria and bakery since 1905, is one of many New Orleans Italians—particularly those who grew up in the French Quarter—with childhood memories of enjoying lemon ice scooped up with a wedge of United twist bread. Flamboyant Quarter restaurateur Diamond Jim Moran would send his son down to Brocato's on summer mornings with a glass water pitcher, and the boy would return with it filled with lemon ice to be eaten with twist bread for breakfast. John Perrone's grandmother would thin slice leftover twist bread "by hand, put it on cookie sheets, and put it in a low temperature oven until it dried out really well. Then she would let it come to room temperature and let it sit until it was absolutely dried out and cool and . . . put it in a cookie jar. And it was like a Melba toast."[27]

According to veteran baker John Gendusa, United's singular twist bread resulted from a special process that involved an enormous amount of hand labor: "You take some day-old dough, and I mean, it's all holey and bubbly and airy and you can barely pick it up—it's going to go through your fingers. Put it down . . . and it's just like you're starting from scratch. You add a little salt . . . a little yeast . . . a little of everything that you put in it, you add it back and you run it through [a roller called a dough break] *fifty-four times.*" At the end, the dough "comes out in a nice slab." He continued, "It's not going to come out airy, it's going to be really tight, . . . like an Italian bread should be." Gendusa ultimately got rid of the machine because he felt it was unsafe—"people were sticking their fingers in it"—and too expensive.[28]

The muffuletta sandwich is arguably the single-most-recognized manifestation of Sicilian New Orleans food culture in America, and the debate over who "invented" it reveals much about the decline of the French Quarter's Italian flavor in the 1970s. Although there are competing theories about the sandwich's origins, Central Grocery on Decatur Street has consistently made the strongest claims to having devised the sandwich. In 1976, Maria Lupo Tusa wrote unequivocally, "It was definitely established by my father and his brother-in-law, Gaetano DeMajo in 1906. . . . Some imagine it originated elsewhere because others imitated it. They used it as an enticement to attract customers. This amused my folks at our store." As food journalist Gene Bourg has pointed out, however, no one can "document a claim" to having originated the sandwich. As discussed earlier, there is no definitive documentation that Lupo and DeMajo were in business as grocers in 1906, and although they certainly sold the sandwich by 1938, a display ad from that year did not list the muffuletta among Central Grocery's specialties, which included imported spaghetti and "drinking water crystals" from the thermal springs at Montecatini. In fact, rather than claiming the muffuletta, they touted themselves as having been "the originators of Italian antipasto in 1906"—another dubious claim, since the term itself dates from the sixteenth century and English baron John Cam Hobhouse wrote that he encountered olive salad while traveling in Turkey in 1809–10. In the absence of additional evidence, it appears impossible to determine who put together the first muffuletta, but that information may not really be important. Rather, what is significant is the fact that the muffuletta unquestionably emerged out of the commercial synergy of Decatur Street in the first decades of the twentieth century and the fact that it was never more important to the financial survival of Central Grocery than in the 1970s, when the mercantile life of Decatur Street, the store's original raison d'être, ceased to exist.[29]

Montalbano's Delicatessen at 724 St. Philip Street in the French Quarter was possibly the most memorable place to obtain a muffuletta. There, bathed in the glow of holy candles and under the watchful eyes of saints, customers might wonder whether they had drifted into a deli or a devotional shrine. In 1917, Biggio Montalbano and his in-laws, the Sciambras, opened the deli and grocery in a long, narrow building that probably began its life as a stable in the early nineteenth century. A relatively recent immigrant from the ethnically Albanian Sicilian enclave of Contessa Entellina, Montalbano was twenty-seven years old at the time. Visitors to the site today will have difficulty believing that ten adults and three children once lived at this address, a fact that reflects both the collective business efforts of early twentieth-century immigrant families and our contemporary disconnect from that era. Passers-by today will see a structure that has received "historically sensitive" restoration work in the 1990s, but a 1956 photograph, taken only two years before cinematographer Russell Harlan filmed Elvis Presley in *King Creole* across the street at McDonough School No. 15, reveals a squat, featureless rectangular white concrete block facade. Over the darkly painted screen door, a weather-beaten sign announces the "Angel of Peace Italian Delicatessen" of B. Montalbano. The image not only captures what people who are now in their seventies remember from childhood but also offers a view of the Sicilian section of the French Quarter before the full implementation of the preservationist imperatives that led to the portrayal of the Quarter as a studied affectation of the mid-nineteenth century.[30]

Author Lyle Saxon entered Montalbano's unprepossessing establishment in 1940 as part of a Works Progress Administration Writers' Project piece on St. Joseph's Day, a religious holiday that the sandwich shop took to proportions even more epic than its muffulettas. According to Saxon,

Entering a screen door from the banquette, you find yourself in a narrow room, furnished with a long counter, shelves and a glass showcase, and on the shelves, among jars of antipasto and anchovies, cheeses and sausages imported from Italy, are numerous statues of saints, crucifixes and holy pictures. Statues, too, occupy half of the counter, and at the far end is an altar in which burn crimson vigil lights and on which repose statues of the Holy Family. Another third of the counter is colorfully occupied by an array of at least fifty gaily decorated highball glasses, filled with oil and floating tapers, some always burning, having been lighted by those who came here to make a wish.[31]

To kids growing up in the French Quarter in the 1930s, 1940s, and 1950s, Biaggio Montalbano represented a fascinating enigma. "He was very military—you know, he was an old military guy—and he was interesting as can be," explained restaurateur Joe Segreto. "And he was ... real Sicilian, had fought in the Sicilian army, and ... knew Garibaldi.... All kind of tales you would hear when you were a little kid and you went there. Spoke very little English." Montalbano may have been a veteran of the Italo-Turkish War of

1911–12, drafted alongside so many of his countrymen and emigrating after the armistice. Montalbano's establishment was also unique in that he sold sandwiches by the pound, allowing his customers to determine both the size and contents of their creation. Remembered Segreto, kids would "put our nickels and pennies together, we'd go there and say, 'Mr. Montalbano! Mr. Montalbano!' And he'd, say, 'Well, well, let me see what you got.' And then we'd show him what we had, he'd make the sandwich according to how much money we had in our hand—you know, would gear it to how many slices of this or that and say 'Give me another six cents.' [And we would say,] 'Give us another slice of Swiss cheese' . . . if we came up with a little more money." Montalbano called his creation the "Roma" or "Greco Roman" sandwich, but sitting on the round loaf, it became a *muffuletta* to those who enjoyed it. In addition, Montalbano sliced all the meats and cheeses with a long, razor-sharp knife, a task that required such skill that it amazed everyone who watched him work. All of the cured meats, cheeses, and oils—as well as, of course, the signature olive salad—gave the crowded shop a unique aroma. "It had a great big giant wheel of cheese on the counter and it smelled so good and it looked so good. . . . It was just oozing oil. . . . Smelled like heaven in there . . . Italian heaven."[32]

Another Sicilian New Orleans institution, Brocato's bakery and gelateria was once a landmark in the French Quarter and since 1981 has been a popular destination on North Carrollton Avenue in Mid City. New Orleans was not very good to Angelo Brocato, at least early on. His father, Salvatore Brocato, had brought the family to the city not long after Angelo's birth in 1875. They left behind the medieval town of Cefalù, located on the western rim of Sicily's Conca d'Oro and long admired for its ancient Norman cathedral and rocky shores overlooking the aquamarine waters of the Tyrrhenian Sea. A cobbler, Salvatore Brocato might well have plied his trade among the numerous Cefalutana who had already migrated to New Orleans, but in the summer of 1878, he and more than four thousand other residents of Orleans Parish died during one of the region's deadliest yellow fever epidemics. Angelo's mother brought the family back to Palermo, where Angelo and his brother, Salvatore, apprenticed in the pastry and gelato trade. When they reached adulthood, the brothers returned to Louisiana seasonally aboard the citrus fleet to work in the cane fields around Donaldsonville and to save money. They came for what they thought would be a final time in 1905 to open a small ice cream parlor on Decatur Street near Ursulines. Yet yellow fever again intervened, claiming the life of Angelo's wife. While his brother carried on the business, Angelo returned to Cefalù and remarried. He did not cross the ocean again until 1907, when he returned to the gelato business.[33]

In 1913, the city passed an ordinance requiring that all ice cream contain at least 10 percent butterfat. Because Angelo Brocato made his gelato with very little milkfat, he landed on the wrong side of the law. Despite these challenges, Brocato's gelateria eventually prospered, moving to 623 Ursulines, just one block downriver from St. Philip Street. The enterprise subsequently expanded into the building next door, which featured a tiled parlor, and in 1924, Brocato hired Italian craftsmen to decorate the interior with archways and place a mosaic with the family name on the threshold. His delicacies were popular in the local neighborhood. He became a member of the "respectable class" of Italians in the French Quarter. Located just around the corner from St. Mary's Italian church, the shop became a gathering place for the neighborhood after Sunday mass, and in the early twentieth century, Italian was usually the only language spoken there. Diamond Jim Moran was not the only resident of the Lower Quarter who enjoyed breakfasting on Italian bread dipped in Brocato's lemon ice: Angelo's son, Roy Brocato, remembered patrons doing just that while sitting at tables in the gelateria with warm loaves purchased from the sales window of Lombardo's bakery around the corner. In the 1930s, Brocato's even offered carhop service to customers parked on Ursulines Street.[34]

Although Brocato's enjoys significant fame today for its cannoli, they were not always central to the menu. Instead, the business sold the vastedda sandwich, another Sicilian food featuring ricotta cheese. A hundred years ago, Italian restaurants commonly featured tripe and other sorts of offal not typically encountered today, and the vastedda generally included boiled cow's spleen and ricotta cheese lightly fried in lard, placed on a focaccia-style bun, and perhaps sprinkled with grated caciocavallo cheese. Today, the likeliest place to find the vastedda is on the streets of Palermo, though a few places in the States still serve it—Joe's of Avenue U and Ferdinando's Focacceria, both in Brooklyn, New York. Like many other foods kept alive mostly for tradition's sake, the vastedda is not universally appreciated. One critic has described it as "like a fictional creature butchered and left to rot in an ogre's cellar." Even Arthur Brocato prefers them without the meat.[35]

At Brocato's, the vastedda inadvertently provided the gateway to cannoli fame. In the early 1920s, Angelo Brocato received deliveries of ricotta cheese for the vastedda from the same dairy that supplied the confectionary of Philip Glorioso, who made and sold cannoli nearby. One day, according to family lore, Glorioso decided that he needed all of the fresh ricotta, infuriating the normally quiet Brocato, who vowed to make cannoli to compete with Glorioso. He succeeded, and in 2013, *Saveur* magazine listed Brocato's cannoli among the magazine's one hundred best food items.[36]

Today, a pleasant patisserie, Croissant d'Or, occupies the address where Angelo Brocato once served gelato in the French Quarter, but the shop still bears the imprint of its former owners. Nowhere is this more conspicuous than the mosaic tile work that demarcates the threshold of the *Ladies Entrance*. An artifact of the nineteenth-century tradition of separate dining spaces for ladies and families, the sign reflects a custom long abandoned in most places by 1924, when the tile was set. But Angelo Brocato was a man of an earlier era, and according to his grandson, Arthur, "there were a lot of young boys in the area who would taunt the single girls." Angelo and the other "old Italians did not believe in young ladies venturing off by themselves.... They always had to have a chaperone if they were going someplace." Even when Angelo installed his special doorway for unescorted young ladies, it would have seemed oddly out of step with post–World War I social mores, but as Arthur noted, "the tile has lasted so much longer."[37]

The last generation of children who grew up in the French Quarter's Italian Colony are today entering their seventies. Their experiences probably bear a closer resemblance to life in the Quarter a century ago than to life there today. "It was a paradise for children," remembered Joe Pacaccio. The vendors "knew all about you, ... so when you walked through the French Market and you wanted a piece of fruit, all you had to do was stop and look at it, and whoever owned that stand sooner or later would come up to you and say, 'Go ahead and take it, kid.'" He recalled "a fun place to live. It was a clean place to live, virtually crimeless. Today, today it's a different ballgame." Though others echo Pacaccio's nostalgia, the Quarter was also a tough place back then, especially along the working waterfront of Decatur Street and the French Market. According to John Perrone, his father encountered a tourist who wanted to know what the word *cafuda* meant, since "every time I hear this word *cafuda*, it seems like somebody hits the deck, ... somebody gets punched." Perrone's father explained that the word meant "Hit him!": the tourist was seeing "the young gangs." Nick Loguidice, who moved into 1001 Chartres when his uncle bought the property in 1956, remembered the French Quarter as "really a bunch of drunks. It was a skid row." In particular, he recalled, Decatur Street was home to a broad range of taverns that catered to the sailors of various ethnicities who came ashore along the working waterfront bearing cards with the addresses of their countrymen's preferred watering holes.[38]

Few people under age sixty remember another important New Orleans and French Quarter institution, A. M. & J. Solari, known more popularly as Solari's Grocery. While some of the vendors on Decatur Street dealt in large volumes of produce and imported goods, Solari's had the most evolved retail operation, in part because it was by far the oldest. When Genoese immigrant J. B. Solari opened his doors at the corner of Iberville and Royal, where today the Brennans' Mr. B's Bistro now stands, for the first time in 1864, his establishment likely resembled many of the era's other groceries and import houses—somewhere between an import wholesaler and a retailer. Wines were a big part of Solari's business from the start, and by the 1880s the grocer had matured into a respected retailer with a robust delivery service and a satellite location on St. Charles Avenue. In essence, Solari's had collected in one place all of the wonderful foodstuffs that flowed through the port of New Orleans from abroad or from the countryside. By the turn of the twentieth century, Solari's had become a food department store, a three-story food paradise that retailed what it called "fancy and staple" groceries in the same way that its contemporaries Maison Blanche, Marshall Field's, and Macy's sold fashions and home goods. Solari's also marketed foodstuffs nationwide via mail order catalog.[39]

While Solari's was not Sicilian and was only Italian in the sense that its founders belonged to the community of Mediterranean traders that flourished in nineteenth-century New Orleans, it played a crucial part in French Quarter life for almost a century, the place where the Uptown world intersected with the Quarter's Sicilian community. In 1950, food writer Clementine Paddleford visited Solari's and shared her experiences in the pages of *Gourmet* magazine. If Paddleford recognized the store's Italian roots, she gave no hint of it in her column. Instead, her fascination rested on the "Creole" nature of specialties for sale, a culinary marketing ploy that had already reached an advanced level of maturity. She described Creole seafood sauce, Creole mustard, Creole salad dressing, and the like. In fact, the word *Creole* appears nineteen times in an essay barely a thousand words in length. She offered a detailed description of a praline gift box called "Old Creole Days," a comestible delight offered with presumably no royalties or apologies accruing to George Washington Cable. Solari's was the grocer of choice for the city's elites. As journalist Carolyn Kolb later observed, "Having your groceries delivered by Solari's was not only a sign of your good taste; the delivery itself was an event," with an implausibly shiny delivery wagon announcing the purchase to neighbors.[40]

But Solari's was also a destination for several generations of Italian kids who grew up on the far side of St. Ann Street. Recalled Joe Pacaccio, "We *lived* at Solari's. That's where all the kids in the French Quarter got their snacks. And they always had samples out. Samples of olives, samples of spreads, samples of crackers, so as kids, we knew we could go to Solari's and get a sample." Maria Impastato, who shopped at Solari's with her aunt, remembered that "they baked their own bread. . . . You could smell all the smells, it was very fresh. All the bins full of either beans or rice or nuts . . . truly like an old-time . . . Sicilian market." Joe Segreto remembered visiting the "hustling" and "bustling" store with his mother, who "took us there all the time for breakfast and for little things at the counter." Arthur Brocato's aunt managed the pastry counter, and "there was a smell in that place that I can still remember. And it was a mixture between the fruit and the pastry and the coffee and the chocolate—all that." It was an aroma that "you could not duplicate." Moreover, according to Brocato, Solari's carried products unavailable anywhere else, among them cans of chocolate-covered ants.[41]

Omar M. Cheer bought the enterprise from the Solari family in 1924 and spent the next thirty-five years building a national reputation as a gourmet store. Cheer lived on an upper floor of the building, and in a routine belonging to a bygone era, ate breakfast every morning at his reserved spot at the lunch counter. Yet after his death in 1959, his heirs decided the real estate was more valuable than the business. A group of Texas investors bought the building in 1961 and promptly razed the structure that had housed Solari's since 1873. Though another investor built a new building in the same location and the store operated there for another four years, it never regained its old magic. The same company later bulldozed the Regal Brewery and the Vieux Carré Inn and replaced them with a Hilton hotel, as the Canal side of the Quarter began to assume its modern appearance. "That was a loss, I think, in the French Quarter," observed Maria Impastato. "People in the French Quarter *really* miss that. When that changed, I remember daddy talking about it, because all my aunts that lived in the Quarter and their families, . . . that was their market, and that was a big loss for them. They didn't have to go out, way out to the suburbs, you know, to get groceries. That was a big, big change."[42]

Another large Italian-owned grocery on the edge of the French Quarter, Puglia's Quality Food Store, opened in 1948 at 1100 North Rampart Street in a brick structure originally built in 1840. Though it was not New Orleans's first modern supermarket, it was the first one in the Quarter. A relatively recent immigrant who had arrived in 1923, John Puglia lived near the Magazine Market and worked as a butcher, priding himself on his special rendition of Italian sausage, which he marketed under the Pisa brand in the 1950s and 1960s. He always harbored a desire to open a true grocery store and brought this dream to fruition at the corner of Ursulines and Rampart Streets. Spacious by French Quarter standards and with a rare covered parking lot next door, Puglia's establishment catered to modern realities, stocking many of the name-brand products that customers increasingly expected and pairing them with a first-rate meat counter and extensive wine selection. "You still had a unique clientele at Puglia's supermarket, it was all the local people. And then some people came from other parts of the city just to shop," remembered Joe Pacaccio. This formula would do remarkably well in the quarter today, but Puglia's was ahead of its time.[43]

At the time of Puglia's founding, the Quarter's dynamics had already begun to change, though those changes are much more visible in hindsight. By the 1980s, the city had entered a bleaker period, and businesses all over the Quarter felt the pinch. By 1984, John Puglia's sons decided to sell the business—building, stock, and all. None of their children had any interest in running the store, and the brothers decided that the time was right to retire. Their timing was actually quite poor from a business standpoint. Although they still did a good business in prepared foods and muffulettas, the demographics of the Quarter had long since changed. "This used to be an area for families with children coming in here. We used to do a heckuva Easter egg business at Easter time," Peter Puglia noted in 1984. "Now the Quarter is full of single people, young professional people. Things change." The store sat diagonally across from Armstrong Park, which the city fenced off to keep people from being victimized by criminals after dark. That same year, the World's Fair lost money throughout the summer, and oil companies recalled staff to Houston. The Puglia brothers were never able to sell the business, and the building remained vacant for decades. After a 2011 fire, preservationists worried that the building itself would no longer stand. Eventually restored, it is now part of the contemporary French Quarter's booming luxury housing sector.[44]

The Sicilian French Quarter that once existed now remains only in memories. What thrives in the Vieux Carré today is almost entirely the product of conscious changes implemented in the 1970s by the mayoral administration of Maurice "Moon" Landrieu. These plans constituted a reaction to the profound demographic, technological, economic, and social changes that had rendered obsolete the life patterns that had once governed the Italian-dominated end of the Quarter. Some observers might criticize this effort to reimagine the life of the French Quarter as unchaining the storied neighborhood from its working past, but in reality, by 1965, most of that history had already gone elsewhere or evaporated entirely. The Italian kids growing up in the Quarter during the 1950s could not have known that they belonged to the last generation of New Orleanians to witness firsthand the commercial dialogue that had governed life in the city's oldest sector since the day that Bienville first stepped ashore on the banks of the Mississippi.

CHAPTER 6

Making Groceries

The Bloodline of Sicilian New Orleans

On a particularly cold February morning in 1982, *New Orleans Times-Picayune* reporter Joan Kent made a final visit to Von Der Haar's Grocery, a cherished landmark at 4238 Magazine Street. "Miss Lucy" Ventura Von der Haar, the store's mainstay for the past three decades, had died the previous month, and her daughter, who was never terribly excited about being a grocer in the first place, had made the tough but inevitable decision to close the business. A somber mood prevailed as longtime customers came to say their final good-byes, while employees, including a butcher who had worked at the store since the closing of Solari's in 1965, contemplated all that seemed to have died along with Miss Lucy. "The closing of Von der Haar's really does mark the ending of a way of life," noted Kent, "that may have lasted longer in New Orleans than in most American cities. A style by which the ladies of some houses never had to stand in line at grocery stores. They called Von der Haar's, accepted the deliveries, and instructed the help in the kitchen in the preparation of the meal." The old customers of Von der Haar's would now have to join the herd at faceless supermarkets, she added, and "may even have to load the bags into the trunks of their cars."[1]

The closing of Von der Haar's grocery was newsworthy primarily because of its upscale clientele but also because it represented one of the last holdouts of a dying breed of food retailers that had once played a ubiquitous role in the city's neighborhood culture. Corner stores operated by Sicilian immigrants had both sustained families and served as hubs of social activity prior to rapidly disappearing from the city in the 1960s and 1970s. These businesses belonged to a particular moment in time, both sustained and later destroyed by grand historical processes that originated with forces beyond any one person's control. The next generation's move away from small corner groceries, fundamental changes in the wholesaling and retailing of food, and profound demographic shifts in New Orleans itself all contributed to the decline and eventual disappearance of corner stores. Yet the mark that they left on the urban landscape remains visible today, even if these spaces have, with few exceptions, been converted to other uses. The few family groceries that continue to operate serve as an important touchstone of cultural memory, a connection to the cherished yet mostly disappeared past for those living in a postdiluvian city that is rapidly evolving into the next iteration of itself.

Although prominent among such groceries, Von der Haar's fit a pattern across the economic spectrum among the generation of Sicilians immigrants who built lives in New Orleans. Lucy Ventura was born in 1892, the fourth of Giuseppe and Josephine Ventura's seven daughters. The Venturas had come to New Orleans from Sicily in 1883, and like so many of his generation, Giuseppe plied the streets of the city as a fruit peddler until he had saved enough money to open his own grocery store at Magazine and Jena Streets at the start of the twentieth century. Lucy was the only one of his children to go into the business. She married Frank Von der Haar in 1915, and two years later, the couple set up their own shop in the newly constructed Jefferson Market at the corner of Magazine and General Pershing Streets, where they cultivated a following by selling poultry, fruits, and vegetables. Perhaps because of her independent nature or because she was raised in a family blessed with only girls, she found freedom to take the leading role at the market, even if the business carried her husband's name. Frank Von der Haar was far more occupied by his job as state fire marshal, a position he gained and held for many years as a supporter and "very close friend" of Governor Huey Long. According to the Von der Haars' son, also named Frank, Lucy believed in the existence of the Black Hand and wanted "nothing at all" to do with St. Joseph's Day; her children never learned to speak Italian. Groceries were her only tangible cultural legacy from her heritage, but she carried forth that legacy in grand fashion.[2]

The 1886 Sunday Law prohibited not just bars and restaurants but also groceries and public markets from selling their wares on the Sabbath, and Miss Lucy's reaction to this unpopular governmental intrusion illustrated her independent streak. "My mother used to tell me that the biggest time was after church on Sunday," explained her son, "when people would come in to buy chickens." By 1919, the law had grown so unpopular in New Orleans that the butchers and grocers in the Jefferson Market, including Von der Haar, advertised that "for the convenience of our customers and the public," their stands would open on Sunday. Legislators from the southern part of the state sought to make this hot-button issue a local option in what became the Louisiana Constitution of 1921, and although they failed, the flurry of enforcement that ensued for the next few years did not last. In 1933, as Prohibition collapsed, the New Orleans Retail Grocer's Association attempted to pressure officials to enforce the Sunday Law, prompting a warning from the city's safety commissioner to housewives "to buy week-end supplies without delay." "My mother was really upset when the city closed groceries on Sunday [because of] the blue law," Frank Von der Haar remembered. "She had to stay home on Sundays. She loved to be with people in the store."[3]

Von der Haar's built its reputation as a supplier of quality fresh goods. Delivery was an important part of the business. After initially using a mule and cart for deliveries, Miss Lucy switched to trucks, raising her "house so that they could park the vehicles underneath it," Frank Von der Haar remembered. She charged for deliveries, and her son credited that service with placing Von der Haar's in increasing competition with Solari's, the grande dame of French Quarter grocery stores. Von der Haar's delivered to restaurants as well as homes, and her produce earned such a positive reputation that a 1937 advertisement for Commander's Palace advertised that its fruits and vegetables came from her market.[4]

Lucy Von der Haar took particular pride in filling difficult orders for special customers. Corrine Dunbar's Restaurant, which opened in 1935 and had its heyday in the decade after World War II, was one of the city's best restaurants of that era. Opened by a socially prominent woman who had fallen on difficult financial times, Dunbar's was a fine-dining establishment of the old school. Even after it had declined in the late 1960s and early 1970s, critics still regarded its most famous dish, Oysters Dunbar, as a work of art. Barry Becnel, a friend of the Von Der Haar family, described it as "absolutely marvelous," and versions of the recipe are now available online from such famous chefs as John Folse and Emeril Lagasse. The dish required a steady supply of artichokes: after they were boiled, the leaves were scraped by hand, and the artichoke and the heart were mixed with oysters. Frank Van der Haar recalled it as "a fantastic dish. It was very rich, of course." Consumers today have grown accustomed to having a wide variety of produce available year-round, but in the 1940s, consistently acquiring artichokes required some planning: Miss Lucy "would order the artichokes and have them stored in cold storage in California and have them shipped on a regular basis to New Orleans," her son explained.[5]

The end of World War II brought sweeping changes to the grocery business in general and posed some very real challenges to Von der Haar's position in the Jefferson Market. Miss Lucy had always leased her space from the city, but in 1948 the city signed a new lease with a growing Nashville-based supermarket chain, H. G. Hill, which planned to evict all of the current tenants and convert the cavernous market into a modern self-service grocery store. Forced to move, Frank Von der Haar purchased the stand-alone building at 4238 Magazine Street diagonally across the street from the Jefferson Market. Today, this location is home to the elegant La Petite Grocery, run by chef Justin Devillier, but from the turn of the twentieth century until 1942, it was a grocery store run by F. W. Mackie. Remaining so close to the shiny new supermarket was a bold move, but Lucy Von der Haar believed—correctly—that her customers would remain faithful to her particular brand of personal service.[6]

When H. G. Hill opened in October 1948, the juxtaposition could not have been more jarring. The chain encouraged customers to "register often" for a drawing to win a new Frigidaire icebox or a Westinghouse "Laundramat" automatic washing machine, two great innovations of the modern postwar home. Orders over $250 received a free twelve-piece cookware set (a $70 value!). A cardboard sign dangling on wires from the store's ceiling advertised "REGULAR EVERY DAY LOW SUPER MARKET PRICES." Innovations included "open-air food lockers" that enabled shoppers to pluck milk and eggs from refrigerated cases without the bothersome impediment of doors, an idea still in its infancy; steaks and chops could be purchased at a "self-service meat market." It was a glimpse of the future—everything that Von der Haar's was not. In spite of—or perhaps because of—these differences, Miss Lucy thrived. The two stores coexisted for the next thirty-five years, with Hill's eventually becoming a Winn-Dixie that, like Von der Haar's, closed its doors in the early 1980s. The old Jefferson Market building now houses the gymnasium of St. George's Episcopal School.[7]

In contrast to H. G. Hill's, Von der Haar's grocery evolved into an establishment popular with the "very Uptown ladies" who arrived in chauffeured automobiles and emerged from the store with their drivers carrying brown-paper-wrapped bundles of purchases. Von der Haar's was built around the idea of personal service, a dying concept in the 1950s and 1960s that reflected Miss Lucy's defiant spirit and probably endeared her to her customer base and enabled her to flourish. Von der Haar's embodied a "New Orleans thing" or at the least "an Uptown thing"—that is, the Uptown universe's ability, even today, to insulate itself from those normalizing and homogenizing paradigms that govern the rest of America, hewing steadfastly to anachronisms either out of an appreciation for tradition or out of sheer stubbornness. The house-labeled glass jars of old-fashioned mix sold at Langenstein's or a cashier calling a customer *Dawlin'* are vaguely reminiscent of this worldview. It is expressed surprisingly far down the socioeconomic scale but is realized most fully at its upper reaches, and it is embedded in a thousand homey quirks seldom seen elsewhere that betray a sometimes unhealthy addiction to the good life, like cocktails at a Tuesday lunch, casually and silently expressing a disregard for how things are done in Chicago or Atlanta. A full-service grocery that stocked the sort of specialized items unavailable on the shelves of Hill's or the A&P fit neatly with this Uptown mind-set. Von der Haar's might not have survived competition with a chain store had it been located elsewhere in the city.

The localized nature of this special grocery took many forms. Miss Lucy's delivery orders always included the old New Orleans tradition of a lagniappe—a bouquet of parsley or perhaps spring onions slipped into the package. Decorative fruit gift baskets were a popular item at holiday time. The grocery employed a man to shuck oysters for customers, and as Frank Von der Haar noted, "Of course, oysters for Thanksgiving was a very, very big thing. Everybody had to have oyster dressing, and they would start shucking oysters almost a week ahead, full-time." The store would also deliver call-in orders of oysters on the half shell. Becnel remembered skilled butchers who could prepare "things like crown roast of lamb" and other "items that were out of the ordinary. I remember [Miss Lucy] carrying a wonderful melba sauce. At this time, this was an exotic item." In the twenty-first century, "making groceries" often entails an automobile ride to a modern supermarket that may be clean, friendly, and efficient but lacks any sort of personal touch. But the individual service and attention to detail offered by Lucy Von der Haar's store meant a lot to her customers. According to Frank Von der Haar, Lysle Aschaffenburg, who built and subsequently owned the Pontchartrain Hotel during its heyday in the 1940s and 1950s, called Miss Lucy one afternoon and said, "I was going through some of the things that were left over when my wife died. And . . . I have a slip from Von der Haar's groceries from an order that my wife called in to you many, many years ago. Could you fill that order again for me? . . . I want to remember my wife." And Lucy did. Such personal connections not only made Miss Lucy famous and beloved but sustained corner groceries and tied them to the communities they served.[8]

Only two short New Orleans blocks down Magazine Street from Von der Haar's stood Ortolano's Grocery. The presence of two substantial grocers in such close proximity reflected not only a fundamentally different era in procuring foodstuffs and broadly differing clienteles but also Uptown's high population density in the early twentieth century. Many large Catholic families lived shoehorned into shotgun doubles, with one family in each five-room half—without air-conditioning.

Thomas Frank Ortolano had immigrated to the United States sometime around 1890, when he was a small child, settling in the Sicilian colony at White Castle, at the time a bustling hamlet nestled in the cane fields of Iberville Parish. Though the beauty of the natural landscape endures, White Castle, like so many other towns in the region, is now an impoverished area, an indistinguishable wasteland of payday loan offices and fast-food joints. However, unlike its neighbors, White Castle maintains a claim to notoriety—the stylish resort complex on the grounds of Nottoway Plantation, "the South's largest remaining antebellum mansion." An impressive structure, Nottoway celebrates an era when planters squeezed fortunes from cane and toil, with much of that labor provided by Sicilians. T. F. Ortolano made a dangerous living in this country as a young man by painting water towers, but by the First World War he had moved forty miles downriver to Vacherie, where he worked as the assistant engineer of a sugarhouse, a position that took advantage of the mechanical aptitude that he later passed on to his sons. In 1918, however, the thirty-five-year-old Ortolano moved his wife and six children to New Orleans, and two years later, he used the family's accumulated savings to open a grocery at the corner of Magazine and Constantinople, a section of Uptown that had recently received an influx of other former residents of White Castle.[9]

A photograph from the late 1930s depicts a bespectacled T. F. Ortolano, the sleeves of his white button-down shirt rolled up to his elbows and a necktie disappearing behind a snowy white grocer's apron. He stands proudly beside a tidy display of Lux soap while rows of neatly stacked canned goods and a tin sign for Eagle Beer tacked to a post behind him round out an image of a prosperous and clean neighborhood grocery. Ortolano's Fresh Foods had two particular specialties—thin-sliced ham and hot Italian sausage. "He did such a business in thin-sliced ham that on Saturday night, . . . he would be there until midnight slicing whole hams in the wire stands, where he could slice it so thin you could look through it," remembered his grandson, Ronnie Sciortino. "He'd slice it around the entire ham and take off each slice intact, leaving the hole in the center, and everyone would come to get his ham. And he would have it pre-packaged, so when they came in, it was ready for them." Ortolano made his unique sausage with an old cast-iron sausage machine, but instead of twisting the meat into links, Ortolano and his son, Russell, would tie off each sausage by hand with a thin jute string. Both of these products reflected the kind of service that would one day mostly vanish under a wave of super-market efficiencies.[10]

As the operator of a tobacco company, Philip Quaglino made deliveries to dozens of groceries and bars run by Italians, including Ortolano's Grocery. Born in Corleone, Sicily, in 1863, Quaglino, like the Ortolanos, migrated to White Castle in the last quarter of the nineteenth century. He moved to New Orleans in 1900 to open a grocery in the Irish Channel but eventually found far greater fortune in tobacco. Starting with one delivery truck in 1920 and housing his stock in a storage shed behind his residence at 5015 Camp Street, Quaglino developed multimillion-dollar operation by the time of his death in 1942. "As a little kid, I would go with my grandfather as he peddled tobacco from store to store," remembered Philip Sciortino. "He'd get an order and tell me, 'Go get this out of the truck: . . . two Lucky Strikes . . . one Chesterfield . . . a Camel, maybe some gum.'" On one of these visits, while his grandfather and Ortolano discussed business in Italian, Philip met Ortolano's youngest daughter, Regina.[11]

Some years later they met again, a reunion that encapsulates the encompassing influence of family, neighborhood, and business in the lives of New Orleans Italians in the years between the two world wars. Philip Quaglino's son, Angelo, was the leader of the Blue Parody Orchestra, a popular big band that was often heard on New Orleans radio stations of the 1930s and that played dance music on the lakefront at the new Pontchartrain Beach casino building, following in the tradition of the earlier bands that had played at Spanish Fort. Regina Ortolano's older brother, Russell, played tenor saxophone in the band, while Philip Sciortino's brother, Jack, played trumpet. A generation after the Sciortinos, Quaglinos, and Ortolanos had begun their American journeys in White Castle, the younger set arrived at the Ortolanos' spacious raised double cottage at 912 Constantinople, just across the street from the family grocery, and pushed aside all the dining room and living room furniture to make room for the fifteen-piece orchestra's rehearsal. An aspiring stand-up bass player, Philip Sciortino came to listen, and he and Regina would sit in the open windows as the sounds of Glenn Miller's popular compositions spilled out onto the streets of Uptown. Shortly thereafter, Philip saw Regina at a wedding reception at the American Legion Hall on Royal Street in the French Quarter and resolved to ask her out that evening. "So that night I called her [and] said, 'Would you like to go out tonight?' She said, 'Why not?' So I went over, picked her up." Philip soon left for military training, but the couple resumed dating while he was home for two weeks prior to being shipped overseas. When he returned from fighting in World War II, he recalled, "We picked up where we left off and got married." Regina Ortolano Sciortino went on to make her own mark on the New Orleans food business as a caterer, while their son, Ronnie, ran the kitchen at the culinarily ambitious Steven and Martin's restaurant in the early 1980s.[12]

The Ortolano family's most enduring legacy was not groceries, however, but their role in the popularization of the New Orleans–style snowball and the SnoWizard stand. For anyone to claim to have "invented" the snowball is a bit of a stretch. Shaved ice as a concept was hardly revolutionary in the 1930s. As early as 1887, a drugstore at the corner of Magazine and Thalia Streets advertised "spoon soda," a "more refreshing" version of ice cream soda. "Our ice shaver is so easily manipulated," the store promised, "that it is but the work of a moment to shave ice, which is dispensed in each glass of soda water, making it truly frigid." Home versions of hand-held ice shavers or scrapers were also popular at the time, when refrigeration did not yet exist and households kept food cold via large, heavy blocks of ice that were delivered by the iceman and placed in the icebox. When people wanted to reduce this block into usable bits for beverages, they could chop off a chunk by hand or, after the advent of the ice shaver, scrape off some "snow." In fact, the shaver had been invented for precisely this purpose: touted one late-nineteenth-century home advice column, "After you have used [the shaver] once you will realize how much ice you might have saved in the days gone by, not including the wear and tear of your temper." Ironically, shaved ice is far more difficult to make at home today than in 1920 because large blocks of ice are no longer common.[13]

Before long, people recognized the epicurean merits of combining shaved ice and fruit syrup. As one ladies' column observed, "The mixture will be quite stiff and suitable for eating with a spoon." Corner stores in New Orleans and elsewhere began selling flavored ice by 1910. Brocato's Store in Raceland has a century-old handheld ice shaver that made countless frozen treats during Vincenzo Brocato's time. The snowball stand as we know it did not appear until after World War II, when the iceman and his wagon exited the urban landscape in the wake of technological innovation, improved infrastructure, and the development of consumer products that altered life in the American home.[14]

The road to SnoWizard began at a small grocery operated by George Ortolano at the corner of Delachaise and Magazine Streets, just eight blocks downtown from his father's store. The snow cone, which featured crushed ice, had become popular nationally after its introduction at the 1919 Texas State Fair. Crushing ice was not practical until the introduction of the portable electric motor, but these treats were perfect for bringing in extra revenue for corner stores. George Ortolano, however, modified the idea. In 1936, the mechanically inclined grocer designed a machine that shaved a fluffy long strip of "snow" from a block of ice. Two years earlier, Ernest Hansen had patented a mechanically different machine that produced similar results, leading to a still-unresolved debate over who deserves credit for the concept. As with the question of who "invented" the muffuletta, more significant than which machine came first are the social and economic processes that led to its appearance. Hansen's invention gave rise to the Sno-Bliz stand at 4801 Tchoupitoulas Street, a beloved New Orleans landmark where residents queue up each spring to buy their favorite flavors from what is now the third generation of Hansens to make snowballs. Not content to simply make snowballs, however, Ortolano also went into the business of making the physical machinery and organizational infrastructure that helped make the confection ubiquitous, a process that reveals much about changes in postwar America.[15]

George Ortolano's move toward franchising and selling turnkey operations came about in an organic way. He spread to more than one location by hand-building snowball machines and placing them in corner groceries owned by kinfolk, much in the way that his cousin, Philip Quaglino, expanded his tobacco business. Ortolano's good Sicilian family offered him quite a few locations for expansion. After World War II, however, the business truly began to take off. The oldest Ortolano son, Frank, had worked during the war at Rheem Manufacturing on Jefferson Highway, which had originally made water heaters but converted temporarily to bomb casings. Frank gained a familiarity with these tanks that led directly to the pressurized cylinders of flavoring syrup used at SnoWizard stands. Also a graphic designer, Frank helped George come up with the original artwork for SnoWizard, turning it into a recognizable brand. Another key element was the postwar phenomenon of prefabricated structures, which were perfect for the seasonal snowball business. According to Ronnie Sciortino, Frank "built these little portable knock-down SnoBall businesses out of plywood, and they consisted of seven different sections: the floor, four sides, an interior shelf, and the roof. And they were designed to be assembled simply by bolting together in a matter of thirty minutes to an hour. And at the end of the season, when it was over, they could be disassembled, laid flat, and then put into storage until the following season." SnoWizard's trademarked SnoBall Stand had been born, and it would long outlast the Ortolano Grocery on Magazine.[16]

The collective memory of Von der Haar's and Ortolano's groceries has been more enduring than most, in large part because of their prominence and contributions to food culture. The legacies of the vast majority of corner stores are much more difficult to trace, though they continue to shape the city. For example, Giovanni Bellone came to New Orleans in 1903 from the rural Sicilian settlement of Piana dei Greci, one in a string of villages populated by Albanian or "Greek" ethnics. It is unclear whether he was commuting seasonally on the citrus fleet to work on the truck farms or in cane fields outside New Orleans, but he lived in Waggaman for a while before 1910. He married Vita Maria Plescia in New Orleans in 1906, when he was twenty-seven and she was just fifteen. The Bellones made their way from Chartres Street in the Quarter to the Dryades area sometime during the First World War and opened a small grocery at 1740 Terpsichore Street. Never terribly elaborate, their store offered delicacies such as cold cuts and imported items obtained through Central Grocery. The Bellones did not deliver or sell alcohol, but they did a steady business supplying the needs of their immediate neighbors at a time when most people did not own cars.[17]

The Bellones' granddaughter, Betty Bellone Unsworth, remembered that Vita "could not read or write, but she was fabulous with numbers," while Giovanni "sort of ran the business, the books and things," making everything work. Far simpler than the operations of Von der Haar and Ortolano, the Bellone grocery was much more typical of the New Orleans corner grocery. Unsworth remembered her childhood trips to the store: "When you got off on St. Charles Avenue . . . it was fun, because all the neighbors knew you as you were coming down the street. Everybody was looking out for everybody else. Everybody was sitting on the stoops. I remember the Parthamores and other people. And when you walked to the grocery store, the first thing was the drink machine on the left," which contained Big Shot red. "I remember this warm comfortable feeling going there. . . . And there was always food going."

She also enjoyed accompanying her grandfather when he went to stock his store: He "was a lot of fun to go to Central Grocery with, because he knew exactly what he wanted."[18]

Also more typical was the fact that the Bellone grocery did not involve multiple generations of the family. The Bellones' only son, Christopher Francis Bellone, graduated from Tulane's medical school in 1933, a remarkable accomplishment considering his modest upbringing and parents' limited education. As an obstetrician and surgeon, Bellone maintained his ties to the neighborhood, and according to his daughter, when the Italian merchants of the French Market got sick or injured, they trusted him to help. On one such occasion, Dr. Bellone left his daughter with friends in the Market while he attended to a patient. Though she was afraid "to be left with these two burly men," he told her, "Believe me, nothing is going to happen to you. You are totally safe." And of course she was. Christopher Bellone's path to college and a profession reflected the immigrant generation's aspirations for their children. A corner grocery could supply a solid living, but it was not always an easy life, and New Orleans's Italians wanted their descendants to have more. Moreover, whether or not the immigrants knew it, the corner grocery was not a sustainable business model in the vast majority of cases.[19]

As the Dryades neighborhood became less financially stable in the 1950s, the Bellone grocery's business prospects faltered. Family tradition continued to draw the children and grandchildren there for Sunday dinner despite the area's escalating crime. After her husband's death in 1960, Vita Bellone carried on alone at the store: "She had great staying power and she ran that grocery store until she was eighty-three," when she had to chase a robber away "with a broken bottle," according to her granddaughter. The store closed after she died in 1972, but an elderly aunt continued to live at 1740 Terpsichore Street, despite the neighborhood's decline and the "problems [it created] for people coming over there." As her nephew recalled, "Some of her family got beat up" when they visited. After the aunt moved out, the family rented the property for a time, but difficulty with tenants led to the reluctant decision to sell the building.[20]

In 1979, the building was purchased by Henry Byrd, better known by fans of New Orleans music as Professor Longhair. He died a few months later, and the structure continued to deteriorate until Steve Armbruster of the Tipitina's Foundation sought to restore the home in the hope of one day opening a museum there to the musician's memory. According to Professor Longhair's daughter, Pat Byrd, the Bellones are remembered fondly in the neighborhood, and today the home stands nicely preserved amid persistent blight despite its location just a few short blocks from St. Charles Avenue and an evolving revitalization of nearby Oretha Castle Haley Boulevard (formerly Dryades).[21]

Still thriving in twenty-first century New Orleans, Terranova Brothers Superette, located at 3308 Esplanade Avenue in the picturesque Faubourg St. John neighborhood, sits just a few blocks from the entrance to the Fairgrounds. Visitors from around the world converge there in late April for the New Orleans Jazz and Heritage Festival, perhaps the most conspicuous symbol of the contemporary city's modern fest-driven tourism engine. Terranova Brothers has survived the push toward suburban supermarkets less by innovating and making concessions to modernity and more by remaining determined and shrewdly prioritizing the qualities that have always mattered to family-run business. For more than a century, since founder Benjamin Terranova operated a butcher's stall in the Treme Market, Terranova's has been known for its meat. The Treme Market and the Poydras Market were the only two other public markets that approached the scale and scope of the French Market. At its height, the Poydras Market stretched along that street's neutral ground between Tchoupitoulas and Basin Streets, while the Treme Market at one time occupied the two blocks between Robertson and Marais Streets along the Orleans Avenue neutral ground. Both were built in the 1830s and demolished a century later when they had outlived their usefulness. The area where the Treme Market formerly operated has been completely transformed. When Benny Terranova sold meat there after World War I, it was only two blocks from the Carondelet Canal's turnaround basin, within sight of Congo Square, a landscape subsequently erased when the canal was filled in and Mahalia Jackson Theater and Armstrong Park were constructed. Benny lived nearby at 2239 Ursulines Avenue, where his uncle operated a grocery in a classic two-story corner store building that still stands today, restored though no longer used as a commercial space.[22]

In 1924, about a decade before the butcher stalls of the Treme Market fell completely silent, Benny Terranova rented out a storefront on Esplanade Avenue (since the 1990s home to Lola's Restaurant). Here, on a hot July afternoon in 1926, on a table in what is now Lola's open kitchen, Benny's wife, Lena, gave birth to the couple's second son, Anthony. Benny, Lena, Anthony, and his older brother, Michael, lived upstairs until the house next door became available.

Then, in a classic New Orleans architectural move, the Terranovas decided to raise the existing house an entire story and build their grocery on the ground floor. Here it remains, painted roughly the color of lima beans, on a desirable pie wedge of ground between Esplanade and Ponce de Leon Street.[23]

Anthony and Michael eventually took over Terranova Brothers Superette and kept it afloat. Anthony met his wife, Lorraine, at nearby Easton Park, where her father took her to watch the boys play baseball. After first becoming friends, she and Anthony "got closer." When they decided to get married, there was no doubt that they would go into the grocery business. She recalled, "I liked the idea of it. In fact I was thrilled that I was going to come into a grocery that I partly owned." At about this time, in January 1951, the A&P Supermarket opened right across the street, where Canseco's Market is today. Although the Terranova family cooperated with cousins who were also in the grocery business in other parts of the city, they had nowhere near the purchasing power of A&P. Yet they also had something that A&P did not—blood: according to Lorraine Terranova, "I would work, say, in the morning shift, and then I was off in the evenings, and then my . . . brother-in-law's wife, she would come in the evening and work, and then the next week we'd reverse. We'd do that constantly until one got pregnant. Then we had to double up a little bit, but it was always either her or myself that used to run the register." Because everyone in the family contributed, overhead remained low. Their biggest strength was their understanding of their customers as well as the fact that they delivered. As Lorraine Terranova put it, "We had some nice customers all through the years, customers that really stayed with us."[24]

As in so many success stories, the key to survival for the Terranova family was cooperation and sacrifice. On holidays, when the store was closed, the extended family would sometimes gather at a fish camp on Lake Catherine and play cards. Anthony and Lorraine Terranova took a grand total of two vacations in the forty years that they ran the grocery: a 1984 visit to the World's Fair while it was in town and a big anniversary trip to Italy. "Because all of us were working and everyone had to pitch in, . . . it was hard for one to leave . . . just was sort of impossible. And as far as mixing with a lot of people, having a lot of friends, . . . my friends were my cousins. When we left, we would go upstairs, we would just relax. And you know, it was just my husband and I and the children." Lorraine Terranova also saw customers as like family: "If you needed somebody to pick up somebody at the airport [and] you didn't have

a way of getting there, suddenly the customers would go out of their way—
'I'll do it! I'll do it!' You know, it was like they were always glad to give you a
helping hand."[25]

Anthony's son, Benny, and his wife, Karen, run the store today, with their
son, Anthony, planning to take over one day. Whole Foods Market eventually replaced the A&P before outgrowing the space. Canseco's Market subsequently moved in. Despite these challenges, Terranova Brothers has continued to offer specialized attention that allows them to remain in business. New
parents still bring their babies in to be weighed on the scale at the meat counter, and the store's predictions regarding the Saints' football fortunes are not
easily dismissed. Along with their hogshead cheese and stuffed artichokes—a
specialty introduced by Karen—the most popular long-standing item is the
Italian and green onion sausage. According to Lorraine and her son, Benny,
the recipe for the sausage involved throwing "a little bit of this" into an "old
washtub," tasting it, and then throwing "in a little bit more of this, and it was
ready."[26]

If there were a mid-twentieth-century analogue to the Sicilian French
Quarter of an earlier generation, it would have to be the development of Gentilly in the decades around World War II. Sicilian immigrants and their children had settled in all parts of the city from the start, and the more prosperous
families in the French Quarter had by the turn of the century begun buying
larger residences in the Creole Faubourgs, particularly up Esplanade Avenue
toward the bayou. But expansion along Broad Street and particularly the Gentilly Ridge was something new, and in the 1920s and 1930s it became so pronounced that one might call it the suburb of choice for the children of those
who had first settled in the Quarter below St. Ann Street.

One of the many families who left the French Quarter for new homes in
Gentilly were the Uddos, whose Uddo-Taormina company imported olive oil,
pasta, and canned goods and had grown to national importance by the 1920s.
At the start of that decade, thirteen family members crowded into a brick
townhouse at 1222 Decatur Street. By 1930, each nuclear family had moved
into its own home on North Broad Street. Meanwhile, the French Quarter
property was turned over to production of the family's growing Sure-Klean
Bleach business, in keeping with what had become the neighborhood's increasingly industrial character. Rosemary Uddo Testa grew up at 1815 North
Broad in a frame-raised double cottage. Both her grandparents and her uncle's family had houses in the 1600 block, and all three subfamilies had moved

there when she was very little, maintaining the familial social patterns that had originated in the Old Country and had remained alive and well during the Uddos' time in the Quarter. Testa recalled that after her grandmother's death, "my grandfather used to walk every day from 1615—he walked every morning to our home, and my mother would give him coffee. He just loved my mother, he really did. . . . He missed his wife, and I guess he would come to talk to my mother. . . . He'd come in [and say], 'Angelina!'" Many years later, Testa still had "sweet" memories of him walking up the driveway to her family's home.[27]

Even though Tommy Tusa's family ran Central Grocery, they, like the Uddos, lived in Gentilly in the 1940s and 1950s, "when it was the place to go." The area offered "new opportunities, a lot of green space to build houses," observed Tusa. "I lived on Elysian Fields and Robin. It was close to Fillmore, which is a big street, and went to St. Raphael for grammar school . . . and went to Cor Jesu [today Brother Martin] for high school." Both were on Elysian Fields Avenue, though in opposite directions from the Tusas' home. Maria Impastato's family "lived . . . in what you would actually call Old Gentilly, which was about two blocks from the Fairgrounds." Her paternal grandparents remained in the apartment above the family business, the Napoleon House in the Quarter, but Maria lived with her parents on one side of a shotgun double, with her maternal grandparents on the other side. She and her siblings went to school in Gentilly, while "for years and years," her father "took a bus from Gentilly all the way to Royal Street . . . and came to work. We didn't have a car . . . until I was in high school. That was his first car. He walked almost everywhere and took the bus. We did too."[28]

On a May afternoon in 1980, Joseph Maselli stopped by the Bruxelles Street home of Joseph and Rosemary Zuppardo, not far from the intersection of Gentilly Boulevard and Elysian Fields Avenue, where Joseph and his older brother, Anthony, had started Zuppardo's Economical Grocery in 1934. Like many of New Orleans's other prominent Italian American families, the Zuppardos knew Maselli well, though he was not originally from the Crescent City. A native of Newark, New Jersey, Maselli arrived in New Orleans courtesy of the U.S. Army, which stationed him there during World War II. After marrying a local girl, he got into the retail and then wholesale liquor business. He subsequently developed a passion for documenting Italian immigrants' contributions to the United States, founding New Orleans's American Italian Renaissance Foundation and American Italian Cultural Center.

In the mid-1970s and early 1980s, Maselli recognized that the stories of members of the immigrant generation were becoming lost, and he began tape-recording interviews with many of his friends. Though the quality of the audiocassettes is often poor and his interview techniques were those of an interested amateur, his enthusiasm and insight have resulted in a priceless collection of dozens of oral histories that offers a treasure trove of irreplaceable knowledge. With the wheels of Maselli's tape recorder turning slowly as it sat on the kitchen table between them, Zuppardo recounted his father's journey from the small Sicilian enclave of Camporeale to prosperity in New Orleans's food and grocery business. Interspersed with Zuppardo's recollections, listeners hear a rooster crowing just outside the window, offering a reminder that even in the twenty-first century, Old Country traditions are not as far removed as we may sometimes think.[29]

Anthony and Joseph Zuppardo's father, Peter, first arrived in the United States in 1903, when he was a young teen and he, his father, and his uncle left their farm in Sicily to work on the railroad. The cold Wyoming winter was more than they cared to endure, and in 1907, Peter Zuppardo returned to Camporeale, where he was conscripted into the Italian army. Boarding the train to leave Camporeale, Zuppardo sat down next to Frank Taormina, a young man from Partanna, a small town further up the line still known today for its groves of olive trees and the oil pressed from their fruit. This chance meeting developed into a lifelong friendship that eventually shaped the lives of children yet to be born in a city situated on the other side of the globe.

In 1913, after finishing his military service, Zuppardo returned to America, where family ties and a deepened appreciation for tropical weather kept him in New Orleans. Looking for work on the docks that fronted the French Quarter, Zuppardo met Luca Vaccaro, one of the brothers who ran the powerful Standard Fruit and Steamship Company. According to Peter's son, Roy, during World War I, "Lukie Vaccaro gave him a couple of cars of bananas and made him sell them to the peddlers to keep the peddlers off the wharf. . . . My dad was afraid to take [the bananas] because he didn't have any money to pay for them. Lukie said, 'You go ahead and sell them. When you get done,' he said, 'you bring me the money.'" By the start of World War II, Peter Zuppardo had become the largest wholesaler of bananas in the country.[30]

Joseph Zuppardo and his brother, Anthony, eleven years older, followed their father into the culinary arena, though they did not merely step into the business that Peter had built. The brothers started at the bottom, working together to peddle fruits and vegetables in the French Quarter and surrounding neighborhoods. "I'd get out of school," remembered Joseph, and Anthony would "take me. I was always with my brother." Like many Italian entrepreneurs, their father invested a substantial portion of his savings in real estate, and Peter eventually gave his sons two adjacent lots on old U.S. 90 (Gentilly Boulevard), where it intersected with Elysian Fields Avenue. In 1932, eighteen-year-old Anthony Zuppardo began constructing a permanent open-air fruit stand to serve customers heading in and out of town on what was then the main east-west artery. According to Joseph, the brothers would bring goods to patrons sitting in their cars, "open oysters . . . sell stuff right there." At the time, Gentilly was still the country, with cow pastures and open spaces, but in 1937, H. G. Hill's began building a supermarket right across the street from the Zuppardos' stand. Tony Zuppardo realized the necessity of progress and began enclosing the fruit stand, transforming it into the Economical Supermarket.[31]

Zuppardo patterned his store on what he considered the first true supermarket in New Orleans, George Puglia's place at 5523 St. Claude Avenue. The two men were friends, with shared cultural and business ties, and Puglia encouraged the Zuppardos and offered tips that helped the new enterprise become a success. Puglia had started in the grocery business in the French Quarter during the 1920s, but like a lot of immigrants' sons, he saw a growing future in the city's Seventh and Eighth Wards. The grand opening of Puglia's supermarket early in the summer of 1938 reflected the general trend away from the old public market system and dry-goods-oriented corner stores and toward one-stop shopping. The store was an angular machine-age rectangular structure measuring fifty feet by eighty feet. The conveniences included "modern refrigeration facilities," although fruits and vegetables remained in an adjacent building—a holdover from an era when grocers sublet the produce business to an outside vendor.[32]

Despite the closeness between Joseph and Tony Zuppardo, it was not entirely clear that the younger brother would follow in the older's footsteps when the Economical Supermarket opened, although because half of the store rested on Joseph's property, he certainly had a stake in the operation. Beginning in 1939, Joseph attended seminary on the north shore of Lake Pontchartrain with an eye toward becoming a Catholic priest. He changed his plans in 1943 and enrolled at Louisiana State University but was almost immediately drafted into the U.S. Army, where he eventually earned a Bronze Star while fighting in the Pacific. He was discharged on Good Friday, and on "Easter Saturday I came over [to the store] and worked in my [army] uniform. I didn't have any [street] clothes that would fit me." Shortly thereafter, he went into partnership with his brother and got married, and he never returned to his studies at Louisiana State.[33]

In America, Peter Zuppardo's good friend, Frank Taormina, formed what would become a giant wholesale food operation, Taormina Brothers, better known today as Progresso Foods. The Taorminas and their children lived on Broad Street in Gentilly, not far from the Uddos, and the two families remained personally and professionally close. Joseph Zuppardo recalled frequent visits to the Taormina Brothers' pasta factory and wholesale business on the corner of Jackson Square, where Muriel's Restaurant is today. He and Rosario Taormina's son, Frank, were "friends all of our lives, from little kids growing up in the grammar school." Shortly after Joseph got out of the army, Frank Taormina's cousin got married "right next door to us [on Bruxelles Street]. I wasn't invited to the wedding, [but Frank] came to see me [and] we were sitting out in front" when Joseph spied Frank's sister, Rosemary, whom Joseph remembered as "a little fat girl." She had changed, and soon after Joseph said, "Frank, *that's* your sister?" Rosemary and Joseph married.[34]

In some respects, the Zuppardo Brothers kept one foot in the past even as they stepped into the future: the grocery distribution system had not modernized alongside their retailing. Joseph's son, Roy, remembers them going to the French Market for produce. "He'd wake me up before the sun got up and we'd go—and we only lived in Gentilly, so it was a five-minute drive—and we'd go and there'd be guys there with truckloads of cauliflower or watermelons or tomatoes or corn, and we'd go through the French Market every day and he'd say, 'Okay, I like that. . . . Come meet me at the store, here's my address,' or if they knew him already, 'Come send me twenty of those.' . . . That was fun." Anthony specialized in meats, and early in the morning, he would venture out to Cuddahay Meat Packing Company on Poydras Street, across from what is today the Superdome. "It was just this huge, huge warehouse of beef that was hanging up, and he'd walk by and say, 'Give me that piece, give me that piece, give me that piece'—he'd tag the ones he wanted." It took a trained eye to buy meat that way. "He wouldn't just say, 'Give me five hindquarters and five fronts.' He'd go pick them out himself cause he knew what he wanted," explained Roy Zuppardo.[35]

If the procurement of wholesale fresh goods had stayed comparatively static through the 1960s, changes on the dry and packaged goods side of the business had begun as early as the 1920s and only accelerated after World

War II. Memphis businessman Clarence Saunders had launched the first grocery chain in 1916, pioneering the idea of the self-service store with Piggly
Wiggly. Both A&P and H. G. Hill had a significant presence in New Orleans
by the 1940s, and in 1948 John Schwegmann, the son of a German immigrant
grocer, began modernizing his store, a plan that ultimately made his name
synonymous with self-service groceries in New Orleans. Despite the Louisiana Grocers Association's efforts to support "fair trade" pricing that fixed
the minimum price at which merchandise could be sold, discount supermarkets continued to win the fight against price controls, often by filing law-
suits that challenged trade restrictions as unconstitutional price fixing. When
these protections were struck down, the corner stores could not compete,
since they lacked the supermarkets' ability to buy in bulk and thus offer lower
prices. Independent supermarkets such as Zuppardo's and Dorignac's eventually fought back by pooling their buying and advertising efforts under the
cooperative Bell Stores label. The grocery business underwent a revolution
between 1920 and 1960, and it has subsequently continued to change under
homogenizing forces.

Adele Chopin Uddo, who married into the Uddo-Taormina family in 1945,
saw the transition from the wholesale producer's side. Her family's canneries
produced the Giardiniera brand tomato paste and other goods that were marketed in the Northeast by Frank Taormina: Frank and his brother, Vincent, operated a wholesale business in Brooklyn, New York, supplying corner grocery
stores. According to Chopin Uddo, when a broker approached Frank and said,
"I want to put you into the supermarket," Frank initially refused "to desert his
family-owned grocery stores." But the reality was that stores like Zuppardo's
and Schwegmann's and Puglia's as well as large chains such as Hill and A&P
were already dominating the market by the 1940s, and Frank ultimately was
convinced "because the supermarkets were coming in and the family grocery
stores were dying out."[36]

Nowhere was the changing face of New Orleans more apparent
than in the French Quarter, once the heartbeat of the city's food supply. The
municipal government's plan to transform the old Decatur Street marketplace
into a full-fledged tourist zone in the early 1970s may have been a prescient
effort to adjust to the inevitable realities of a dawning era, but the changes
were jarring for those who watched the curtain come down on a shipping and
commodity-trading system that had been governed more or less by the same

assumptions for the past two and a half centuries. In the twenty-first century, the old Sicilian families still own considerable real estate in the city's oldest neighborhood, but they lease it out to a range of businesses that would have been unimaginable when their forebears first carved out a life there in the late nineteenth century.

A visit to the French Market in December 1972, normally the busiest time of year in the grocery business, revealed how the once-bustling landmark had fallen into disuse. The French Market Corporation's decision to reimagine the bazaar's predominantly vacant buildings dominated the conversation of the few vendors who remained. All of the butchers had left, as had all but one seafood wholesaler and one seafood retailer. In the produce market, two Italian vendors still stacked fruit into colorful pyramids, but both knew that their time was coming to an end. To head the redevelopment of the market, Mayor Maurice "Moon" Landrieu appointed Clay Shaw, a highly regarded New Orleans businessman who had founded the International Trade Mart after serving in World War II. Shaw was also an ardent preservationist who had personally restored numerous historic properties, including sixteen in the French Quarter, and had recently been targeted by Orleans Parish district attorney Jim Garrison in his quest to secure a conviction in an alleged conspiracy to assassinate John F. Kennedy. Shaw relished the opportunity to lend his talents to the overall resurrection of the French Quarter, noting that the market had changed since "the old days when women shopped daily for fresh produce. That was when the French Market was the jewel of markets."[37]

Decatur Street soon took on a new appearance as parking meters disappeared, making it almost impossible to find spots near the businesses that had been located there for decades. These changes had the greatest impact on the lower part of Decatur, the heavily Sicilian stretch between St. Ann and Barracks. The overall plan favored tourist foot traffic over vehicle-driving locals intent on purchasing wheels of cheese or cases of olive oil. Customers at Sam Finazzi's G. & F. Wholesale Tobacco, for instance, would pull in and place their orders while keeping a watchful eye out for city tow trucks. According to John Perrone, "It was very difficult to get into the French Quarter.... You couldn't park.... Everybody got tickets. You had to have a real good reason to come down. And I just ... I said to myself, 'I wouldn't do it.' And people didn't." Echoed Tusa, "The French Quarter got harder and harder to come to and park.... You had to make an effort to get here." Sales fell off at both Central and Progress Groceries as well as at most businesses along the strip. As longtime customers died or moved away, their children now made groceries by pushing carts through the fluorescent-lit aisles of Zuppardo's Economical Grocery or the many locations of Schwegmann's, all of which featured convenient parking lots. The entire Decatur Street scene had grown culturally, geographically, and economically untenable.[38]

"I could see it happening" at Progress Grocery, remembered John Perrone. "There were those days when all you heard spoken in the store was Italian. . . . I was twelve years old and [was at the grocery] more just to hang around than to work. . . . My grandfather [spoke Italian], my dad spoke fluent Italian, and a lot of the customer base that came in [did too]." But as the 1960s wore on, "it was supermarket time. The supermarkets also started carrying a lot of the products that we did, and our business dropped off." In addition to the decline in retail sales, the wholesale business fell off with the closing of the corner groceries that had stocked their shelves with imported goods from the Central and Progress Groceries. As the economic realities of running an old-fashioned grocery in the Quarter began to set in, the muffuletta's popularity with tourists proved to be an unlikely savior.[39]

Few people would have predicted what was around the corner for the Quarter's tourist scene and the food business in the rest of the city. In 1976, Perrone remembered, "My good friend, an attorney, Larry Layman, says 'John, you gotta check out this little restaurant right down the street.'" And thus, Perrone was introduced to K-Paul's Louisiana Kitchen. "Paul Prudhomme used to come in [to Progress Grocery], and he would buy his ingredients for his fettuccini and Reggiano Parmesan, things like this, for his restaurant. Nobody knew who he was at the time, and all of a sudden he hit with his blackened redfish." Writers such as Brett Anderson and Tom Fitzmorris have identified the opening of Prudhomme's quirky French Quarter restaurant as a turning point in the New Orleans dining scene, a development that was equally important for the Perrones, the Impastatos, and the other families who continued to sell food in the French Quarter.[40]

On one occasion in the early 1980s, when Prudhomme's popularity was at its height, he ordered about fifty muffulettas from Progress Grocery to feed his staff during JazzFest, which Perrone described as "our absolute best time of the year." Prudhomme himself came to pick up the sandwiches, driving "a three-wheeler [with] about a twelve-foot-long whip antenna with a flag on it to let people know he was coming so he wouldn't get run over on the street." Prudhomme did not get off the three-wheeler but "had somebody open that front door for him, . . . popped that three-wheeler into the store, came up to the counter, [and said,] 'I'm going to pick up the sandwiches for my staff.'" The "store was only around twenty feet wide, with an aisle down the center," and "at the time we had about thirty people in the store, which was just about as many as you could put in." Perrone continued, "While all of this was going on, people were crowding around getting his autograph, and I had to get one too—for the signing of the bill for the sandwiches. And then he turned that thing around and went out the store. And one guy is saying, he says, 'Look, I got Paul Prudhomme's autograph.' I said, 'Yeah, so do I, but mine's worth a little bit more than yours.'"[41]

Such foot (or tire) traffic would have made most business owners ecstatic, but it also caused a dramatic but not immediately obvious transformation of Perrone's grocery: "I saw my restaurant base go from . . . like, let's say, 10 percent to 100 percent [of sales] in a few years' time." Explained Perrone, "Restaurants were opening left and right in the late 1970s through the 1980s, [so] we all of a sudden had a base of restaurants in the French Quarter that we didn't have before. So my business in the wholesale end started to snowball at that time." By the end of the 1970s, the original store functioned primarily as a tourist attraction, selling muffuletta sandwiches, an activity that had grown tangential to the family's core business. Choosing to focus strictly on restaurant wholesale supply, Perrone closed Progress Grocery in 2001, selling the building at 915 Decatur Street to a group of investors who tried but failed to replicate the Perrone family's eight-decade-old business. As the sons of Biaggio Montalbano had discovered decades before, serving a legendary muffuletta was more complicated than it appeared on the surface.[42]

Visitors seeking a French Quarter restaurant that both is "authentic New Orleans" and meets common tourist expectations usually find both requirements satisfied by the Napoleon House, with its shady private courtyard, cool dining rooms with archways, bow-tie-wearing waitstaff, and affordable selection of well-executed New Orleans culinary standards. Yet its connections with the Quarter's twentieth century, though less immediately apparent, reveal far greater historical texture than the period of Mayor Girod's residency or any lore about Bonapartists conspiring to spirit their favorite exiled conqueror to Louisiana. In the hundred years since the Impastato family took up residence there, the Napoleon House has adjusted to the dramatically changing realities of the French Quarter.

Peter Impastato was already in his thirties and had three children when he got out of the army after World War II. His uncle and father had bought the spacious building during the 1910s with money earned from peddling fruit and laboring in one of the Quarter's macaroni factories. The location had already been a grocery for some time, and the Impastato family added a bar. Yet by the late 1940s, the Napoleon House Grocery and bar had become obsolete. In response, Peter Impastato expanded the "Nap House's" bar operation and it soon became a rather bohemian establishment where local artists and college students from Tulane and Loyola came to hang out, drink, and listen to Caruso playing on an old Victrola.[43]

When Peter's son, Sal Impastato, took daily operations in 1971, it was clear that more changes were necessary to keep the business afloat. According to Sal Impastato, "a lot of people would come in, get a drink, and would also bring lunch from somewhere else. So after some thought, I decided to open up a sandwich shop." One of his bartenders was Nick Montalbano, an older man who had been a close friend of Peter and whose family had operated Montalbano's Grocery until it closed. Nick's brother, Martin Montalbano, was in need of work and already had a good recipe for olive salad and knew how to prepare the sandwiches, so the Napoleon House began serving muffulettas. The change coincided with what Impastato characterized as a steady increase in French Quarter tourism. The Impastatos later converted the upstairs of the historic building from a private family residence into a banquet hall that customers could rent for special events.[44]

Running the business required an enormous commitment from many members of the Impastato family: reflected Sal in 2010, "We have a lot of family doing everything that it takes to keep it going . . . and we're all getting to retirement age, or past. . . . I don't know if anybody really wants to do that [any more]. You really need a lot of family helping out if you are going to do this type of business." In early 2015, after lengthy negotiations, New Orleans restaurant magnate Ralph Brennan bought the Napoleon House, planning to keep as much as possible the same while applying the restaurant management techniques honed at his other numerous successful houses.[45]

Today, what was once the heart of the Italian Colony in the French Quarter has become a predominantly gay neighborhood. On Mardi Gras Day, the intersection of St. Ann and Bourbon Street is now home to the well-known drag beauty pageant. The Quarter's gay scene began developing as early as the 1950s, when the last of the Italian kids were still growing up in the neighborhood. Young Nick Loguidice lived in an upstairs apartment at 1001 Chartres, where he would stand on the balcony, "always looking down" at the neighborhood goings-on, though not fully comprehending. In 1954, the New Orleans City Council revoked the liquor license of the Starlet Lounge, which rented space at 943 Chartres (at the intersection with St. Philip) from Loguidice's uncles, Nick and James Evola. In what had since the 1880s been an overwhelmingly Sicilian immigrant neighborhood, the bar had become an avantgarde hangout for cross-dressing men such as the head bartender, who went by the name "Louise" and was "dolled up in female garments." The city council's attempt to stamp out the gay establishment had little success: a sign on the door at 943 Chartres announced, "Moved to 435 Esplanade. Come see me, Louise." As the gay community began to grow in the blocks surrounding St. Philip and St. Ann Streets, it supplanted another culture living on the margins of the American mainstream. It also changed the streetscape. Population densities dropped, and the area became home to far fewer children. Like the Sicilians before them, members of the gay community sought affordable rents and like-minded culture; in addition, however, they were drawn to the neighborhood in a self-conscious pursuit of New Orleans character and charm—qualities that have continued to sustain the Quarter into the twenty-first century.[46]

CHAPTER 7

Meatballs, Mafia, and Memory

*The New Orleans Italian Restaurant in
Myth and Reality since 1945*

After decades of failing to get their man, in the summer of 1981 the U.S. Department of Justice finally secured a meaningful conviction against Carlos Marcello in an ambitious undercover sting operation. The FBI's Brilab (a combination of *bribery* and *labor*) operation involved a phony Beverly Hills insurance company and extensive wiretapping to ensnare Marcello and various Louisiana politicians in a racketeering scheme. Veteran journalists Jim Amoss and Dean Baquet covered the trial for the *New Orleans States-Item*, and their regular columns detailed the complex dealings that led to Marcello's eventual incarceration. But as they listened to hour after hour of court-released tapes in pursuit of the story, the reporters realized another fundamental truth: Marcello and company "frequently had food on their minds" and spent much of their time "talking fettuccine, eggplant dishes, wine—and where to get them."[1]

"Marcello, like many of his fellow New Orleanians, forever is talking about what to eat," observed Amoss and Baquet. He "has a predilection for pasta," they continued, and "tends to favor restaurants that specialize in so-called Italian-Creole cooking." Among his favorites were "Mosca's in Waggaman; Broussard's and La Louisiane in the French Quarter, and Impastato's and T.J.'s in Metairie." Marcello's voice, often sounding disinterested and distant during the most damning of conversations, suddenly brightened when it came time to decide where and what to eat for dinner or when he learned that one of the Mosca brothers had dropped off a package of hogshead cheese. When codefendant Vince Marinello called to say that he had some homemade caponatina for Carlos and his brother, Marcello joked, "Forget about Joe. Give me mine." Baquet, a New Orleans native who in 2014 became executive editor of the *New York Times*, recalled Marcello as "a Louisiana-style mob boss:

he mainly planned lunches and dinners, and he griped that he couldn't get a table at Mosca's." At one point, after noticing that Marcello "had gotten tired of his lawyers and his constantly weeping family," Baquet "sidled up to him in the corridor of a Los Angeles courthouse, and he talked and talked. And what I learned was that the feared mob boss, Bobby Kennedy's Public Enemy No. 2, the boss of all bosses, was actually a Yat"—local slang for a regular guy of modest education who, like many New Orleanians, found his greatest pleasure in the simple charms of the local culture.[2]

Baquet's characterization of the wealthy mob boss squares with French Quarter character and Marcello driver Frenchy Brouillette's account of Marcello as obsessed with braciole, which he pronounced as "something resembling *booshaloni*." The boss would park his Cadillac outside of Hyp Guinle's Bourbon Street eatery, the Spot, and wait for hours for the cook to prepare the dish, despite the conspicuousness of Marcello's car and his desire to avoid the appearance "that he had nothing better to do with his time." Such accounts are at odds with the usual mythology that surrounds Carlos Marcello, the tomato salesman turned feared chieftain of Gulf Coast organized crime allegedly involved in complicated plots to assassinate President John F. Kennedy. Indeed, the mostly sealed forty-five-thousand-page transcript of the Brilab wiretaps has become the basis for a thriving cottage industry of conspiracy websites. Yet Amoss and Baquet's *New Orleans Times-Picayune/States-Item* metro editor, Jack Davis, recalled his reporters howling with laughter at the sheer banality of the reams of Brilab transcripts released to the media: Marcello opined on birds ("Herons, dat's something like a crane. You find 'em on garbage dumps. But dey ain't no good to eat") and Governor Edwin Edwards ("a sonofabitchin' *man*"). Old-fashioned historical source analysis reveals that many of Internet "facts" about Marcello can be traced to a 1970 *Life* investigative piece by David Chandler, an avid journalistic promoter of the Marcello myth who subsequently lost a defamation suit filed by one of the article's subjects. "Anybody who tells you that Carlos Marcello plotted the Kennedy assassination," observed Dean Baquet, "is a moron."[3]

The Marcello myth, particularly in its more specious dimensions, has also distracted us from the significant contributions that the Marcellos and other Sicilians made toward building New Orleans into the food and entertainment destination that it is today. Their influence was most profound during the half century from the end of Prohibition to the late 1970s, when the defining characteristics of our current era of dining began to take shape. The high-end

Creole Italian restaurant represented the fullest manifestation of all that had gone before it, from the nineteenth-century oyster saloons and turn-of-the-century spaghetti houses to the elaborate tables set by the lakeside resorts at West End and the early jazz cabaret nightclubs of 1920s Bourbon Street. The underworld influence on these houses was less the stuff of Mafia fantasy fiction than the prosaic reality of financing restaurants in a city with lending institutions whose conservative stances on credit bordered on the reactionary. And as the Brilab tapes taught us, the wise guys harbored a deep cultural affinity for traditional Louisiana "Creole" seafood dishes in general and Sicilian specialties in particular. In New Orleans, this interest gave life to more than one memorable culinary landmark.

If the period between 1830 and 1900 saw the oyster saloon mature into the Sicilian-run grand restaurant and dance hall and the next thirty years saw another set of oyster saloons and taverns evolve into spaghetti houses and nightclubs, then the post–World War II Creole Italian restaurant represented a final maturation of these concepts that reached its apex circa 1970. At a formative moment in the city's mid-twentieth-century cultural life, the Creole Italian restaurant stood among the very finest of New Orleans institutions. But during the 1980s, the rules of the restaurant game began to change, undermining many of the assumptions under which these establishments operated. Most were unprepared for the coming embrace of casual dining, the emergence of modernized corporate service-industry structures, expanding and changing tastes and the embrace of "new" ethnic foods, and the phenomenon of the "name" chef. That this older style of Creole Italian restaurant persists today results in no small measure from the city's deep affinity for both cultural tradition and anachronism, with kitchens and diners alike holding at arm's length the paradigm that governs the rest of the modern restaurant world.

The best-known Sicilian restaurants in New Orleans today are two very different long-running institutions. For over a century, Pascal's Manale has operated not far from the familiar paths trod by out-of-town tourists, nestled neatly in Uptown under the shady live oaks of Napoleon Avenue. Mosca's, in contrast, has since 1946 occupied an unadorned roadhouse on a largely featureless stretch of U.S. 90 on the Mississippi River's west bank. Diners can arrive at Manale's via the picturesque St. Charles Avenue Streetcar; visiting Mosca's requires a seventeen-mile automotive odyssey from the French Quarter. But despite these enormously different settings, Mosca's and Manale's are alike in that they are rare survivors among an arguably dying breed of New Orleans restaurant, informed by cultural assumptions and management philosophies that might be unsustainable in a different context.

Frank Manale opened his Uptown restaurant in 1913, just as the appetite for red-sauce-style Italian food began to take off in New Orleans. The unusual grammar of its present name traces to 1937, when Manale died and his nephew, Pascal Radosta, took over the business. It remains family-run today. The "barbecued shrimp" in Manale's most famous dish are not barbecued at all but instead are broiled in butter and pepper and are so messy to eat that they come with a large paper bib. The restaurant's first-rate oyster bar and ably mixed old-school cocktails are commendable in a town where such things are crucial. But regular diners do not necessarily frequent Manale's for the fare, which can be delicious but is almost never adventurous, and although normally gracious, staff members are not above periodic episodes of combativeness—and they certainly have not been trained to exude the corporate artifice of "the customer is always right." Patrons go there almost out of habit, to see friends and be seen by friends. With white tablecloths and black-vested waiters in the pleasant dining room and the wood-paneled bar studded with autographed portraits of celebrities, the Manale's experience is somehow more than the sum of its parts, an impression only intensified by regular patronage. Its vibe is defiantly New Orleans.

Across the river, Mosca's is housed in a small, white, nearly windowless edifice defined primarily by its lack of defining characteristics—ignoring the modest signage outside, one might think it was a lawnmower repair shop. Mosca's remains a popular destination for locals as well as out-of-town diners who believe that through some error of judgment, they have been let in on a treasured secret—despite the fact that said "secret" has been featured in the *New Yorker*, the only Italian restaurant in New Orleans to receive that honor. Yet Mosca's enduring success is about more than good press. Diners return generation after generation to get their fill of Chicken a la Grande or Oysters Mosca, garlic-infused dishes that issue forth from the kitchen on family-style platters with care and consistency. Numerous homey touches remain as much part of Mosca's appeal as the food, and the restaurant clings to the once-common custom of accepting only cash. Like Manale's, it is defiantly New Orleans, but in an entirely different way.[4]

A crucial element that differentiates Mosca's from Manale's is the dark lore of supposed Mafia activity that routinely surfaces during conversations about Mosca's history, a notion reinforced by its remote location, the Marcello family's ownership of the land on which the building sits, and the mostly unfounded rumors of gangsters dumping bodies in the forbidding swampland that trails out behind the restaurant. Yet like many enduring mythologies, this one contains a kernel of truth. The Mosca's myth had its genesis on a cool fall morning in 1943, when two rabbit hunters stumbled across a badly decomposed body half buried in a shallow grave "in a desolate wooded section just off the Boutte highway near Willswood." Within a week, authorities had identified the corpse as someone known locally as Gene Mano whose real name was Constantino Masotto. He had been operating a butcher's stall in the French Market for about a year and had a costly habit of betting on losing horses at the Fairgrounds, a high-flying lifestyle brought to ground when unknown parties shattered his skull with a hammer and sprinkled the body with quicklime on this lonely Westbank stretch of U.S. 90.[5]

Mano's wife had run personal ads inquiring about his whereabouts not long after her husband disappeared the previous August but had somehow failed to call the police about the matter before moving back home to Washington, D.C. After the discovery of his body, Theresa Mano came back to New Orleans and told investigators about two men with whom she and her husband had shared an early Sunday dinner the night he disappeared. Tommy Siracusa was a dark-haired, jowly New Orleans tavern owner, while Salvatore Vitale (or Vittali) was a deadly looking Italian citizen who wore small round glasses with darkened lenses. The foursome had gone to dinner at the Willswood Tavern, the predecessor of Mosca's, not far from where Mano's body was later found. Returning to the French Quarter around 4:00 in the afternoon, Siracusa and Vitale dropped the Manos off at their St. Ann Street residence before heading over to Italian Hall on Esplanade to play cards. But a little before 8:00, according to Theresa Mano, her husband asked for a clean shirt, kissed her several times, and said "'he was going to the corner' to see 'a couple of fellows' of whom he said he was 'suspicious.'" He never returned.[6]

"And that's where, in the Mafia's stories, they tell you they take you to dinner and you don't come home—that's where it came from," explained Nick Loguidice, who grew up on St. Philip Street in the 1950s and from whom I first heard the tale of Gene Mano's disappearance. Masotto had fled New York, where he had been under investigation in the bludgeoning death of his sister in early 1942, and according to Loguidice, Mano/Masotto's killing had resulted after Sylvestro "Silver Dollar Sam" Carollo received a telephone call from a New York boss. "That's where that shit come from," explained Loguidice. Carollo, the reputed head of organized crime in New Orleans, lived in the 600 block of St. Philip, the heart of the Sicilian French Quarter, just doors from Loguidice and his family. Carollo's headquarters was the St. Charles Tavern, which never closed, and he owned Willswood and the property around it.[7]

The police arrested Siracusa and Vitale but failed to find the evidence necessary to hold them despite an extensive investigation using techniques both legal and illegal. In February 1944, still under indictment but out on bond, Tommy Siracusa disappeared. His car was found, keys still in the ignition, parked in front of a home on Elysian Fields Avenue. Police found a naked, badly decomposed body in the river weeks later and suspected that it was Siracusa but were unable to confirm his identity because the corpse had been embalmed and all the teeth had been removed. The wiseguys did a more convincing job one month later when a dairy farmer came across a headless skeleton in a rural area near Downman Road and Lake Pontchartrain. The skeleton was neatly dressed in Siracusa's clothing, and the pockets contained "$65 in currency, a pawn ticket for $81.60 on a diamond stick pin dated July 31, 1943, a driver's license, a draft registration card, a 3-3 draft classification card, a social security card, an Italian Union Club membership card, and a memorandum book, all in Siracusa's name." When police showed the body and some of the effects to Siracusa's widow, she declared herself "satisfied it's my Tommy." Then she collected ten thousand dollars in life insurance. For his part, Vitale never served time for either homicide. Although Siracusa and Vitale were supposedly dead, Loguidice noted that both men attended his christening some years later. The last time anyone made any attempt to determine who killed Constantino Masotto was 1951, when the House Un-American Activities Committee asked Carlos Marcello, "Do you know Salvatore Vittali?" He declined to answer that question, along with many others. Marcello acquired the Willswood Tavern property from Carollo and rented to Provino Mosca in 1946, not long after the chef relocated from Chicago Heights. Contrary to popular lore, Mosca had not been Al Capone's chef.[8]

Mosca's success has resulted not from its colorful past but from modern critical restaurant reviews beginning in the early 1970s. In the 1950s, Mosca's was more of a local family place where people went after Sunday mass or on a special weeknight. Indeed, through the 1960s, Mosca's remained the province of food writer Calvin Trillin and others were who were indeed in on what was truly a secret. In 1970, however, Richard Collin placed it in the front section of his revolutionary restaurant review guide, *The New Orleans Underground Gourmet*, a place reserved for what he deemed the city's "Grand Restaurants." Even today, to look at Mosca's exterior and place it in the same category of Galatoire's might seem like a stretch to those unfamiliar with local prevailing cultural standards. "This is one of New Orleans' most glorious restaurants," wrote Collin in a revised version of his book published in 1973. "The kitchen is one of the most original anywhere. Mosca's is the prototype of the great little restaurant no one knows about that serves the best food anywhere."[9]

Publisher Simon and Schuster probably did not anticipate the impact that Collin's book would have on New Orleans's food culture. Bearing the provocative subtitle, "Where to Find Great Meals in the City and Environs for Less Than $3.75 and as Little as 50¢," the first volume in the Underground Gourmet series covered San Francisco and appeared in 1969, with volumes for Los Angeles; Washington, D.C.; New York; and New Orleans released the following year. Targeted at tourists, with distances measured based on their proximity to the French Quarter, Collin's exhaustive guide generated enormous buzz in a local culture that disproportionately emphasized conversations about eating.

A history professor by day, Collin offered extensive and sometimes biting subjective judgments that stood in stark contrast to earlier written restaurant reviews. Beginning with the Works Progress Administration's 1938 *New Orleans City Guide*, publications had from time to time offered airy and uncritical descriptions of notable dining landmarks. Likewise, Lucius Beebe and other food writers produced glowing testimonials about Antoine's and some of the city's other notable eateries in the pages of *Gourmet* or *Holiday* magazines during the 1950s. Such reviews differ not at all in substance from the always positive observations of contemporary restaurants found today in *Food and Wine*, *Garden and Gun*, and other publications that aim more to inform readers about style and cultural currency and fuel modern food tourism than to highlight areas that might benefit from improvement.[10]

In 1971, Collin's restaurant review column began appearing weekly in the *New Orleans States-Item*, bringing his influential and sometimes acerbic observations to a much wider audience. In our contemporary food culture, afflicted by Urban Spoon comments and oversaturated by media from every conceivable origin, it is hard to imagine that the first meaningful restaurant reviews in a city that takes its food so seriously appeared less than half a century ago. But newspaper restaurant reviews had been popularized only in the late 1950s by Craig Claiborne in the *New York Times*. Observed Charles Ferguson, the *States-Item* editor who hired Collin, "Eating out in New Orleans was considered synonymous with eating at Antoine's or Galatoire's or Commander's—and what [Collin] did was say, 'No, eating out in New Orleans may be that, but it's also eating paella at España,' which was under the Broad Street overpass, which he thought was the prototypical underground restaurant." Diners weren't the only ones paying attention: according to Ferguson, Collin "had the power to make or break. He couldn't break an Antoine's, but . . . I think he put small places out of business. He was read avidly by people who were interested in eating out." When Collin gave up writing the column, noted Ferguson, the paper's average daily circulation dropped by ten thousand.[11]

Collin's reviews had an almost immediate but not always welcome impact on the city's restaurant scene. As culinary matriarch Ella Brennan observed, her family owed some of its early success with the Vieux Carré restaurant and flagship Brennan's on Royal Street in the 1950s to the friendly pieces that Beebe and others penned for the era's most popular glossy magazines. And Collin's negative review of Commander's Palace, published in 1974, not long after the family had taken over daily operation the culinary landmark, "certainly got our attention, to put it mildly," she recalled forty years later, characterizing Collin's review as "low and underhanded." In contrast to the beloved Gene Bourg, who took over restaurant reviews for the *States-Item*, Brennan declared that "everybody disliked [Collin] intensely."[12]

But Collin offered effusive praise for the "incalculable" imprint that the city's Italians left on New Orleans cuisine. In so doing, he was perhaps the first to articulate in writing what diners and restaurateurs had known to be true since at least the early 1920s: "Bringing with them a long culinary tradition of their own and a love for seafood, the Italian chefs understood and readily adapted to the local cuisine. They also extended it with innovations of their own." Collin's authority gave weight to his assertion that "some of the greatest local cooking in recent years has been done in restaurants run by Italians." Italian cuisine, he noted, had "blended into specialties which have become New Orleans favorites." Indeed, Collin coined the term *Italian Creole* (more commonly *Creole Italian* today) in a 1975 review of the Restaurant Sclafani that the restaurant reprinted in its entirety as an advertisement in the competing *New Orleans Times-Picayune*.[13]

Despite (or perhaps because of) their centrality to the city's evolving cuisine, Sicilian-descended restaurateurs often demonstrated a paradoxical blend of ethnic pride and public self-deprecation. For example, "Wop Salad" persisted on menus well into the 1980s, arguably symbolizing the narrow-minded idea that Italian restaurants could never truly be considered "fine dining." The use of a racial slur to define this garlicky course often deeply offended outsiders. During the 1970s, one New York couple followed the advice of their cab driver and dined at T. Pittari's, an unusual Creole and Italian restaurant on Claiborne Avenue known for its flamboyant advertising and bizarre offerings of exotic wild game dishes such as lion and elephant. When the cabbie returned to fetch the couple and take them back to their hotel, they berated him: "How could a good Italian boy send us to a restaurant like that where they have a 'wop salad' on the menu?" But as Betty Bellone Unsworth noted, to "everybody in New Orleans at the time, it was a wop salad. [We] didn't think anything of it."[14]

This casual acceptance of "Wop Salad" might have resulted from New Orleans's studied culture of anachronism. It is easy to imagine Richard Collin waving a hand dismissively in the air as he wrote in the early 1970s how the appellation "illustrates the easy and informal recognition of the Italian contribution to New Orleans." Yet its tolerance by the city's Sicilian Americans, not entirely unrelated to a similar acceptance of unwarranted Mafia innuendo, bears exploration. Sociologists, anthropologists, and folklorists who study such phenomena acknowledge that an ethnicity's embrace or at least toleration of ethnic humor and derogatory terminology often flows from seemingly contradictory impulses. For some, otherwise denigrating terms such as *Wop* lose their force as insults over time, while other émigrés may see in placid acceptance a pliable strategy for survival in a foreign land. "Wop Salad" eventually faded from menus as that brand of 1980s hyphenated ethnic pride finally melted into the cracks in change-resistant New Orleans during the 1990s, but the Internet still offers a plethora of recipes for dishes by that name.[15]

The appearance of Collin's observations about the New Orleans dining scene coincided with dramatic changes in Americans' expectations for eating out, a process fueled by the sort of growing critical dialogue of which Collin was a part. He quit writing his weekly column for the *States-Item* in 1980, in part because he and Ferguson had an agreement that Collin would eat at a restaurant at least three times before giving it a bad review: according to Ferguson, Collin said that the "bad restaurants are killing me." By that time, casual dining had begun taking root even in hidebound New Orleans, where restaurants frequently held the riffraff at bay by requiring gentlemen to wear jackets despite the seasonally oppressive tropical heat. The rise of casual dining was not the least of the transformations of the 1980s that began separating the city's past dining scene from its present.

An important local and national structural shift that occurred during the 1970s also changed the way that diners perceive a restaurant's value, linking its currency to the reputation of a "name" chef in the kitchen. As with most transformative cultural movements, it is difficult to identify a single distinct episode that served as its genesis, but in New Orleans, one event that signaled the gradual yet inexorable drift toward this new restaurant model was the emergence of Paul Prudhomme as the executive chef at Commander's Palace. Chef Paul, whose rendition of blackened redfish became so popular nationally that it threatened to depopulate the Gulf of Mexico of its namesake species, went on to become a national culinary celebrity in the same league as Julia Child.[16]

Several theories seek to explain why "cooks" became "chefs" in America during the late 1970s, with most citing the ideas that diners who were more educated about culinary matters wanted to know who made their meal, that restaurant work was becoming increasingly respectable, and that the United States experienced a cultural transference from Europe, where the French chef reigned supreme. Before this era, however, a restaurant's identity coalesced around the magnetic personality of its proprietor, who often fulfilled the role of maître d' and host. No matter how involved a proprietor might be in ensuring culinary excellence in the kitchen, a restaurant's reputation rested on his (or sometimes her) front-of-house presence. A superior host ensured a special night out. This concept is foreign to today's diners, lured by the reputation of a particular celebrity chef and paying scant if any attention to the staff who greet them at the door. The highlight of a meal in the twenty-first century dawns when the executive chef walks through the dining room, not unlike General Montgomery touring the British front lines at El Alamein, stopping at tables to dispense words of goodwill and posing for the obligatory selfie.[17]

A fundamental operational problem arose from relying on the presence of a noted maître d', and the emergence of the celebrity chef entirely solved that problem. Owner/hosts could only be in one place at a time, and the essence of their personalities was their status as notable individuals. That status could not be replicated or transferred, making it difficult for restaurateurs to own and operate multiple successful high-end restaurants. Chefs, however, could be created, as restaurateurs and the emergent corporatized restaurant industry began to realize.

Among the innovators of this now common model was Joe Baum, who in

1955 helped found Restaurant Associates, considered one of the premiere hospitality corporations of its kind, though it is now thirty years past its heyday. When Baum's Four Seasons opened in 1959, it became the first fine dining "theme" restaurant that subsumed the personality of the host to the cuisine, style, and service within. It was a model primed for growth and expansion even if Four Seasons itself was hardly ever profitable. In New Orleans, the first restaurateurs to recognize the importance of this model were arguably the Commander's Palace branch of the Brennan family, led by siblings Ella and John Brennan. Their "chef" of the 1950s and 1960s, Paul Blangé, was of the old kitchen paradigm—"No more of a chef than I was," remembered Ella Brennan. Blangé worked closely with the owner to build a menu, right down to the tasting. Prudhomme, in contrast, was hired more as a cook than a chef, but the sweep of culinary history transformed him into the prototypical chef, and he went on to a level of success that the Brennans certainly did not anticipate. His successor, Emeril Lagasse, whom Ella Brennan defined as a *chef* because of his formal culinary training and sent to New York early in his tenure at Commander's Palace to study under Baum, went on to redefine the role of celebrity chef and eventually to create his own modern corporate restaurant empire.[18]

Few of the pre-1970s Sicilian restaurants that aspired to fine dining—places such as Restaurant Sclafani, Moran's La Louisiane, and Elmwood Plantation—survived very far into this new age, and propositions built on that model today would be unlikely to succeed. In addition, the Marcello family, which had taken such an active role in capitalizing and operating some of the city's more memorable institutions, withdrew from its involvement in the New Orleans food scene, which was also affected by broader trends, including a shrinking local economy that depended less on petroleum and shipping and more on tourism. The changes of the 1980s significantly diminished but did not entirely eliminate Sicilian influence in New Orleans dining.

If Manale's and Mosca's are the most famous Italian restaurants in New Orleans today, in the 1950s the same would have to be true of Turci's, then located on Poydras Street, and the sprawling Restaurant Sclafani, which Peter Sclafani opened on Palmyra Street in 1945. Sclafani's, a restaurant of the white-tablecloth-and-silver-plate-service variety that is now all but extinct, represented a broad expanse of the twentieth-century Sicilian immigrant experience in the Lower French Quarter. Peter Sclafani's father, Frank, came to the city in 1898 at the age of twenty-two. Having trained as a blacksmith and a veterinarian during his youth in Palermo, the young immigrant had no trouble finding steady work in New Orleans at a time when many goods still moved through the city in wagons pulled by draft animals. Not long after his arrival, he and a partner opened a blacksmith shop at 911 Chartres. Frank rode his cutting horse down to the nearby French Market to collect mules, a job that exposed him to a broad range of dialects spoken by the city's Sicilian immigrants. "A lot of times they would pay half in money, and half in produce," remembered his grandson and namesake, Frank. Like other professionals and tradesmen who offered critical services to distinct immigrant subcultures, the Sclafanis became well known and respected in the Sicilian French Quarter.[19]

Frank Sclafani could see that veterinary blacksmithing was a dying trade, so he saved his money and bought real estate, including a large house at the foot of Esplanade Avenue where he and his wife, Jenny, would host neighborhood residents on special feast days. Because Frank was frequently paid with food, he "had a lot more food than he could ever eat," and the elder Sclafani eventually converted their home into a restaurant. Here, in Jenny Sclafani's kitchen, her eldest son, Peter, would help out by "lifting the pots and bringing in stuff and going in to get what they wanted." Peter went on to work at his father's restaurant and bar, receiving a unique education in Sicilian cuisine as he picked up various specialties that reflected the "different styles and different regional cooking all over Sicily."[20]

Yet Peter Sclafani possessed a free-spirited nature that sat poorly with his father, who hoped to pass on his habits of steady work and financial accumulation. Peter liked to put on boxing exhibitions on French Quarter cross streets, prompting Frank to quip, "It's better to be kicked in the head by a mule for a quarter than to box for nothing." Undeterred, Peter sought further adventure as a cook and butcher aboard one of the Vaccaro family's United Fruit steamers, where he learned the intricacies of fine-dining service. According to Peter's son, Frank, "They had the white starched linens . . . elaborate silverware and plating. They wanted the finest of service, so he learned this fancy service that he eventually brought back to Palmyra Street." By the 1950s, people had come to expect a certain dining experience—"white starched tablecloths and silverware and tuxedoed waiters and people that knew how to serve. . . . You couldn't give them stainless steel. They'd have thought they were in prison if you gave them stainless steel." On one occasion, Frank recalled overhearing a boy say, "Mother, I can't eat the salad." When she asked why not, he said, "I don't have a salad fork." So Frank "told the busboy, 'Get that gentleman a salad fork right away!'"[21]

Collin placed Restaurant Sclafani alongside Mosca's among the "Grand New Orleans Restaurants." In the 1950s, Sclafani's occupied nearly an entire block on Palmyra Street in Mid City and a menu featuring more than 150 items. Sometimes people would order a dish by an unfamiliar name, and Frank Sclafani "would go back and ask my dad" because he had such encyclopedic knowledge of regional variations. Late in the decade, Sclafani's became one of the first major Italian restaurants to move to Metairie, where the family built a sprawling building on what was then a mostly empty stretch of Causeway Boulevard. It remained there until the 1980s, when it closed. The building was subsequently demolished.[22]

Offering a similar style of New Orleans Italian cuisine in a much more casual style, Tony Angello's was until very recently a Lakeview landmark. Beloved by regular patrons for its plentiful "feed me" specials, this restaurant embodied the sort of Sicilian cooking that Italian-descended New Orleanians remembered their grandmothers making. Angello, however, hailed not from New Orleans or from Sicily but instead from Pueblo, Colorado, on the high plateau that stretches east from the Rocky Mountains. Nevertheless, Angello followed a familiar path on his way to becoming a beloved New Orleans restaurateur, guided by friendships and blood relations forged on the Gulf Coast. His father, Calogero "Carlo" Angello, had emigrated from Sicily to New Orleans in 1910 and in the following year married Rosa Latino, a young woman who had migrated to the city in 1904 from Villafranca, a tiny Sicilian agricultural village, and whose family operated two spaghetti restaurants on Decatur Street. The young couple soon left for Colorado, with Carlo finding work in a steel mill before becoming section chief for the Santa Fe Railroad. While in Pueblo, Rosa gave birth to two daughters and two sons, the last of whom was Tony. The Angellos returned to New Orleans in 1932, possibly to be closer to their Latino kin, and moved into a house on Marshal Foch Street in Lakeview, then the outer vanguard of the city's suburban rim.[23]

The Lakefront of the late 1940s and 1950s in which Tony Angello came of age was only a few miles from the French Quarter but was culturally and historically a world apart. Instead of the Quarter's ancient narrow buildings and cobbled streets soiled by mud and the leavings of draft animals, Lakeview had newly paved streets dotted with new bungalows featuring driveways and that rare New Orleans luxury, lawns. The turn-of-the-century pleasure zones of West End and Spanish Fort had long since disappeared under heaps of mud dredged during an ambitious land-reclamation project completed in 1934. By the 1950s, the area had become popular with young people who enjoyed cruising, especially along Lakeshore Drive, which led to Pontchartrain Beach, the latest iteration of lakefront resort, with amusement rides and a bandstand. The Angello men found work in nearby bars that catered to this clientele. Carlo became a "watchman" at the Rockery Inn, a popular drive-in joint that served as something of a landmark on Robert E. Lee Boulevard, while young Tony became a partner in the Two Tony's Lounge on Canal Boulevard. A generic strip mall has now replaced the Rockery Inn's neon sign, which beckoned motorists to enjoy fried chicken and cocktails.[24]

In 1955, Tony joined his older brother, Joseph, in opening the Black Orchid Lounge at 2100 Foy Street in the inner suburb of Gentilly, near the intersection of Elysian Fields Avenue and Gentilly Boulevard, a neighborhood whose Craftsman and Spanish Revival bungalows had since the 1920s attracted large numbers of aging Sicilian immigrants and their American-born offspring. The origins of the Black Orchid's name are unclear, although a popular horse by that name won at the nearby Fairgrounds during the 1942–43 racing season, and the bar served as home base for more than one "Gentilly mathematician"—or devotee of pari-mutuel betting—in its day. Upstairs from the Black Orchid one found the Angellos' Il Ristorante, where Joseph and Tony's mother, Rosa, and sisters, Frances and Catherine, produced Sicilian favorites for what became a devoted clientele. Joseph's death in 1961 at the age of forty-four left Tony in charge. "The Black Orchid was open late at night so the musicians who played in the Quarter and the people who worked in the Quarter would have a place that they could go," recalled Philip Sciortino. "And what I remember is he had that spinach bread. . . . We used to go there often, and we took all the kids." Collin deemed the fare "polite and palatable" but ultimately "unexciting," though even the sometimes-difficult-to-please Collin declared the Crabmeat Tina worth the trip.[25]

In 1972, Angello opened the doors to his eponymous restaurant on Fleur de Lis Avenue, a quiet residential street in a Lakeview neighborhood full of brick ranch houses that, like Gentilly a generation before, were increasingly occupied by the descendants of Sicilian immigrants. Tony and his sisters had refined the menu items that defined their cuisine and, more important, had cultivated a following, particularly within the city's Sicilian-descended community, whose third-generation members were eager to connect with their heritage in an age when such meals might only be had at home on important holidays. Tony Angello was something of a hybrid in this era of restaurant transition. He was the chef, responsible for the wonders produced by the kitchen, but he was also the personality and host. Although "best restaurant" rankings certainly do not reflect objective reality, it is noteworthy that food columnist Jack Du Arte declared Tony Angello's the tenth-best place to eat in New Orleans in 1976, so popular that it was "almost impossible to get into." More in line with Collin's earlier observations, Gene Bourg opined in 1994 that the restaurant served good and sometimes excellent food but that the flavors "flatter the tastebuds rather than challenge them."[26]

Like many restaurants owned by Sicilian Americans in New Orleans and elsewhere, Tony Angello's gained a reputation as a mob hangout primarily because it was a favored dining destination of reputed crime bosses. Like many New Orleans institutions, Angello's restaurant was never open to the public on Mondays, though Tony Angello occasionally used the downtime to hold special invitation-only luncheons and dinners. On one September 1976 afternoon, Angello's guests included Carlos Marcello (who arrived at the restaurant with federal agents on his tail) and Arthur Tedesco, a prizefighter during the 1940s who went on to work for New Orleans bookmaker Sam Saia. By the mid-1970s, Tedesco was working as a beer salesman in New Jersey, and he had arrived in New Orleans via Greyhound bus only a few days earlier; short on funds, he had slept in the restaurant's upstairs office. The day after the luncheon, local media reported that a great Mafia meeting had taken place at Tony Angello's, describing Tedesco as the "New Jersey Beer Baron." Retorted Tedesco, "If I'm such a big shot from New Jersey, why am I riding a bus?"[27]

The event also had political implications. Also in attendance was Joseph V. DiRosa, who was running for reelection as an at-large member of the New Orleans City Council and who found himself in the uncomfortable position of having to deny that he had known that Marcello would be there. The incident resurfaced the following year, when DiRosa ran for mayor against Ernest "Dutch" Morial, prompting one editorialist to declare that DiRosa "cannot expect to attend a luncheon also attended by Marcello without some questions being asked"—even if that luncheon was, in essence, a routine social gathering.[28]

As silly as the conclusions drawn from this 1976 luncheon may have been, it is also true that underground and often illegal economies played a role in the operation of restaurants and nightclubs. Long after the end of Prohibition, its legacy persisted through a series of restaurants that had some degree of association with individuals who had built both legitimate and illegal business empires during the first half of the twentieth century. In fact, the roots of the relationship between restaurants and gambling, alcohol, music, showbiz, and other illicit activities in New Orleans stretch back to at least the 1830s and continued to nurture the emergent corporatized structure that in the 1970s took over the way most Americans ate out.[29]

Salvatore "Joe" Segreto was the dapper and gracious host of a series of restaurants, the last of which, Eleven79, operated from 2000 to 2015 at 1179 Annunciation Street. His grandfather and namesake, Salvatore Segreto, came to America from the Sicilian village of Monreale through the Port of New York in 1892. Salvatore later collected his wife, Gerolama, and his brothers, Philip and John, who opened saloons in the tough neighborhood surrounding the intersection of Liberty and Perdido Streets. Salvatore opened his own establishment at 833 Decatur Street, opposite the bustling French Market. The first two decades of the twentieth century were violent ones for the Segreto brothers, and in the spring of 1916 they became entangled in a feud over local control over alcohol and vice. One of their adversaries, Andrew Henry Pons, operated a saloon and cabaret directly across the street from John Segreto's establishment at 1401 Perdido Street (now part of Duncan Plaza, across the street from City Hall), in an area considered such an irredeemable slum that it was bulldozed in the 1950s to make room for the current modernist city government complex. John Segreto's bar was located not far from Jane Alley, the boyhood home of Louis Armstrong, whose 1954 autobiography offers a somewhat unreliable account of the affray between Segreto and Pons.[30]

On April 8, 1916, Philip Segreto's sons, Joseph and Vincent, and three friends entered Pons's saloon and became embroiled in a verbal altercation that spilled over into violence when Joseph Segreto drove a knife blade into Pons's shoulder. "Bleeding profusely," Pons retrieved a shotgun from behind the bar and, moving to the sidewalk, fired both barrels at the five men fleeing on foot down the street, though they escaped unharmed. Three weeks later, Salvatore Segreto was standing on the sidewalk in front of his Decatur Street saloon talking to a cigar salesman when a slender Italian man in a gray suit came quickly toward him and fired a revolver at Segreto, wounding him in the thigh. Segreto received treatment at Charity Hospital but told police detectives that he could not identify his assailant. In early May, a trio of men ambushed and killed Philip Segreto, firing buckshot from sawed-off shotguns in broad daylight on the sidewalk of Perdido Street. The attack was so brazen that it warranted front-page headlines in the newspapers of a city somewhat inured to news of Sicilian violence. That one of the attackers was a recent immigrant who had come to New Orleans by way of New York suggests that the bloodshed had broader implications.[31]

The advent of Prohibition in 1920 changed the career trajectory of Salvatore Segreto, who as a saloon operator was already rather familiar with the rough world of alcohol and vice. According to his grandson, Joe, "Probably the best and the biggest of his interests [was] the wine and liquor business." Sometime in this era, Segreto met Joseph Marcello Sr. and by extension his sons, Carlos and Joseph Jr., who ultimately went on to greater fame. According to Joe Segreto, the elder Marcello "was a farmer and would bring things to the French Market, and my grandfather was in the market. So, you know, it was a long family friendship." A family photograph from the 1930s shows an older Salvatore Segreto sitting in the sun on the sidewalk outside his bar at 833 Decatur Street. Behind him stands a much younger, much shorter man, his right foot propped up on the curb and his right arm casually leaning on Segreto's chair. Though the man's square jaw and tight mouth are shaded by the brim of his fedora, he is almost certainly Carlos Marcello.[32]

Salvatore and Gerolama Segreto's oldest son, Joseph, born in 1909, became much more of a public figure than his father, playing a role in the creation of institutions whose names enjoy a storied place in what some term "the golden age of Bourbon Street." But he endured a rocky start. In 1935, Joseph Segreto and twelve other men were arrested for participating in a complex narcotics ring operated by gangsters Sam Alonze and Sylvestro Carollo. Smugglers paid Honduran revolutionaries with machine guns and other small arms in exchange for heroin, much of it carried through Louisiana's porous coastline in oyster luggers. The scheme began to unravel when federal agents bought fifteen ounces of dope at Alonze's restaurant at City Park Avenue and Dumaine Street. Segreto pled guilty in January 1936. Because he was a convicted felon, he could not hold a liquor license, so Ola, his wife and business partner, did so in his stead. These were hardly the last of his troubles. An ongoing feud with another ex-convict, Frank Poretto, boiled over in 1943 when Segreto gunned down Poretto inside his Dauphine Street bar, the Cat and the Fiddle, an act deemed self-defense by a criminal district court judge.[33]

In September 1944, however, Joseph and Ola Segreto took over the management of Masera's, a thriving restaurant and nightclub that had originated as a late-nineteenth-century oyster saloon at 809 St. Louis Street. Under Joe Segreto's parents, Masera's became "a favorite place for all of the visiting musicians and entertainers, [who] came to the Blue Room." These connections brought young Joe into contact with numerous "interesting entertainers as a young man. . . . Oftentimes we would go to Louis Prima's mother's house on Canal Boulevard, and as guests there would be Harry James and Betty Grable." Segreto also got to know other New Orleans music greats, among them Louis Prima's brother, Leon; Sharkey Bonano; Santo Pecorra; Tony Almirico; Frank and Freddie Asanto; the Dukes of Dixieland; and the Basin Street Six, with George Girard and Pete Fountain."[34]

In 1945, Masera's was renamed Segreto's, and around this time, the restaurateurs developed a relationship with a young African American Creole chef, Nathaniel Burton. Born in Mississippi in 1914, Burton arrived in New Orleans in 1939 and worked bussing tables at the Hotel New Orleans. Working in the hotel's kitchen and memorizing Escoffier at night, Burton quickly amassed an education that he put to use as kitchen manager at the Naval Hospital during World War II. After the war, Burton began preparing more elevated cuisine for diners at Segreto's. In those days, no black chefs and very few white ones ever went by anything but "cook," and it is doubtful that diners at Segreto's would have known the name of the man who prepared their dinner. Yet Burton went on to become one of the era's premiere Creole culinary authorities, with a long tenure during the heyday of the Pontchartrain Hotel's famous Caribbean Room. Burton's culinary talent and the colorful maître d' helped make Segreto's a dining destination, and in 1946, Joseph Segreto joked that the restaurant's signature dish, Chicken Cacciatore, was a "boon to the shortage-ridden world."[35]

In the spring of 1947, Joseph Segreto made a move that led directly to the creation of two memorable New Orleans institutions. According to his son, he "got interested in the business across the street . . . and called Leon Prima, who was in Memphis . . . to come home, bring his band," and the two men founded the 500 Club burlesque bar. In addition, Segreto sold his namesake restaurant to Diamond Jim Moran, who changed the name Moran's Restaurant. Moran and Segreto had been close friends and business associates. Born James Brocato, Moran changed his name to avoid embarrassing his family when he began a boxing career. He subsequently became "involved in the slot machine business. Frank Costello sent a lot of slot machines down here, and Jimmy handled a lot of slot machines for Frank. . . . Frank was a friend of my grandfather's, a friend of a lot of guys down here in New Orleans, and Jimmy, as well as my wife's family, the Geigermans, handled a lot of the things for the slot machines. And Jimmy Moran was well known in . . . political circles also, . . . being in the gambling business." Sixty years earlier, John Astredo and Terry Tranchina had built a similar empire on a foundation of food, alcohol, gambling, sports, celebrity, and family relationships.[36]

The primary attraction at Moran's Restaurant, popularly known as Diamond Jim Moran's, was always its flamboyant host. Explained Joe Segreto, "Diamond Jim was just a man about town in those days, you know? He became sort of like a . . . gadfly . . . always well dressed [and wearing] diamonds everywhere." Diners entered the restaurant's plush, dimly lit interior and encountered walls tiled with autographed celebrity photos and Diamond Jim himself. Perhaps the restaurant's most famous publicity stunt was its occasional placing of a diamond inside a meatball for discovery by a lucky diner. (Perhaps not coincidentally, one of Diamond Jim's sons became a dentist.) Moran's became known for offering the particular style of Sicilian cooking that had emerged in New Orleans in the first half of the twentieth century. Diamond Jim's wife, Mary, was also Sicilian and "was a fabulous cook [who] made all the meatballs and sauces." Reflecting the geographic dynamics of the Sicilian French Quarter's twilight in the 1950s and juxtaposing Moran's high-flying celebrity world and authenticity of the restaurant's cuisine, the Morans "would go to their house right on Royal Street . . . right off Esplanade with the station wagon to pick up those big pots full of sauce and meatballs and bring them to the restaurant."[37]

While Diamond Jim continued on at 809 St. Louis and later took over La Louisiane, a Creole restaurant on Iberville Street that dated back to the 1880s, Segreto ended his partnership with Prima at the 500 Club after just two years and opened Sloppy Joe's Haven, a nightclub at 231 Bourbon Street. Here, in 1949, amid a halfhearted effort to clean up the vice flourishing on Bourbon Street, Joseph and Ola Segreto found themselves at a hearing of the Louisiana Board of Alcoholic Control, charged with "permitting a lewd and immoral dance to be performed by" Evelyn West, a well-known burlesque performer who once had her breasts insured by Lloyds of London for fifty thousand dollars. At Sloppy Joe's, West had performed "with the aid of a dummy," the *Esquire Magazine* mascot, "Esky, the G-String Thief." Attorneys for the Segretos feigned ignorance about "some of the words used in the act" and suggested that one of the policemen clarify matters by acting out the routine with a mannequin. As the courtroom descended into equal parts mirth and acrimony, the commissioner from Alexandria asked Ola Segretto, the stenographer, "and a third woman to leave the courtroom so he could ask a witness to describe the dummy."[38]

Speaking in her defense, Ola Segretto told the board that she was the mother of two children and did not find West's act objectionable: "Evelyn was a high-class girl. I think her act was a comedy dance. I think that every policeman on the force saw her do it, and they complimented me." Frank Matranga, whose office was next door, said he had twice taken his daughters, ages twenty-seven and thirty-four, to see the act: although West "disrobed," he considered it "nothing. . . . That's nature." Bert Adam, the manager of the Flamingo Lounge, suggested that West's dance was "clean entertainment." Moreover, West's routine was far from unusual on Bourbon Street: "Just because a girl dances with a guy in a brassiere and holds him tight," observed Adam, "I don't think that's lewd." The Alcohol Board disagreed, ordering a fifteen-day ban on liquor sales at Sloppy Joe's—one day shorter than West's run at the venue. But Sloppy Joe's Haven never recovered and closed less than two years later. Joseph Segreto's subsequent clubs became less impressive as his fortunes declined, although his son, Joe, carried the family name forward with greater success, helping to shape the New Orleans dining scene that we know today.[39]

Growing up on Bourbon Street gave Joe Segreto a fascinating education as a restaurateur. He bussed tables at the Court of the Two Sisters before beginning work at Brennan's not long after it moved to Royal Street in 1956. "My dad knew the Brennans" and helped him get a job first as an assistant waiter and then as a waiter. Segreto also received culinary training from Paul Blangé, who ran Brennan's kitchen, and was influenced by headwaiter Frank Strauss and maître d' Bill Strauss. Dottie Brennan saw Joe as "like a brother." Indeed, Segreto and Ella and Dottie Brennan all matured together as restaurateurs as the 1950s became the 1960s. Moreover, the Masera brothers, who had sold their restaurant to Segreto's father in 1944 but continued to work for him and then Moran at Bourbon and St. Louis, took over the Old Absinthe House after Owen Brennan's death in 1955. In the evenings, Joe kept his hand in the world of entertainment by tending bar at Sharkey Bonano's Dream Room on Bourbon Street. At the age of twenty, he moved to Las Vegas, where he reunited with Louis Prima, who had by that time become an entertainment mainstay of the strip, and became his manager.[40]

Joe did not return to New Orleans until the late 1960s, when during a visit home he had a conversation with his old friend Carlos Marcello. "We had discussed doing a business together," recalled Segreto, "and I said, . . . 'I'm going to go back to Vegas, and I'll come back and we'll start putting it together.' He said, 'Okay—just let me know when you get back.'" By the time Segreto returned, however, Carlos was in the midst of legal troubles, and his brother, Joe, stepped in and suggested, "In the meantime . . . why don't you come to work for me at Elmwood Plantation? You can help train some of my waiters and improve the service."[41]

Elmwood Plantation's ancient live oaks still greet visitors to its River Road site, but instead of framing the fabled West Indian–style mansion, the branches now offer midafternoon shade to the lawns of a compact development of new luxury homes. Although pleasant, they are just as detached from the thoroughfare's history as the warehouses and other semi-industrial outposts that have sprouted up in the area over the last thirty years. Built by Nicolas de Chauvin LaFrenière in 1762, Elmwood Plantation was once billed as the oldest house of its kind along the Lower Mississippi. A devastating 1940 fire reduced the rambling two-story structure nearly to rubble, but its owners salvaged the ground-floor brick colonnade and made it the basis for a low-slung, single-story plantation house. It remained a residence for the next two decades, home to such notables as Australian soprano Marjorie Lawrence and New Orleans businessman (and supposed conspirator in the JFK assassination) Clay Shaw. In 1960 the property sold to a restaurant operation, with "hostesses Jeannine Matranga and Oneida Steekler" greeting guests of the sort who attended garden club and ladies auxiliary luncheons and dined on plantation-style "home cooking."[42]

Elmwood Plantation might have gone on peddling its Louisiana version of an Old South fantasy had it not been for the 1962 death of Provino Mosca, the patriarch of the Mosca family. His sons, Nick and John, had been running the Waggaman landmark under the guidance of their parents since 1946, but Provino's death led to a family split in which John and mother Mary Jo continued on with the original family business and Nick took his extensive culinary talents into a partnership with front-of-the-house man Joe Marcello. The two men bought Elmwood, only a short distance across the river from Mosca's, nine months after the death of Provino Mosca, and by the spring of 1963, they had opened their newly reimagined Elmwood Plantation.[43]

The cover of an elegant color menu from that time depicts an ancient live oak, towering in its verdant glory and draped with lacy ropes of Spanish moss that stretch lazily earthward from its dark limbs, framing a broad expanse of lawn that leads to Elmwood's long, low form. The dishes featured on it expressed the cultural parity enjoyed by Italian and Creole dishes at New Orleans's top white-tablecloth restaurants. Pasta offerings included spaghetti and ravioli made in-house. In the "Fowl" section, Chicken Cacciatore appeared just above Squab with Wild Rice. Diners might also select from an array of New Orleans Creole staples such as turtle soup and gumbo, Trout Meunière, and a variety of vehicles for lump crabmeat. Nick Mosca also brought some of his family specialties to Elmwood, including Oysters Mosca and Chicken a la Grande. But the menu also included such far more ambitious fare as Lobster Thermidor.[44]

In 1970, Joe Segreto joined a young man from Florida, Nino LoScalzso, as co–maître d's at Elmwood Plantation. Marcello and Mosca benefited from Segreto's experience as well as from the friendships that he had cultivated over his decade-long partnership with Louis Prima, an association that brought extra buzz to the restaurant. Four years later, Segreto took his talents to Broussard's on Conti Street in the French Quarter, where he and partners Joe Marcello Jr., Clarence Greco, and Joseph C. Marcello (son of Carlos Marcello) breathed new life into a careworn Creole restaurant. The first chef that Segreto hired was Nathaniel Burton, who had many years earlier been Joseph Segreto's chef on St. Louis Street. At Broussard's, however, Burton assumed a much more public role, reflecting Joe Segreto's awareness that diners had begun to care about the chef as much as the host. The Marcello brothers' search for a gifted and well-connected maître d' had brought Joe Segreto back from Vegas, but Burton's experience at the fabled Caribbean Room began to attract attention to Broussard's. Segreto also brought in another African American chef, James Evans, who had overseen the kitchen at Commander's Palace since 1942. This deep reservoir of experience in Broussard's back of the house brought accolades to the restaurant by the late 1970s. A photograph from that era shows Joe C. Marcello, Segreto, and their wives arm in arm with Sammy Davis Jr. and Burton. All are smiling widely, enjoying the moment with each other, except for Burton, who stands stiffly and offers the camera a tolerant expression. In another generation, he might have more fully participated in the fun, a celebrity chef in the making. His coworkers at Broussard's harbored a deep love for Burton, with Joe C. Marcello describing him as "laid back" and a "gentleman" who trained his staff to run a kitchen with precision and care. But the photograph was taken at the twilight of an era.[45]

In the wee hours of the morning, just a week before Christmas 1978, a faulty water heater burst into flames in an attic room of Elmwood Plantation. Employees quickly noticed the growing conflagration, but the phones had already stopped working. By the time that someone had run down River Road and called for help, Elmwood Plantation was well on its way to once again being reduced by fire to its distinctive brick colonnade and foundation walls. Several months later, Joe Marcello and Nick Mosca attempted to resurrect "Elmwood in Exile" by moving all seventy-four members of the staff to the dining room of La Louisiane, run as an Italian restaurant by Diamond Jim Moran until his 1958 death from a heart attack and thereafter by his sons. La Louisiane's most notable dish, Fettuccine Alfredo, so loved by the men whose voices fill the Brilab tapes, had by the 1960s become a novelty whose tableside preparation had become as much theater as entrée. When Marcello and Mosca took over, however, Moran's La Louisiane had fallen on difficult times as a consequence of its failure to adapt to the rapidly changing restaurant landscape, and half of the building had been partitioned off to house the equally doomed Playboy Club. Marcello and Mosca's attempt to keep Elmwood afloat at La Louisiane soon foundered, a victim not only of the oil bust and rising crime in the French Quarter but also of the fact that the high-end Creole Italian model, from menu to management philosophy, had not changed along with the times. Ownership of La Louisiane changed hands many times during the 1980s, but none of the subsequent operators met with success in the historic space.[46]

When Joe Segreto opened Eleven79, he offered an elegant tribute to restaurants past, an approximation of the style of dining offered at Elmwood Plantation in the mid-1960s. Neatly dressed, Segreto himself almost always greeted patrons at the door, and his celebrity friends often turned up in the softly lit dining room. An old-school kind of house, Eleven79 seldom advertised. As at Elmwood, the kitchen was almost comically small, yet the cuisine that emerged from it was carefully executed. After Eleven79 closed, the space it occupied was taken over by a pleasant dessert bar operated by a woman who started off her career baking doberge cakes part-time in her home.

For the last five years of their lives, Joe Segreto and Tony Angello regularly met for Tuesday morning coffee at Dorignac's grocery store on Veterans Highway in Metairie, a short distance from Angello's restaurant. I often ran into Joe at Dorignac's—it's the kind of place where such things happen. When I saw him there in the spring of 2015, I was shocked by his poor health, but he smiled when I mentioned that I'd seen that his friend Tony Bennett was coming to JazzFest to perform with Lady Gaga. "I had a little hand in making that happen," he brightened. "In fact, I was just on the phone with Lady Gaga this morning." In October, Joe died, having outlived his friend Angello by less than three months. At the end of 2016, the doors to Tony Angello's restaurant closed for good. It has been difficult to see the passing of these men and the world that they had created as anything other than announcing the end of an era.

As the second decade of the twenty-first century comes to a close, New Orleans remains one of the world's prime destinations for food tourism. Dining constitutes an economic engine fueled by the presence of more restaurants than the local population could ever hope to support. In a variety of contexts, Sicilian immigrants and their descendants were responsible for creating this vital sector. They began in the 1840s with modest port city oyster saloons and had by 1900 created several restaurants of national significance. The next generation capitalized on the economics of Prohibition and by the postwar era guided the transformation of dining and entertainment into a significant segment of the city's tourist-based cultural economy. It is hard to believe that as recently as 1973, eight of the eighteen "Grand Restaurants" listed in Richard Collin's *Underground Gourmet* were either run by Sicilians or were Sicilian in origin.[47]

But few of these old-school Creole Italian restaurants remain with us today. Most of them succumbed to the dining revolution that unfolded in the early 1980s, failing to adjust to fundamentally different expectations about going out to eat. Elements of their legacy remain, though less in gustatory style than in the scale and ambition of what they hoped to achieve. The Morans, Marcellos, Segretos, and other families played an important part in the city's maturation as a dining destination. They trained waitstaff, cultivated talent in the kitchen, financed expansion, and used their many connections in media and showbiz to market their creations to a national audience. In the process, they helped define New Orleans as we know it today.

Notes

INTRODUCTION. Uncovering the Sicilian Past in the Creole City

1. Faber, *Building the Land of Dreams*, deftly chronicles the material origins of the Anglo-Creole divide. Charles Gayarré and Grace King were among the most prominent promoters of Creole cultural hegemony in the late nineteenth century. See Gayarré, *Creoles of History*; King, *Creole Families of New Orleans*. For a systematic analysis of the construction of Creole identity see Fertel, *Imagining the Creole City*. The literature on the city's significant German population is quite scant. See Nau, *German People of New Orleans*. Germans are interesting where they intersect with slavery, as in the case of John Bailey, *Lost German Slave Girl*. The most insightful scholarship into the plight of German immigrants comes in Schafer's study of abused children (*Brothels, Depravity, and Abandoned Women*, 47–55). Likewise, despite the importance of the Irish in New Orleans, book-length treatments of the subject are few. See Niehaus, *Irish in New Orleans*. Somewhere between popular and scholarly history, one finds Kelley, *Irish in New Orleans*.

2. Maurice "Moon" Landrieu, interview by Jack Davis and Justin A. Nystrom, September 24, 2013, transcript, Making Modern New Orleans Collection, Documentary and Oral History Studio, Loyola University New Orleans.

3. One area of twentieth-century New Orleans that has received some thoughtful scholarly consideration is tourism. See Stanonis, *Creating the Big Easy*; Souther, *New Orleans on Parade*. Souther also takes direct aim at the French Quarter's constructed fantasy in "Disneyfication of New Orleans." The battles over race and place ongoing in America today have precedent elsewhere. Holocaust studies arguably led the reappraisal of historical consciousness in the twentieth century; for an overview, see Bourguignon, "Memory in an Amnesic World."

4. Many of these observations stem from my ongoing oral history collaboration with veteran journalist Jack Davis, which focuses on recording the memories of key players in New Orleans during the 1970s.

5. Scholarship on New Orleans clusters around both chronological and thematic bases. The eighteenth and nineteenth centuries dominate the historiography.

For recent works on the eighteenth century, see Dawdy, *Building the Devil's Empire*; Powell, *Accidental City*. The chronologically brief Louisiana Purchase era in New Orleans has a fine recent political study in Faber, *Building the Land of Dreams*. More books may have been published about free people of color than any other topic in the New Orleans historiography. For a recent work, see Emily Clark, *Strange History*. The intersection of the nineteenth-century sex trade with race has also received great attention. See, among others, Schafer, *Brothels, Depravity, and Abandoned Women*; Long, *Great Southern Babylon*; Landau, *Spectacular Wickedness*. The literature on Creoles is voluminous, much of it precipitated by Logsdon and Hirsch, *Creole New Orleans*. Slavery and the central role New Orleans played in the system have rightly received significant attention. For the most prominent work, see Johnson, *Soul by Soul*. Great expanses of twentieth-century New Orleans lack any mature works of history, though the civil rights era features two prominent works: Germany, *New Orleans after the Promises*; Arend, Austin, and Jones, *Showdown in Desire*.

6. Peirce F. Lewis, *New Orleans*, 4–5, 10. Inspired by Lewis's study, Richard Campanella, *Bienville's Dilemma*, comes the closest to making a systematic study of the city, albeit from the geographer's perspective. For an insightful analysis from the sociological perspective, see Fussell, "Constructing New Orleans, Constructing Race." Brothers's relation of Armstrong's boyhood in *Louis Armstrong's New Orleans* treads slightly further than Armstrong's ghostwritten memoir, *Satchmo*. Dated but compelling, Hair's *Carnival of Fury* is the most insightful work on Protestant black New Orleans at the turn of the twentieth century. The leading work of economic history on New Orleans is Marler, *Merchants' Capital*, which focuses entirely on the mid-nineteenth century. Powell's *Accidental City* was intended to be a single-volume history of New Orleans, but he was lured away by the compelling story of Bienville and only reached 1815.

7. For representative perspectives on the Hennessey lynching, see Gambino, *Vendetta*; Nelli, *Business of Crime*; Hunt and Sheldon, *Deep Water*; Baiamonte, "'Who Killa de Chief' Revisited." The sort of sensational popular writing one finds about organized crime in New Orleans is best characterized by John H. Davis, *Mafia Kingfish*.

8. Gabaccia, *Militants and Migrants*; Scarpaci, "Immigrants in the New South"; Margavio and Salomone, *Bread and Respect*. The one book-length treatment of Prima, Boulard, *Just a Gigolo*, it is not an analytical biography.

9. Work on the intersection of food and ethnicity continues to grow in quality. I found particularly insightful Ray, *Ethnic Restaurateur*. See also Diner, *Hungering for America*. For a recent analysis of food and culture among Italians in New York, see Cinotto, *Italian American Table*. Recent books exploring Prohibition expand the circle of food commodity into ethnic and political analysis: see Marni Davis, *Jews and Booze*; McGirr, *War on Alcohol*. Much of the literature on food remains in the realm of sweeping trade narratives, such as Kurlansky, *Salt*. Popular trade work can also offer deep insight: see Beahrs, *Twain's Feast*.

10. Smart food writing pieces on New Orleans Sicilians are limited. For two of the better examples, see Roahen, "Red Gravy"; Trillin, "No Daily Specials."

11. See Nystrom, *New Orleans after the Civil War.*

CHAPTER 1. Sicily Lemons and Sugarcane

1. Louis Prima, Jack Zero, and Ben Jaffe, "Please No Squeeza Da Banana" (Leeds Music Corp., 1944); Boulard, *Just a Gigolo*, 73–77; "Advertisement (Louis Prima)," *Billboard*, May 12, 1945.

2. For an account of the contributions of early "Italians" in New Orleans, see Magnaghi, "Louisiana's Italian Immigrants."

3. Tolkowsky, *Hesperides*, 115–16; Depew, *1795–1895*, 602–3; "Sicily Lemons" (advertisement), *New Orleans Daily Picayune*, May 24, 1838; "Lemons! Lemons!! Lemons!!!" (advertisement), *New Orleans Daily Picayune*, August 20, 1843. Depew was a lawyer for Cornelius Vanderbilt who consequently possessed an intimate knowledge of commercial markets.

4. Alvarez, "March of Empire," 29.

5. "Citrus Fruits in Sicily," 266–68.

6. Chace, "Manufacture," 18–27. For examples of recipes using lemons, see Tipton-Martin, *Jemima Code.*

7. *Official Report*, 85; "Californian Fruit Industries," 221; Crist, "Citrus Industry in Florida," 4; "Citrus Fruits in Sicily," 266.

8. Seftel, "Government Regulation," 371–73.

9. *American Economist* 44 (1909): 81; U.S. Congress, House Committee on Ways and Means, *Tariff Information*, 1936; Basile, "Agricultural Sicily," 112.

10. *New Orleans Daily Picayune*, June 14, 1846; "Lemons—Lemons," *New Orleans Daily Picayune*, April 7, 1850; "Cargo of the Bark Rover," *New Orleans Daily Picayune*, January 23, 1853.

11. "R. Tramontana & Co.," *New Orleans Daily Picayune*, December 27, 1860; U.S. Internal Revenue Service Tax Assessment Lists.

12. Giuseppe Grande, in U.S. Census, 1860; Angelo Cusimano, in U.S. Census 1900; "Arrived on Sunday," *New Orleans Daily Picayune*, April 9, 1872; Morrison, *Industries of New Orleans*, 74.

13. "Imports," *New Orleans Daily Picayune*, February 25, 1882; Morrison, *Industries of New Orleans*, 33–34. Unlike lemons, the tropical commodities of coffee and bananas entered the port duty-free because they lacked domestic competitors.

14. Roland and Keyssar, *Way of the Ship*, 190–92. Shipping costs are measured today as they were a century ago—by dollar per ton per sea mile.

15. Wright, *Old South, New South*, 76

16. Jung, *Coolies and Cane*; Scarpaci, "Immigrants in the New South," 172.

17. Margavio and Salamone, *Bread and Respect*, 71–72; Gabaccia, *Militants and Migrants*, 108.

18. Nelli, *From Immigrants to Ethnics*, 23–25.

19. "Custom-House Notes," *New Orleans Daily Picayune*, November 13, 1890; "The Manila's Immigrants the Last of the Season," *New Orleans Daily Picayune*, November 22, 1902; *New Orleans Daily Picayune*, November 22, 1902 (emphasis added).

20. Scott, *Degrees of Freedom*; Hair, *Carnival of Fury*; Hair, *Bourbonism and Agrarian Protest*.

21. Scarpaci, *Italian Immigrants*, 107; "Two Ships Loaded With Immigrants," *New Orleans Daily Picayune*, October 22, 1900; "Italian Immigrants," *New Orleans Daily Picayune*, May 4, 1896. According to Scarpaci, it is difficult to determine a precise figure for immigration to Louisiana from Sicily in this period because of the prevalence of reverse migration.

22. Bakker, *Sugar Cane Cultivation and Management*.

23. Latrobe, *Southern Travels*, 38.

24. Heitmann, "Organization as Power"; Coons, "Sugar Beet"; Galloway, "Botany"; Scarpaci, "Immigrants in the New South," 165.

25. "Homeward Bound," *New Orleans Daily Picayune*, January 31, 1895; Gabaccia, *Militants and Migrants*, 86.

26. Paul Leslie, interview by Justin Nystrom, July 17, 2010, videorecording, Creole Italian Collection, Documentary and Oral History Studio, Loyola University New Orleans.

27. Romero, *Louisiana Strawberry Story*, vi–2, 20.

28. Ibid., 3–4.

29. Ibid., viii, 3–4; Van Syckle, "Preserving the Louisiana Heritage Strawberry"; "Our History," *Independence Sicilian Heritage Festival*, http://www.indysicilianfest .com/our-history.html.

30. Anne Brocato Parker, interview by Justin Nystrom, July 9, 2010, transcript, Creole Italian Collection, Documentary and Oral History Studio, Loyola University New Orleans. Jean Ann Scarpaci interviewed Brocato in the mid-1960s for *Italian Immigrants*, her seminal work about Sicilian immigrants in the cane fields.

31. Parker, interview.

CHAPTER 2. A Road Paved with Oyster Shells

1. "Documentation for Commander's Palace: A Camarda Family Legacy," available at http://www.ustica.org/san_bartolomeo/catalog/commanderdocs.htm.

2. Influential in my thinking on the linkages between historical consciousness and collective memory has been Funkenstein, "Collective Memory and Historical Consciousness." For the best treatment of the conscious construction of "Creole New Orleans," see Fertel, *Imagining the Creole City*.

3. The ubiquity of game and oysters was also apparent in nineteenth-century New York. See Freedman, "American Restaurants and Cuisine." Lobel, "'Out to

Eat,'" suggests that early New York restaurants clustered around the city's business district and served lunches. For a general view of the importance of game and wild-caught fish in even late-nineteenth-century America, see Beahrs, *Twain's Feast.*

4. Lobel, "'Out to Eat.'"

5. Williams, *New Orleans,* 97; Guste, *Antoine's Restaurant,* 6–7; Haley, *Turning the Tables,* 23–30.

6. Campanella, *Geographies of New Orleans,* 149–50; Hastings, *Lakes of Pontchartrain,* 51; advertisement, *New Orleans Daily Picayune,* March 16, 1839.

7. "New Restaurant," *New Orleans True American,* October 20, 1838; U.S. Census, 1840; "All Sorts of a Place," *New Orleans True American,* October 16, 1838. Canonge's restaurant was only two doors down from home of Edward Gottschalk and his family, which included twelve-year-old piano prodigy Louis Moreau Gottschalk, who made his performing debut that year at the nearby St. Charles Theater.

8. "Card," *New Orleans Daily Picayune,* April 16, 1839; *New Orleans Annual and Commercial Register of 1846.*

9. Sokolov, *Fading Feast,* 242–49; Rees, *Refrigeration Nation,* 5–8; Pillsbury, *From Boarding House to Bistro,* 26–27; Kurlansky, *Big Oyster;* Beahrs, *Twain's Feast,* 113–47; Tucker, *New Orleans Cuisine,* 66–67.

10. Rees, *Refrigeration Nation,* 16–22; Oscar E. Anderson, *Refrigeration in America;* "Advertisement: Ice! Ice! Ice!," *New Orleans Daily Picayune,* June 10, 1868; "Ice-Making in New Orleans," 67.

11. *New Orleans Annual and Commercial Register of 1846,* 546; advertisement, *New Orleans Daily Picayune,* October 26, 1847.

12. Advertisement, *New Orleans Daily Picayune,* December 31, 1852; Christovich and Toledano, *New Orleans Architecture,* 46.

13. *New Orleans Business Directory, 1858;* "Lightning Ends Two Useful Lives," *New Orleans Daily Picayune,* August 2, 1901; "An Old Veteran Sinking," unidentified newspaper clipping, in possession of Michael Dauenhauer, New Orleans.

14. Marie Adrien Persac, *Port and City of New Orleans* (painting), 1858, Historic New Orleans Collection. For an thorough overview of the nineteenth-century commercial economy of New Orleans, see Marler, *Merchants' Capital.*

15. *New Orleans Business Directory, 1858;* "Lightning Ends Two Useful Lives," *New Orleans Daily Picayune,* August 2, 1901; "An Old Veteran Sinking," unidentified newspaper clipping, in possession of Michael Dauenhauer, New Orleans; advertisement, *New Orleans Daily Crescent,* June 5, 1856.

16. *New Orleans Daily Picayune,* October 19, 1853; advertisement, *New Orleans Daily Picayune,* October 18, 1854; advertisement, *Plaquemines Parish Gazette and Sentinel,* January 5, 1861.

17. "Some Fish," *New Orleans Daily Crescent,* November 17, 1859. Developers razed the old Merchant's Exchange buildings in 1961, making way for the building of what is today part of the Wyndham Hotel. Astredo's Oyster Saloon stood where the en-

trance to the hotel's parking garage is now. Oysters were sold more or less continuously in that spot for a century, with Kopanica's Oyster Bar and Seafood operating there in the 1950s. In the late nineteenth century, it was the location of the Sazerac Bar (Alecia P. Long, *Great Southern Babylon*, 84). Jim Astredo's saloon disappears from the record in 1853, a year before Anthony's establishment opened.

18. "Astredo Branching Off," *New Orleans Daily Picayune*, September 13, 1855.

19. Booth, *Records*, 1:84; "A Card," *New Orleans Daily Picayune*, January 21, 1862.

20. *New Orleans Crescent*, November 17, 1868; *New Orleans Daily Picayune*, August 26, 1876.

21. *Edwards' Annual Directory*; *Soards' New Orleans City Directory*; advertisement, *New Orleans Daily Picayune*, May 27, 1876; advertisement, *New Orleans Daily Picayune*, September 9, 1877. Astredo's residence on Cleveland (Gasquet) Street lies in the footprint of the new Louisiana State University/Veterans Administration hospital complex, while his St. Mary Street home was demolished to make room for the St. Thomas Housing Project, which, in turn, was demolished for the Rivergarden development.

22. Nitti, "Prisoners of Mussolini"; Virgets, "Postcards from Ustica." The descendants of the *usticesi* migrants in New Orleans remain tightly knit, and their cultural activities are documented at www.ustica.org. The official tourism site for Ustica is www.visitustica.it.

23. Niccolino "Peter" Compagno, interview by Joseph Maselli, November 14, 1977, American Italian Research Library, American Italian Cultural Center, New Orleans; *New Orleans Daily Picayune*, January 12, 1902, August 4, 1904. Frank, Anthony, and Charles established bars at 900 Washington Avenue (no longer standing), 4605 Magazine, and the corner of Fern Street and St. Charles Avenue, the present location of Vincent's restaurant.

24. Compagno, interview. The most famous member of the Martina family was "Oyster Joe" Martina, who pitched in the 1924 World Series.

25. New Orleans, Passenger Lists; U.S. Census, 1900; *Soards' New Orleans City Directory* (1876).

26. *Soards' New Orleans City Directory* (1876, 1884, 1896); *New Orleans Daily Picayune*, February 10, 1884; "City Hall," *New Orleans Daily Picayune*, October 15, 1892; "Lafayette Fire Insurance Co.," *New Orleans Daily Picayune*, January 26, 1896.

27. "Oak Cottage," *New Orleans Daily Picayune*, May 29, 1877; Isenberg, *John L. Sullivan*, 105–9.

28. New Orleans Cotton Centennial Exposition, *The World's Industrial and Cotton Exposition* (map) (New Orleans: Southern Lithographic, 1885), David Rumsey Map Collection, www.davidrumsey.com; "Lake House, Lake End," Images of the Month, New Orleans Public Library, September 2000, www.nutrias.org; Twain, *Life on the Mississippi*, 198, 312.

29. "Branch of the Excelsior Restaurant," *New Orleans Daily Picayune*, June 1, 1878; *New Orleans Daily Item*, October 6, 1893; Twain, *Life on the Mississippi*, 445–46.

30. "Branch of the Excelsior Restaurant," *New Orleans Daily Picayune*, June 1, 1878; *New Orleans Daily Item*, October 6, 1893; "West End Hotel," *New Orleans Times-Picayune*, July 22, 1880; "West End Hotel—New Lessee," *New Orleans Times-Picayune*, December 19, 1882; Twain, *Life on the Mississippi*, 312–13.

31. "Solid Columns of Brick and Mortar," *New Orleans Daily Picayune*, September 1, 1895; *Soards' New Orleans City Directory* (1894); "Wymann's Staff," *New Orleans Daily Picayune*, July 19, 1900.

32. "A Minor Key," *New Orleans Daily Picayune*, January 16, 1898; "Roland Reed, the Comedian, Dead," *New York Times*, March 31, 1901; Roland Reed trading card, image available at http://www.flickr.com/photos/boston_public_library /8494779249/.

33. "A Minor Key," *New Orleans Daily Picayune*, January 16, 1898.

34. "Lightning Ends Two Useful Lives," *New Orleans Daily Picayune*, August 2, 1901; "Disastrous Fire Again Sweeps over West End," *New Orleans Daily Picayune*, April 15, 1903.

35. "The City Paid a Million for Land at West End," *New Orleans Daily Picayune*, July 20, 1902; "Status of West End," *New Orleans Times-Picayune*, March 17, 1905; "Tranchina's New Location," *New Orleans Times-Picayune*, December 1, 1910; "West End Sea Wall Accepted by City," *New Orleans Daily Picayune*, August 25, 1912.

36. "Southern Yacht Club," *New Orleans Daily Picayune*, June 6, 1888; "Yachting," *New Orleans Daily Picayune*, May 14, 1900; "Chewink Beats Calypso by Just Three Seconds in the Most Exciting Race Ever Sailed," *New Orleans Times-Picayune*, August 21, 1904.

37. "Society," *New Orleans Times-Picayune*, August 18, 1901; "Italian Colony Beauties," *New Orleans Times-Picayune*, April 3, 1904; "Italian Cruiser's Officers Guests at Patorno Fete," *New Orleans Times-Picayune*, June 7, 1905. For details on 915 Royal Street, see Collins C. Diboll Vieux Carré Digital Survey, www.hnoc.org/vcs. The Cornstalk Hotel trades on antebellum lore and celebrity guests (www.thecornstalk hotel.com).

38. "Documentation for Commander's Palace: A Camarda Family Legacy"; U.S. Census, 1870, 1900; *Soards' New Orleans City Directory* (1872, 1879, 1884).

39. "Emile Commander," *New Orleans Times-Picayune*, August 28, 1906; "1880: Humble Beginnings for Commander's Palace, a Landmark New Orleans Restaurant," *New Orleans Times-Picayune*, September 14, 2011; Beebe, *Lucius Beebe Reader*, 261; *Soards' New Orleans City Directory* (1886, 1889, 1891); "Building Permits," *New Orleans Item*, November 2, 1892; advertisement, *New Orleans Item*, December 19, 1892; "Official," *New Orleans Item*, January 27, 1893; advertisement, *New Orleans Item*, November 14, 1893.

40. *Soards' New Orleans City Directory* (1886, 1893, 1894); "Lady Bugs to Save the State's Orange Industry," *New Orleans Times-Picayune*, August 24, 1904; "Little Journeys to Realty Row," *New Orleans Times-Picayune*, May 19, 1929; "A Saloon Burglar," *New Orleans Times-Picayune*, August 2, 1902. The city had numerous Sazerac

Bars during the late nineteenth century, all named for the popular French brandy rather than the now-popular cocktail originally made with that brandy. During the 1870s, Handy's Sazerac was located at 16 Royal Street, the same location where Anthony Astredo's Oyster Saloon operated two decades earlier.

41. Craig LaBan, "Food and Spirits—A Network of Family and Friends Was Nurtured for 102 Years at Delmonico," *New Orleans Times-Picayune*, March 2, 1997.

42. "Auction," *New Orleans Times-Picayune*, September 20, 1903; advertisement, *New Orleans Times-Picayune*, January 27, 1904; Craig LaBan, "Food and Spirits—A Network of Family and Friends Was Nurtured for 102 Years at Delmonico," *New Orleans Times-Picayune*, March 2, 1997; Haley, *Turning the Tables*, 24–26; Soards' *New Orleans City Directory* (1887).

CHAPTER 3. Blood and Macaroni

1. Jen DeGregorio, "Port Proposal Raises Opposition from Marigny Residents," *New Orleans Times-Picayune*, December 12, 2008; Peter T. Leach, "New Cold Storage Warehouse Opens in New Orleans," *Journal of Commerce*, July 19, 2012.

2. Nelli, *From Immigrants to Ethnics*, 62; "The Immigration Season Started," *New Orleans Daily Picayune*, October 19, 1901.

3. "The Immigration Season Started," *New Orleans Daily Picayune*, October 19, 1901.

4. "Facilities Here for Immigration," *New Orleans Daily Picayune*, March 19, 1896; "The Manila's Immigrants the Last of the Season," *New Orleans Daily Picayune*, November 22, 1902; Beck, "Myth That Would Not Die."

5. "Italian Immigration," *New Orleans Daily Picayune*, August 12, 1904; Beck, "Myth That Would Not Die."

6. Baiamonte, "'Who Killa de Chief' Revisited"; Botein, "Hennessy Case"; Gambino, *Vendetta*. Hunt and Sheldon, *Deep Water*, are most adamant about the scope and organization of a nineteenth-century Mafia in New Orleans. See also Nelli, *Business of Crime*. The most recent scholarly work on the development of the Sicilian Mafia and its overseas ties is Fentress, *Rebels and Mafiosi*, which documents that the Monrealesi Mafia entered New Orleans and had ties to the Matranga clan but stops well short of suggesting greater organizational collaboration. See also Baiamonte, *Spirit of Vengeance*. Perhaps the strongest argument against truly "organized" crime as late as the 1920s comes from Vyhnanek, *Unorganized Crime*.

7. Bauer, "From Burnt Canes to Budding City."

8. *State v. Gebbia et al.*, No. 16,931, 121 La. 1083, 47 So. 32 (1908); "Several Sensations in Trial of Gebbias," *New Orleans Daily Picayune*, November 15, 1907.

9. Hughes, *Yale's Confederates*; "Several Sensations in Trial of Gebbias," *New Orleans Daily Picayune*, November 15, 1907; "The Awful Crime for Which Gebbia Paid with His Life," *New Orleans Daily Picayune*, July 17, 1909; "The Alleged Serio Dyna-

miters Heard," *New Orleans Daily Picayune*, July 3, 1908. Joseph Lawrence Federico operated L. Federico and Brothers Macaroni at 1000 Chartres Street. In 1900, he lived at 812 North Rampart Street and would have walked to and from work down St. Philip Street. By 1920, Vincent Taormina was operating a cannery in Riverside, California, for the growing Uddo-Taormina corporation. See U.S. Census, 1900, 1920.

10. "Giaconas Held without Bond," *New Orleans Times-Picayune*, June 19, 1908; Scarpaci, "Immigrants in the New South," 171.

11. Morgan Whitney, *1113 Chartres*, glass plate negative, April 1906, N-1051, Special Collections, Tulane University Libraries; Richard Anthony Lewis, *Robert W. Tebbs*; Laughlin, *Ghosts along the Mississippi*.

12. U.S. Census, 1910; "The Surviving Italian of Chartres Street Tragedy Puts a New Light on Triple Killing," *New Orleans Daily Picayune*, June 18, 1908; advertisement, *New Orleans Daily Picayune*, April 25, 1907. *Vini passiti* can now be bought straight from Palermo at vinisicilia.com.

13. "The Surviving Italian of Chartres Street Tragedy Puts a New Light on Triple Killing," *New Orleans Daily Picayune*, June 18, 1908.

14. "Rich Italian Slays Blackmailing Guests," *Pensacola (Florida) Journal*, June 18, 1908; "Death to Black Hand," *Bemidji (Minnesota) Daily Pioneer*, June 19, 1908; "Three Italians Shot To Death," *Los Angeles Herald*, June 18, 1908.

15. "Telephone Call Brought Baraccas to Death Here," *New Orleans Times-Picayune*, June 20, 1908; "Giaconas Held without Bond," *New Orleans Times-Picayune*, June 19, 1908.

16. "Dangerous Attack upon the Home of Peter Giacona," *New Orleans Times-Picayune*, September 10, 1909.

17. "Giacona Attack Suspects Go Free," *New Orleans Times-Picayune*, March 17, 1910.

18. "Pepitone on Trial for Slaying Rival," *New Orleans Times-Picayune*, July 21, 1910; "Old Man Pepitone Gets Twenty Years," *New Orleans Daily Picayune*, August 10, 1910.

19. "Barracca Fiendish Vendetta Victim," *New Orleans Times-Picayune*, April 14, 1910.

20. "Di Martini, Blonde Italian, Killed in Real Mafia Way," *New Orleans Times-Picayune*, June 3, 1910.

21. Fortier, *Louisiana*, 199–200.

22. "Black Hand Widow Vanishes from the Charity Hospital," *New Orleans Daily Picayune*, December 16, 1910.

23. Dickie, *Delizia!*, 149–52.

24. Evans, *Confederate Military History*, 566; *New Orleans City Directory* (1832); "Destructive Fire," *New Orleans Daily Picayune*, February 21, 1849; "A Midnight Fire," *New Orleans Daily Picayune*, October 24, 1882.

25. "Making Macaroni in New York," *New Orleans Daily Picayune*, June 3, 1894.

26. "Custom-House Notes," *New Orleans Daily Picayune*, May 16, 1894; "A Macaroni Maker Praises New Orleans Enterprise," *New Orleans Daily Picayune*, September 6, 1899.

27. *Soards's New Orleans City Directory* (1901); "Macaroni to Be Made Here by Electricity," *New Orleans Daily Picayune*, July 29, 1903.

28. "Making New Orleans the Macaroni Market," *New Orleans Daily Picayune*, February 10, 1902.

29. "Public Improvements," *New Orleans Daily Picayune*, September 14, 1897; "Jacob Cusimano Taken by Death," *New Orleans Times-Picayune*, May 2, 1930; "Making New Orleans the Macaroni Market," *New Orleans Daily Picayune*, February 10, 1902; "Making Macaroni," *New Orleans Daily Picayune*, August 8, 1902; U.S. Census, 1910, 1930. Details of Jacob Cusimano's life were pieced together using a variety of records. The 1886 *Soards' New Orleans City Directory* shows Angelo Cusimano running a fruit wholesaling business at 144 Decatur Street (now 1238 Decatur). For details regarding French Quarter property owned or occupied by Jacob Cusimano, see Collins C. Diboll Vieux Carré Digital Survey, www.hnoc.org/vcs. At the time of the factory's opening, Cusimano lived at 1227 Dauphine, which was razed in the late 1930s to make room for the Cabrini Playground.

30. Hunt and Sheldon, *Deep Water*, 113–17, 136–37; "Esposito's Suit," *New Orleans Daily Picayune*, December 11, 1881; "Non-Suited: The Case of Esposito against Cusimano and Grande Thrown Out of Court," *New Orleans Daily Picayune*, November 7, 1882. Hunt and Sheldon see Mafia ties everywhere in late-nineteenth-century New Orleans, but their book's complete lack of source notes means that there is no way to determine the quality of their evidence.

31. Romero, *Louisiana Strawberry Story*, 10–15; Van Syckle, "Preserving the Louisiana Heritage Strawberry."

32. Bruner and Carr, *Panic of 1907*; Jeanie Blake, "The Italians: An Immigrant's History Is Part of the Heritage of New Orleans," *New Orleans Times-Picayune*, November 29, 1981.

33. Rosemary Uddo Testa and Adele Chopin Uddo, interview by Justin A. Nystrom, June 14, 2011, videorecording, Creole Italian Collection, Documentary and Oral History Studio, Loyola University New Orleans.

34. Kendall, *History of New Orleans*, 1031; Will Branan, "The Spaghetti District of New Orleans," *New Orleans Daily Picayune*, January 21, 1912; Dickie, *Delizia!*, 154.

35. "Women's World and Work," *New Orleans Daily Picayune*, December 9, 1912; "Women's World and Work," *New Orleans Daily Picayune*, May 20, 1902.

36. "Southern Macaroni Company," *New Orleans Times-Picayune*, January 16, 1914; advertisement for Luxury Pasta, *New Orleans Times-Picayune*, March 22, 1922; *New Orleans Times-Picayune*, June 4, 1969; "Borden Cuts Close Local Pasta Plant," *New Orleans Times-Picayune*, June 5, 1992.

37. Collins C. Diboll Vieux Carré Digital Survey, www.hnoc.org/vcs.

38. Andrew Taormina, interview by Justin A. Nystrom, July 6, 2011, transcript, Creole Italian Collection, Documentary and Oral History Studio, Loyola University New Orleans.

CHAPTER 4. Booze, Red Gravy, and Jazz

1. "National Homesteaders at Spaghetti Feast," *New Orleans Daily Picayune*, March 2, 1908; Masson, "J. N. B. de Pouilly."

2. "National Homesteaders at Spaghetti Feast," *New Orleans Daily Picayune*, March 2, 1908. Messina's was located at 1119 Decatur Street (*Soards' New Orleans City Directory* [1908]).

3. Richard Campanella, *Bourbon Street*, 97–98.

4. Marni Davis, *Jews and Booze*, 6–7. Davis's study of Jewish immigrants in New York puts forth thoughtful conclusions about the connections among cultural cohesiveness, immigrant status, experience in the liquor trade, and illicit booze. For such an important topic, there is surprisingly little professional scholarship about Prohibition. For standards, see Sinclair, *Prohibition*. Locally, the fullest investigation of Prohibition remains Jackson, "Prohibition in New Orleans." For the most recent significant work on Prohibition nationally, see McGirr, *War on Alcohol*.

5. Nystrom, *New Orleans after the Civil War*, 211–13.

6. "Lake Resorts Free from Sunday Law," *New Orleans Daily Picayune*, June 30, 1895; "West End Hotel Must Face the Criminal Court for Violating Sunday Law," *New Orleans Daily Picayune*, September 9, 1896.

7. "The Courts," *New Orleans Daily Picayune*, September 20, 1896; "West End Violation on the Sunday Law Is Turned into a Farce in Judge Gill's Court," *New Orleans Times-Picayune*, September 26, 1901; "Sunday Law Enforced with Greater Strictness," *New Orleans Times-Picayune*, September 5, 1904.

8. Many news stories covering the 1908 legislative session predicted the defeat of the full Prohibition measure and noted the willingness of legislators from dry parishes to support Gay-Shattuck because it promised to raise revenue primarily from Orleans Parish and other wet locales. See, for example, "Next Week Will Bring a Crop of Hot Fights," *New Orleans Daily Picayune*, June 13, 1908. The city did not enact a single ordinance regulating the sale of alcohol until its charter of 1896. Thus, most of the Gay-Shattuck law must have represented a significant departure to a city full of bar owners accustomed to making their own rules. For a contemporary reflection on how much liquor laws had changed with Gay-Shattuck, see "The Gay-Shattuck Law," *New Orleans Daily Picayune*, February 17, 1909. For a complete enumeration of the eleven provisions of the law see "Tests of the New Liquor Statute," *New Orleans Daily Picayune*, January 3, 1909. For a discussion of how Gay-Shattuck affected Storyville, see Alecia P. Long, *Great Southern Babylon*.

9. The definitive work on the Robert Charles riot remains Hair, *Carnival of Fury*. A similar riot occurred in Atlanta in 1906, and four years later, that city passed an ordinance much like New Orleans's that required restaurants to secure segregated business tax certificates. See Mixon, *Atlanta Riot*.

10. "Tests of the New Liquor Statute," *New Orleans Daily Picayune*, January 3, 1909; "Fiery Speeches by the Lawyers," *New Orleans Daily Picayune*, May 30, 1909.

11. Records of the New Orleans District Criminal Court, City Archives, New Orleans Public Library. I thank Greg Osborn, one of the foremost authorities on the treasure trove of materials located in the library's subbasement, for his assistance in combing through several hundred court cases.

12. "Charge of Malicious Prosecution Is Made," *New Orleans Times-Picayune*, July 7, 1917; Alecia P. Long, *Great Southern Babylon*.

13. *State v. Joseph Impastato*, No. 43512B, October 31, 1914; *State v. Anthony Loscasio and Victor Lemane*, No. 45108B, February 28, 1917; *State v. Fortune Salvaggio*, No. 41309A, February 11, 1913, all in New Orleans District Criminal Court, City Archives, New Orleans Public Library.

14. Advertisement, *New Orleans Times-Picayune*, April 2, 1913; "Spanish Fort," *New Orleans Times-Picayune*, May 1, 1913.

15. Charters, *Trumpet around the Corner*, 72, 224–28; Raeburn, *New Orleans Style*, 224; Peter Bocage, interview by William Russell and Richard B. Allen, January 29, 1959, transcript, Hogan Jazz Archive, Tulane University.

16. Bocage, interview.

17. "Guests Grabbed Whisky, Chief Dry Officer Says," *New Orleans Daily Picayune*, July 15, 1924; "Tranchina Guests in Panic as Shot Roars Out in Raid," *New Orleans Times-Picayune*, August 17, 1925.

18. "Tranchina Reopens To-Day," *New Orleans Times-Picayune*, September 30, 1907. Genealogy on the *usticesi* descendants of New Orleans has been lovingly recorded at Ustica.org and proved immeasurably useful in untangling the Tranchina family tree.

19. "Advertisement: The Restaurant You Want to Know," *New Orleans Times-Picayune*, November 4, 1916; "Advertisement: D. J. Tranchina's Restaurant Handicap," *New Orleans Times-Picayune*, January 9, 1917; "Tranchina Restaurant Trophy Handicap Today," *New Orleans Times-Picayune*, January 9, 1917; "No Music in His Restaurant," *New Orleans Times-Picayune*, April 26, 1917; "Cabarets 'Jazz' Their Swansong as Lid Goes On," *New Orleans Times-Picayune*, July 7, 1918; *State ex re. Tranchina v. City of New Orleans*; In re Tranchina, 141 La. 711; 75 So. 683; 1917 La. LEXIS 1565 (Supreme Court of Louisiana 1917).

20. "Monte Carlo of 'Riviera of America' Patronized by New Orleans 'Select,'" *New Orleans Times-Picayune*, July 18, 1925; advertisement, *New Orleans Times-Picayune*, January 1, 1926.

21. "Monte Carlo of 'Riviera of America' Patronized by New Orleans 'Select,'" *New Orleans Times-Picayune*, July 18, 1925; advertisement, *New Orleans Times-Picayune*,

January 1, 1926; "Two Dozen Cafes Now Threatened by Padlock Law," *New Orleans Times-Picayune*, May 29, 1925; "Sues to Possess Beverly Gardens," *New Orleans Times-Picayune*, June 19, 1926.

22. Advertisement, *New Orleans Times-Picayune*, September 17, 1926; "Dahlberg Gem Theft, Werner Murder Linked," *New Orleans Times-Picayune*, May 25, 1927; "Victory Inn Shuts Down 15 Days before Ordinances Go into Effect," *New Orleans Times-Picayune*, August 4, 1927.

23. "Tranchina's Club Threatened with Seizure and Sale," *New Orleans Times-Picayune*, July 18, 1929; "Private Counsel to Be Employed in Gaming Suits," *New Orleans Times-Picayune*, May 10, 1929; "Tranchina Last Rites Set Today," *New Orleans Times-Picayune*, November 2, 1955; Vyhnanek, *Unorganized Crime*, 121–27.

24. "A Spaghetti Fire," *New Orleans Times-Picayune*, February 11, 1899; advertisement, *New Orleans Times-Picayune*, September 1, 1902.

25. "Italian Athletes, on Long 'Hike,' Arrive," *New Orleans Times-Picayune*, May 8, 1914; "Shipping News," *New Orleans Times-Picayune*, March 5, 1879; "Real Estate News: Ursuline Nuns Sell Property Held by Them since 1821," *New Orleans Times-Picayune*, January 20, 1914; *Soards' New Orleans City Directory* (1906, 1913); Advertisement, *New Orleans Item*, September 28, 1902.

26. "Advertisement: La Nasa Italian Restaurant," *New Orleans Times-Picayune*, December 1, 1916; advertisement, *New Orleans Times-Picayune*, January 1, 1917; "Orleans Bakery Sold to NY Firm," *New Orleans Times-Picayune*, December 12, 1949.

27. *Edwards' Annual Directory to New Orleans* (1870); *Soards' New Orleans City Directory* (1886, 1906); advertisements, *New Orleans Daily Item*, May 5, 1901; advertisement, *New Orleans Times-Picayune*, April 26, 1915; advertisement, *New Orleans Daily States*, November 20, 1917; advertisement, *New Orleans Item*, June 24, 1917.

28. "Visitor Describes Figallo's Restaurant," *New Orleans States*, September 18, 1922; "Figallo's Ravioli Can't Be Duplicated," *New Orleans States*, July 7, 1922.

29. Advertisement, *New Orleans States*, January 2, 1916; "Guest Charmed with Toro Restaurant," *New Orleans States*, July 7, 1922.

30. "Fabacher's Rathskeller," *New Orleans Daily Picayune*, August 15, 1915; "Former Singer Expires at 82," *New Orleans Times-Picayune*, August 13, 1970; "N.O. Restaurant Figure Expires," *New Orleans Times-Picayune*, April 8, 1957; "Advertisement: 'Italian Restaurant,'" *New Orleans Daily Picayune*, January 23, 1919. Fabacher's was located at 410–418 St. Charles Avenue, which today is a parking lot next door to the Queen and Crescent Hotel (*Soards' New Orleans City Directory* [1916]).

31. "Caruso's Golden Voice Is Forever Stilled by Death," *New Orleans Daily Picayune*, August 3, 1921; Key and Zirato, *Enrico Caruso*, 356.

32. "Advertisement: Turci's Italian Garden Restaurant," *New Orleans Daily Picayune*, August 22, 1924; "Little Journeys to Realty Row," *New Orleans Daily Picayune*, November 2, 1924; "Perjury Charged in Booze Seizure," *New Orleans Times-Picayune*, April 18, 1922; "City League to Meet at Dinner Wednesday," *New Orleans Daily Picayune*, October 24, 1924.

33. Advertisement, *New Orleans Daily Picayune*, December 28, 1924; "Letters to Elizabeth," *New Orleans Daily Picayune*, December 28, 1924.

34. "Padlock Order Hits Bucktown Cafe, Two Others," *New Orleans Daily Picayune*, February 3, 1926; "Vautrin, Halme Get Six Months on Rum Charge," *New Orleans Daily Picayune*, March 13, 1926; "Turci Gets Term on Liquor Charge," *New Orleans Times-Picayune*, May 31, 1931. For discussion of stiffening enforcement in New Orleans, see Vyhnanek, *Unorganized Crime*, 72.

35. "Business Leases Showing Activity," *New Orleans Daily Picayune*, February 10, 1934; advertisement, *New Orleans Times-Picayune*, September 18, 1935; "Gigli Brings His Spaghetti along on Orleans Visit," *New Orleans Times-Picayune*, January 2, 1939.

36. *Soards' New Orleans City Directory* (1886, 1893); U.S. Census, 1910.

37. "Cabarets 'Jazz' Their Swansong as Lid Goes On," *New Orleans Times-Picayune*, July 7, 1918; Richard Campanella, *Bourbon Street*, 98–99; advertisement, *New Orleans States*, November 22, 1918.

38. "Masera," *New Orleans Times-Picayune*, February 10, 1919; "Prohibition Officers Find Liquor in Four Raids," *New Orleans Times-Picayune*, February 10, 1922; "Owner Claims Seized Cruiser," *New Orleans Times-Picayune*, August 10, 1923; "Girl Dry Agent Signs Fabacher Liquor Charges," *New Orleans Times-Picayune*, January 25, 1924; "Seize $10,000 Car Containing Liquor," *New Orleans Times-Picayune*, February 6, 1924; advertisement, *New Orleans Times-Picayune*, December 5, 1929.

39. Advertisement, *New Orleans Times-Picayune*, January 20, 1934; advertisement, *New Orleans Times-Picayune*, February 21, 1935; "Nut Club Owner Arrested after Liquor Is Seized," *New Orleans Times-Picayune*, July 14, 1935; "Bonnie Hill Found Guilty on Charge of Manslaughter," *New Orleans Times-Picayune*, May 22, 1935.

40. Photo of Panzeca Grocery, in author's possession; "Four Held after Prohibition Raid," *New Orleans Times-Picayune*, May 3, 1928; "Twenty-One Held by Dry Raiders on Rum Charges," *New Orleans Times-Picayune*, February 10, 1929; "Order to Destroy Stills Is Asked," *New Orleans Times-Picayune*, January 5, 1930; "Bourbon Street Curb Service on Liquor Alleged," *New Orleans Times-Picayune*, May 24, 1931.

41. "800–804 Bourbon St.," Collins C. Diboll Vieux Carré Digital Survey, https://www.hnoc.org/vcs/property_info.php?lot=18616; "Up and Down the Street," *New Orleans Times-Picayune*, November 9, 1937; "La Lune Gets National Mention," *New Orleans Times-Picayune*, November 21, 1940.

42. Philip and Ronald Sciortino, interview by Justin Nystrom, July 19, 2011, transcript, Creole Italian Collection, Documentary and Oral History Studio, Loyola University New Orleans; Kolb, "Virgilians."

CHAPTER 5. "Italian Heaven"

1. Despite numerous references to "Little Italy" in current literature to describe this time in French Quarter history, I have found no contemporary evidence of its usage.

2. [Unloading Bananas, New Orleans, Louisiana], 1900, Library of Congress Prints and Photographs Division, https://www.loc.gov/item/det1994013503/PP/; New Orleans, La., a Corner of the French Market], 1900–1910, Library of Congress Prints and Photographs Division, https://www.loc.gov/resource/det.4a19876/; Frances Benjamin Johnston, *1133–1135 Chartres St., New Orleans, Orleans Parish, Louisiana,* 1 1937, Library of Congress Prints and Photographs Division, http://www.loc .gov/pictures/item/csas200801249/.

3. "Commerce and Finance," *New Orleans Daily Picayune,* September 21, 1872.

4. Botein, "Hennessy Case"; Gauthreaux, "Inhospitable Land"; Baiamonte, "'Who Killa de Chief' Revisited." There are many works today about "whiteness studies" and its relationship to the immigrant experience. Influential in shaping this field has been Roediger, *Wages of Whiteness.* For more on the Hennessey affair and the complex factors that led to it, see Hunt and Sheldon, *Deep Water;* Gambino, *Vendetta.*

5. Karnes, *Tropical Enterprise,* 2–15.

6. *City of New Orleans vs. Tony Renfero, Tony Latriglio, Nicola Aranda, Sam Carruso, Emile Martin & Charlie Mayensa,* First Recorder's Court of the City of New Orleans, July 21, 1904; *City of New Orleans v. Fargot,* La. 369 116 (Supreme Court of Louisiana 1906); Louisiana Writers' Project, *Gumbo Ya-Ya.*

7. *City of New Orleans vs. Tony Renfero et al.;* U.S. Census, 1870; Louisiana, Naturalization Records; *Soards' New Orleans City Directory* (1904); advertisement, *New Orleans Daily Picayune,* March 22, 1861; "Yesterday's Afternoon Dispatches," *New Orleans Daily Picayune,* September 23, 1869.

8. Latrobe, *Southern Travels,* 41; Hearn, *Inventing New Orleans,* 23.

9. *French Market, New Orleans, La.,* 1906, Library of Congress Prints and Photographs Division, http://www.loc.gov/pictures/item/det1994011954/PP/.

10. Sauder, "Origin and Spread."

11. "French Market Improvement," *New Orleans Times-Picayune,* July 21, 1934.

12. Tommy Tusa, interview by Justin Nystrom, July 12, 2012, transcript, Creole Italian Collection, Documentary and Oral History Studio, Loyola University New Orleans; Maria Impastato and Salvatore Impastato, interview by Justin Nystrom, August 18, 2010, transcript, Creole Italian Collection, Documentary and Oral History Studio, Loyola University New Orleans.

13. John Perrone and Joe Pacaccio, interview by Justin Nystrom, August 2, 2010, Creole Italian Collection, Documentary and Oral History Studio, Loyola University New Orleans; John Gendusa and Jason Gendusa, interview by Justin Nystrom, August 19, 2010, Creole Italian Collection, Documentary and Oral History Studio, Loyola University New Orleans.

14. Salvatore "Joe" Segreto, interview by Justin Nystrom, August 5, 2010, transcript, Creole Italian Collection, Documentary and Oral History Studio, Loyola University New Orleans.

15. "Legal Notice," *New Orleans Times-Picayune,* September 10, 1903; *Soards' New Orleans City Directory* (1908); "Bartholomew Macaluso," *New Orleans Daily Pica-*

yune, October 22, 1911; "Widow Cries Fraud," *New Orleans Times-Picayune*, August 7, 1912.

16. *Soards' New Orleans City Directory* (1910); "Frank Alfano, Well-Known Orleanian, Influenza Victim," *New Orleans Times-Picayune*, January 12, 1919; "Judge Foster Sentences Two to Year and a Day," *New Orleans Times-Picayune*, May 6, 1919.

17. Tusa, interview; Betty Bellone Unsworth and Buster Unsworth, interview by Justin Nystrom, August 4, 2011, transcript, Creole Italian Collection, Documentary and Oral History Studio, Loyola University New Orleans.

18. Perrone and Pacaccio, interview. Today the family uses the spelling *Perrone*, but in all records prior to 1930, the name is spelled *Pirrone*. Bartolomé Pirrone arrived on March 10, 1907 (New Orleans, Passenger Lists; U.S. World War I Draft Registration Cards; U.S. Census, 1920).

19. Gendusa and Gendusa, interview; Perrone and Pacaccio, interview.

20. Tusa, interview.

21. Perrone and Pacaccio, interview.

22. U.S. Census, 1920.

23. Nick Loguidice, interview by Justin Nystrom, August 2, 2011, videorecording, Creole Italian Collection, Documentary and Oral History Studio, Loyola University New Orleans.

24. Ibid.; "Bread Exposed," *New Orleans Daily Picayune*, August 19, 1909.

25. Loguidice, interview.

26. Elizabeth Williams, interview by Justin Nystrom, July 23, 2010, transcript, Creole Italian Collection, Documentary and Oral History Studio, Loyola University New Orleans; Impastato and Impastato, interview.

27. Arthur Brocato, interview by Justin Nystrom, July 22, 2010, transcript, Creole Italian Collection, Documentary and Oral History Studio, Loyola University New Orleans; Perrone and Pacaccio, interview.

28. Gendusa and Gendusa, interview.

29. Howard Jacobs, "Muffuletta Born and Bread Here," *New Orleans Times-Picayune*, October 10, 1976; Howard Jacobs, "Dads Defended by Daughters," *New Orleans Times-Picayune*, November 5, 1976; Gene Bourg, "'Progress' Means Tradition at Quarter Grocery," *New Orleans Times-Picayune*, May 20, 1988; Broughton, *Journey through Albania*, 1019.

30. Kolb, *New Orleans Memories*, 44–45; Michael Curtiz, *King Creole* (1958); Robert Drew, *718–720, 724, 726–728 St. Philip*, 1956, Negative N-231, Historic New Orleans Collection.

31. Louisiana Writers' Project, *Gumbo Ya-Ya*, 102–3.

32. Segreto, interview; Loguidice, interview.

33. Rosario Brocato and Joseph Brocato, interview by Joseph Maselli, April 5, 1988, audiocassette (transferred to digital), American Italian Cultural Center, New Orleans.

34. "Poydras Market to Be Rebuilt," *New Orleans Daily Picayune*, August 7, 1913; Rosario Brocato and Joseph Brocato, interview; Arthur Brocato, interview by Justin Nystrom, July 22, 2010, transcript, Creole Italian Collection, Documentary and Oral History Studio, Loyola University New Orleans; advertisement, *New Orleans Times-Picayune*, April 27, 1941.

35. Rao, "Spleen Sandwiches"; Roahen, "Red Gravy"; DiStefano, "Joe's Vastedda"; Rosario Brocato and Joseph Brocato, interview; Arthur Brocato, interview.

36. Rosario Brocato and Joseph Brocato, interview; Arthur Brocato, interview.

37. Arthur Brocato, interview.

38. Perrone and Pacaccio, interview; Loguidice, interview.

39. *New Orleans Daily Picayune*, June 22, 1890; Solari, *Fancy and Staple Groceries*; Paterson, "Grocery Matters"; Kolb, *New Orleans Memories*, 29–30.

40. Paddleford, "Food Flashes"; Kolb, *New Orleans Memories*, 31.

41. Perrone and Pacaccio, interview; Impastato and Impastato, interview; Arthur Brocato, interview.

42. *New Orleans Times-Picayune*, January 20, 1959, September 1, 1965; Impastato and Impastato, interview.

43. Ed Anderson, "Vieux Carre Store Owners Ready to Retire," *New Orleans Times-Picayune*, August 8, 1984; advertisement, *New Orleans Times-Picayune*, December 22, 1953.

44. Ed Anderson, "Vieux Carre Store Owners Ready to Retire," *New Orleans Times-Picayune*, August 8, 1984; Danny Monteverde, "Fate of Former Grocery in Quarter Up in the Air," *New Orleans Times-Picayune*, April 8, 2011.

CHAPTER 6. Making Groceries

1. Joan Kent, "Way of Life in New Orleans Dies with Miss Lucy," *New Orleans Times-Picayune*, February 7, 1982. Joan Kent became one of many New Orleanians to leave in this period, moving to La Crosse, Wisconsin, in the 1980s after one too many burglaries at her home. See Joan Kent, "The Stories, The People; A Reporter's Saga Ends," *La Crosse Tribune*, February 20, 2007.

2. U.S. Census, 1900, 1910; Frank Von der Haar and Barry Becnel, interview by Justin Nystrom, July 28, 2011, transcript, Creole Italian Collection, Documentary and Oral History Studio, Loyola University New Orleans.

3. Von der Haar and Becnel, interview; advertisement, *New Orleans Times-Picayune*, March 14, 1919; W. D. Robinson, "Delegate Would Leave Matter Entirely Up to Parishes," *New Orleans Times-Picayune*, January 29, 1921; "Grocerymen Arrested," *New Orleans Times-Picayune*, December 18, 1922; "Grocery Stores, Open Yesterday, Hit by Raiders," *New Orleans Times-Picayune*, August 18, 1924; "Retail Grocery Store Closing on Sunday Ordered: Housewives Warned to Buy Week-End Supplies without Delay," *New Orleans Times-Picayune*, August 12, 1933.

4. Advertisement, *New Orleans Times-Picayune*, January 25, 1937; Von der Haar and Becnel, interview.

5. Von der Haar and Becnel, interview.

6. Advertisement, *New Orleans Times-Picayune*, August 5, 1942; advertisement, *New Orleans Times-Picayune*, October 21, 1948; "Real Estate Transfers of the Week," *New Orleans Times-Picayune*, June 21, 1948.

7. Advertisement, *New Orleans Times-Picayune*, October 21, 1948.

8. Von der Haar and Becnel, interview.

9. "Grocery Changes Cited by Ortolano," *New Orleans Times-Picayune*, November 9, 1950; U.S. World War I Draft Registration Cards; Nottoway Plantation, www .nottoway.com.

10. T. F. Ortolano photograph, in possession of Ronald Sciortino; Philip Sciortino and Ronald Sciortino, interview by Justin Nystrom, July 19, 2011, transcript, Creole Italian Collection, Documentary and Oral History Studio, Loyola University New Orleans.

11. "Philip Quaglino, Tobacco Dealer, Taken by Death," *New Orleans Times-Picayune*, February 24, 1942; Sciortino and Sciortino, interview.

12. Sciortino and Sciortino, interview.

13. Advertisement, *New Orleans Daily Picayune*, July 11, 1887; "Timely Topics," *Honolulu Evening Bulletin*, January 21, 1897.

14. Helen Watts McVey, "The Home Department," *The Commoner*, May 29, 1903.

15. Roahen, *Gumbo Tales*, 36–39; Sciortino and Sciortino, interview.

16. Sciortino and Sciortino, interview.

17. Louisiana, Naturalization Records; New Orleans, Marriage Records Index; Elizabeth Bellone Unsworth and Buster Unsworth, interview Justin Nystrom, August 4, 2011, transcript, Creole Italian Collection, Documentary and Oral History Studio, Loyola University New Orleans.

18. Unsworth and Unsworth, interview.

19. Ibid.

20. Ibid.

21. Keith Spera, "New Orleans Piano legend Professor Longhair's final Home Is Brought Back to Life," *New Orleans Times-Picayune*, February 20, 2014; Pat Byrd, conversation with Justin Nystrom, June 25, 2015.

22. U.S. World War I Draft Registration Cards.

23. Benjamin Terranova and Lorraine Terranova, interview by Justin Nystrom, July 29, 2010, audio recording, Creole Italian Collection, Documentary and Oral History Studio, Loyola University New Orleans.

24. "Advertisement: A&P Grand Opening," *New Orleans Times-Picayune*, January 2, 1951; Terranova and Terranova, interview.

25. Terranova and Terranova, interview.

26. Ibid.

27. Michael Testa and Rosemary Uddo Testa, interview by Joseph Maselli, September 17, 1985, audiocassette (transferred to digital), American Italian Cultural Center, New Orleans; Rosemary Uddo Testa and Adele Chopin Uddo, interview by Justin Nystrom, June 14, 2011, videorecording, Creole Italian Collection, Documentary and Oral History Studio, Loyola University New Orleans.

28. Tommy Tusa, interview by Justin Nystrom, July 12, 2012, transcript, Creole Italian Collection, Documentary and Oral History Studio, Loyola University New Orleans; Maria Impastato and Salvatore Impastato, interview by Justin Nystrom, August 18, 2010, transcript, Creole Italian Collection, Documentary and Oral History Studio, Loyola University New Orleans.

29. Joseph Zuppardo, interview by Joseph Maselli, May 13, 1980, audiocassette (transferred to digital), American Italian Cultural Center, New Orleans.

30. Ibid.; Rosario Zuppardo, interview by Justin Nystrom, July 14, 2010, transcript, Creole Italian Collection, Documentary and Oral History Studio, Loyola University New Orleans.

31. Joseph Zuppardo, interview.

32. "Puglia's Market Will Open Today," *New Orleans Times-Picayune*, June 24, 1938.

33. Joseph Zuppardo, interview.

34. Ibid.

35. Rosario Zuppardo, interview.

36. Testa and Uddo, interview.

37. James H. Gillis, "CPC Approves Phase of Plan," *New Orleans Times-Picayune*, March 3, 1971; "Landrieu Picks Shaw for Board," *New Orleans Times-Picayune*, July 20, 1971.

38. Clarence Doucet, "Decatur-1," *New Orleans Times-Picayune*, January 9, 1974; John Perrone and Joe Pacaccio, interview by Justin Nystrom, August 2, 2010, transcript, Creole Italian Collection, Documentary and Oral History Studio, Loyola University New Orleans; Tusa, interview.

39. Perrone and Pacaccio, interview.

40. Brett Anderson, "The Natural"; Fitzmorris, *Hungry Town*, 49–54.

41. Perrone and Pacaccio, interview.

42. Ibid.; Brett Anderson, "Changing Scenes: Culinary Institute Grad Opens Restaurant in Hotel; Progresso Deli Occupies Former Progress Grocery Space," *New Orleans Times-Picayune*, April 24, 2001.

43. Impastato and Impastato, interview.

44. Federal Writers' Project, *New Orleans City Guide*, 33; Impastato and Impastato, interview; U.S. Census, 1920, 1930.

45. Impastato and Impastato, interview; Dominic Massa, "Ralph Brennan to Buy Napoleon House," *New Orleans Advocate*, April 15, 2015.

46. Richard Campanella, *Bourbon Street*; "Council Revokes Liquor License," *New*

Orleans Times-Picayune, May 6, 1954; Nick Loguidice, interview by Justin Nystrom, August 2, 2011, videorecording, Creole Italian Collection, Documentary and Oral History Studio, Loyola University New Orleans.

CHAPTER 7. Meatballs, Mafia, and Memory

1. "Brilab Jury Convicts Carlos Marcello and Former Louisiana Official," *New York Times*, August 4, 1981; Jim Amoss and Dean Baquet, "Munchies Are Hot Topic in Tapes," *New Orleans Times-Picayune*, June 21, 1981.

2. Jim Amoss and Dean Baquet, "Munchies Are Hot Topic in Tapes," *New Orleans Times-Picayune*, June 21, 1981; Dean Baquet, "From the Big Easy to the Big Apple: An Evening with Dean Baquet," interview by Lee Zurik, videorecording, March 16, 2015, Ed Renwick Lecture Series: Institute of Politics, Loyola University New Orleans.

3. Jim Amoss and Dean Baquet, "Tapes May Be Key in Marcello Bribery Trial," *New Orleans Times-Picayune*, March 29, 1981; Iris Kelso, "Carlos' Tune: Don't Do Nuttin' until Ya Talk to Me," *New Orleans Times-Picayune/States-Item*, May 31, 1981; "Brilab Jury Convicts Carlos Marcello and Former Louisiana Official," *New York Times*, August 4, 1981; David Chandler, "The 'Little Man' Is Bigger Than Ever," *Life*, April 10, 1970; *Emmett E. Batson v. Time, Inc., and David Chandler*, 298 So. 2d 100 (Court of Appeal of Louisiana, First Circuit 1974). For the successful prosecution of Marcello in Brilab, see *U.S. v. Marcello*, 537 F. Supp. 1364 (U.S. District Court, E.D. Louisiana 1982); Baquet, "From the Big Easy to the Big Apple." Although there are more recent works on Marcello, most rehash John H. Davis's *Mafia Kingfish*, which typifies the works that link Marcello to the Kennedy assassination. A more entertaining and possibly more accurate account of Marcello's day-to-day existence appears in Brouillette and Randazzo, *Mr. New Orleans*, 101.

4. Trillin, "No Daily Specials."

5. "Mano's Checking Account Studied," *New Orleans Times-Picayune*, November 13, 1943; "Mano Wanted in Sister's Slaying," *New Orleans Times-Picayune*, November 17, 1943.

6. "Widow of Slain Butcher to Aid in Solving Crime," *New Orleans Times-Picayune*, November 14, 1943; "Alien Examined in Slaying Probe," *New Orleans Times-Picayune*, November 20, 1943.

7. Nick Loguidice, interview by Justin Nystrom August 2, 2011, videorecording, Creole Italian Collection, Documentary and Oral History Studio, Loyola University New Orleans.

8. "Auto of Missing Siracusa Found," *New Orleans Times-Picayune*, February 22, 1944; "Chemical Tested in Body Mystery," *New Orleans Times-Picayune*, March 16, 1944; "Bones of Missing Siracusa Found Hidden in Weeds," *New Orleans Times-Picayune*, April 4, 1944; "Subpoenaed Probe Witness Threatened over Telephone," *New Orleans Times-Picayune*, January 18, 1951.

9. Trillin, "No Daily Specials"; Collin, *Revised New Orleans Underground Gourmet*, 58–59.

10. Federal Writers' Project, *New Orleans City Guide*.

11. McNamee, *Man Who Changed the Way We Eat*; Charles A. Ferguson, interview by Jack Davis and Justin A. Nystrom, April 29, 2014, transcript, Making Modern New Orleans Collection, Documentary and Oral History Studio, Loyola University New Orleans.

12. Ella Brennan, interview by Jack Davis and Justin A. Nystrom, June 25, 2014, transcript, Making Modern New Orleans Collection, Documentary and Oral History Studio, Loyola University New Orleans.

13. Collin, *Revised New Orleans Underground Gourmet*, 31; "Advertisement: Restaurant Sclafani," *New Orleans Times-Picayune*, August 24, 1975.

14. Betty Bellone Unsworth and Buster Unsworth, interview by Justin A. Nystrom, August 4, 2011, transcript, Creole Italian Collection, Documentary and Oral History Studio, Loyola University New Orleans.

15. Collin, *Revised New Orleans Underground Gourmet*, 112. For an exploration of ethnic humor and its various interpretations and analyses, see Shifman and Katz, "'Just Call Me Adonai'"; Boskin and Dorinson, "Ethnic Humor"; Lowe, "Theories of Ethnic Humor"; Zenner, "Joking and Ethnic Stereotyping." For a thoughtful exploration of the theory regarding perceptions of power in food and ethnicity, see Ray, *Ethnic Restaurateur*, 1–17.

16. Brett Anderson, "The Natural."

17. Wurgaft, "Stardom and the Hungry Public."

18. Matsumoto, "Legacy of Joe Baum." Freedman, *Ten Restaurants That Changed America*, 323–63, criticizes Baum's style and what Freedman characterizes as a lack of practicality. In this, he is at odds with Ella Brennan, who has high appreciation for what Baum sought to accomplish. See Brennan, interview.

19. Frank Sclafani, interview by Justin A. Nystrom, August 1, 2011, transcript, Creole Italian Collection, Documentary and Oral History Studio, Loyola University New Orleans.

20. Louisiana Naturalization Records; Sclafani, interview.

21. Sclafani, interview.

22. Ibid.

23. New Orleans, Passenger Lists; Louisiana Vital Records, Marriage Index, 33:622, Louisiana Division of Archives, Records Management, and History. Peter Latino operated the Messina restaurant on Decatur Street (U.S. Census, 1910, 1930, 1940; *Pueblo City Directory* [1917]).

24. U.S. Census, 1940; Calogero Angello obituary, *New Orleans Times-Picayune*, September 15, 1953.

25. *New Orleans Times-Picayune*, April 15, 1955; Joseph Angello obituary, *New Orleans Times-Picayune*, December 24, 1961; William McG. Keefe, "Five Choices out

of Seven Annex Races," *New Orleans Times-Picayune*, December 3, 1942; Philip and Ronald Sciortino, interview by Justin A. Nystrom, July 19, 2011, transcript, Creole Italian Collection, Documentary and Oral History Studio, Loyola University New Orleans; Collin, *Revised New Orleans Underground Gourmet*, 59.

26. Jack Du Arte, "Le Ruth's, Brennan's Head List of Top Restaurants," *New Orleans Times-Picayune*, January 23, 1977; Gene Bourg, "Down Home Italian at Tony Angello's," *New Orleans Times-Picayune*, February 11, 1994.

27. Bill Grady, "Ex-Fighter Earns Moniker over Lunch—'Beer Baron' Knows the Ropes," *New Orleans Times-Picayune*, January 5, 1997.

28. "DiRosa Denies Luncheon Was Meeting with Marcello," *New Orleans Times-Picayune*, September 3, 1976; James H. Gillis, "Marcello and the Mayor's Race," *New Orleans Times-Picayune*, October 27, 1977.

29. Although there is much more scholarship to be done on the economics of organized crime and organized crime generally, Hortis and Jacobs, *Mob and the City*, 155–71, explores the underground economics of nightlife, alcohol, and restaurants in New York.

30. "A Burglar Killed," *New Orleans Times-Picayune*, February 15, 1902; "Duncan Plaza." See Armstrong, *Satchmo*, 57–59. Armstrong's account is full of improbabilities and inaccuracies; his knowledge may have been obtained secondhand and was transmitted through a ghostwriter. According to Armstrong, "Ponce" [*sic*], "one of the biggest operators in the red light district," employed Armstrong to play cornet in his bar during this formative period of his remarkable career. Joseph Segreto later sued Armstrong for libel, but the case was thrown out. See "Trumpet Player Named in Suit," *New Orleans Times-Picayune*, September 24, 1966. Despite its many improbabilities, Armstrong's account of this era is represented nearly intact in Brothers, *Louis Armstrong's New Orleans*, 110–12.

31. "Pons Stabbed in Saloonists' Feud," *New Orleans Daily States*, April 8, 1916; "Three Merchants Shot; Assassins Baffle Pursuit," *New Orleans Times-Picayune*, May 16, 1916; "Italian Barkeeper Seriously Wounded," *New Orleans Times-Picayune*, April 25, 1916; "Bank Swindler in Murder Case Here?" *New Orleans States*, December 31, 1916.

32. Salvatore "Joe" Segreto, interview by Justin A. Nystrom, August 5, 2010, transcript, Creole Italian Collection, Documentary and Oral History Studio, Loyola University New Orleans; Salvadore Segreto and Carlos Marcello photograph, 1930s, in possession of Sophia Segreto.

33. "Carollo, Alonze Convicted, Given Five Years Each," *New Orleans Times-Picayune*, January 14, 1936; "Two Are Cleared in Poretto Death," *New Orleans Times-Picayune*, June 12, 1943.

34. Advertisement, *New Orleans Times-Picayune*, September 21, 1944; "Segretos Now at 809 St. Louis," *New Orleans Times-Picayune*, April 26, 1945; Segreto, interview.

35. Burton and Lombard, *Creole Feast*, 3–8; "Segreto Offers Chicken Cacciatore as Boon to Shortage-Ridden World," *New Orleans Times-Picayune*, June 2, 1946; Segreto, interview.

36. Ibid.

37. Ibid.

38. "Lack of Evidence Thins ABC Docket in Hectic Session," *New Orleans Times-Picayune*, January 19, 1949; "Beverage Board Penalizes Club," *New Orleans Times-Picayune*, January 22, 1949.

39. "Lack of Evidence Thins ABC Docket in Hectic Session," *New Orleans Times-Picayune*, January 19, 1949; "Beverage Board Penalizes Club," *New Orleans Times-Picayune*, January 22, 1949.

40. Brennan, interview; Segreto, interview; *New Orleans City Directory* (1949, 1956).

41. Segreto, interview.

42. Swanson, *Historic Jefferson Parish*, 70–71; "Elmwood Place 178 Years Old, Is Burned to Ground," *New Orleans Times-Picayune*, February 3, 1940; "Newcomer to Get Key to the City," *New Orleans Times-Picayune*, September 23, 1956; Brennan, interview; "Excellent Home Cooked Meals Now at the Elmwood Plantation," *New Orleans Times-Picayune*, December 8, 1960.

43. "Provino Mosca Funeral Today," *New Orleans Times-Picayune*, March 1, 1962; "Property Transfer," *New Orleans Times-Picayune*, December 2, 1962; advertisement, *New Orleans Times-Picayune*, March 6, 1963.

44. "Elmwood Plantation Restaurant Menu," Louisiana Menu and Restaurant Collection, Louisiana Research Collection, Howard-Tilton Memorial Library, Tulane University.

45. Joseph C. Marcello, telephone conversation with author, June 30, 2016.

46. Bruce Nolan, "Owners Plan to Rebuild Fire-Ravaged Elmwood," *New Orleans Times-Picayune*, December 19, 1978; "Quarter Fettuccine King Dies," *New Orleans Times-Picayune*, January 20, 1995; Stella Pitts, "La Louisiane: French Quarter 'Ghost,'" *New Orleans Times-Picayune*, April 20, 1979.

47. Collin, *Revised New Orleans Underground Gourmet*, table of contents.

Selected Bibliography

Oral History Collections

Creole Italian Collection, Documentary and Oral History Studio, Loyola University New Orleans
Hogan Jazz Archive, Howard-Tilton Memorial Library, Tulane University
Making Modern New Orleans Collection, Documentary and Oral History Studio, Loyola University New Orleans
Joseph Maselli Oral History Collection, American Italian Research Library, East Jefferson Parish Library, Metairie, Louisiana

Subscription Databases via Ancestry.com, Provo, Utah

Louisiana, Naturalization Records, 1836–1998
New Orleans, Marriage Records Index, 1831–1920
New Orleans, Passenger Lists, 1813–1963
U.S. Census, 1830–1940
U.S. Internal Revenue Service Tax Assessment Lists, 1862–1918
U.S. World War I Draft Registration Cards, 1917–18
U.S. World War II Draft Cards Young Men, 1940–47

Court Cases and Legal Records

Arrest Records, New Orleans Criminal District Court, Sections "A" and "B," 1880–1918, Louisiana Division, City Archives, New Orleans Public Library
City of New Orleans v. Fargot, La. 369 116 (Supreme Court of Louisiana 1906)
City of New Orleans vs. Tony Renfero, Tony Latriglio, Nicola Aranda, Sam Carruso, Emile Martin & Charlie Mayensa, Louisiana Division, New Orleans Public Library (First Recorder's Court, City of New Orleans 1905)
Emmett E. Batson v. Time, Inc., and David Chandler, 298 So. 2d 100 (Court of Appeal of Louisiana, First Circuit 1974)

Interdiction of Giacona, 158 La. 148; 103 So. 721; 1925 (Supreme Court of Louisiana 1925)

Marcello v. United States, No. 13773 (U.S. Court of Appeals for the Fifth Circuit April 22, 1952)

State ex re. Tranchina v. City of New Orleans; In re Tranchina, 141 La. 711; 75 So. 683; 1917 La. LEXIS 1565 (Supreme Court of Louisiana 1917)

State v. Gebbia et al., No. 16,931, 121 La. 1083, 47 So. 32 (1908).

State v. Joseph Impastato, No. 43512B, October 31, 1914

State v. Anthony Loscasio and Victor Lemane, No. 45108B, February 28, 1917.

State v. Fortune Salvaggio, No. 41309A, February 11, 1913.

U.S. v. Marcello, 537 F. Supp. 1364 (U.S. District Court, E.D. Louisiana 1982).

City Directories

Edwards' Annual Directory to New Orleans. St. Louis: Edwards, 1869, 1870.

Gardner's New Orleans Directory for 1861. New Orleans: Gardner, 1861.

New Orleans Annual and Commercial Register of 1846. New Orleans: Michel, 1845.

New Orleans Business Directory, 1858. New Orleans: Mygatt, 1857.

New Orleans City Directory. Detroit: Polk, 1949, 1956.

New Orleans City Directory, 1832. New Orleans: Percy, 1832.

Pueblo City Directory, 1917. Colorado Springs: Polk, 1917.

Soards' New Orleans City Directory. New Orleans: Soards, 1874, 1886, 1887, 1893, 1895, 1901, 1903, 1904, 1906, 1908, 1910, 1912, 1913, 1914, 1916, 1917, 1918, 1925.

Published Primary Sources and Ephemera

Booth, Andrew B., comp. *Records of Louisiana Confederate Soldiers and Louisiana Confederate Commands*. 3 vols. New Orleans: Louisiana Commissioner of Military Records, 1920.

"Californian Fruit Industries." *Bulletin of Miscellaneous Information* (Royal Gardens, Kew) 1893, no. 80 (1893): 218–22.

Chace, E. M. "The Manufacture of Oil of Lemon and Citrate of Lime in Sicily." *Journal of Industrial and Engineering Chemistry* 1, no. 1 (1909): 18–27.

Chamber of Commerce of the New Orleans Area. *New Orleans: Facts about the City : Alphabetically Arranged*. New Orleans: New Orleans Association of Commerce, 1931.

"Citrus Fruits in Sicily." *Bulletin of Miscellaneous Information* (Royal Gardens, Kew) 1895, no. 106 (1895): 266–71.

"Duncan Plaza: Regional Urban Design Assistance Team, New Orleans, Jan. 17–21." American Institute of Architects, January 17, 1980.

Federal Writers' Project. *New Orleans City Guide*. Boston: Houghton, Mifflin, 1938.

Gayarré, Charles. *The Creoles of History and the Creoles of Romance: A Lecture Delivered in the Hall of the Tulane University, New Orleans*. New Orleans: Hopkins, 1885.

Gelpi, Paul, & Bro. *Catalogue of Fancy Groceries, Fruits, Etc., Etc*. New Orleans, 1874.

Grocery Store Route List. New Orleans: Times-Picayune, 1960.

"Ice-Making in New Orleans." *Harper's Weekly*, January 25, 1890, 67.

King, Grace Elizabeth. *Creole Families of New Orleans*. New York: Macmillan, 1921.

Louisiana Ice Manufacturing Company. *Charter and By-Laws of the Louisiana Ice Manufacturing Company of the City of New Orleans: Chartered February 18th, 1868*. New Orleans: Iiyman Smith, 1883.

Louisiana Restaurant Guide. Louisiana Restaurant Association, 1958.

The New Lakeview: Bounded by West End, Spanish Fort, Lake Pontchartrain, City Park and Metairie; in America's Most Interesting City. New Orleans: New Orleans Land Company, 1928.

"New Orleans, La.: Foodstuffs. Name of Owner Must Be Displayed in Buildings and on Vehicles Containing Foodstuffs or Substances Which May Become Offensive. (Ord. 2566, July 13, 1915)." *Public Health Reports (1896–1970)* 31, no. 22 (June 2, 1916): 1447–48.

Official Report of the Ninth Fruit Growers' Convention of the State of California. Sacramento, Calif.: State Office, 1888.

Pittari's Restaurant. *Tourist's Guide for New Orleans*. 1957.

Solari, A. M. & J., Ltd. *Fancy and Staple Groceries: Importers of Fine Wines and Liquors, Wholesale and Retail*. New Orleans, 1913.

Tourists' Guide to New Orleans: What to See and How to See It. New Orleans: New Orleans Railways Company, 1904.

Twain, Mark. *Life on the Mississippi*. New York: Harper, 1883.

U.S. House, Committee on Ways and Means. *Tariff Information, 1921: Hearings on General Tariff Revision*. Washington, D.C.: U.S. Government Printing Office, 1921.

———. *Tariff Schedules: Hearings before the Committee on Ways and Means*. Washington, D.C.: U.S. Government Printing Office, 1913.

U.S. Department of State. *Correspondence in Relation to the Killing of Prisoners in New Orleans on March 14, 1891*. Washington, D.C.: U.S. Government Printing Office, 1891.

U.S. Department of Agriculture. *Bulletin of Plant Industry* 65 (1904).

Zacharie, James S. *New Orleans Guide: With Descriptions of the Routes to New Orleans, Sights of the City Arranged Alphabetically*. New Orleans: New Orleans News, 1885.

Books, Articles, and Theses

Ackerman, Edward A. "Influences of Climate on the Cultivation of Citrus Fruits." *Geographical Review* 28, no. 2 (1938): 289–302.

Adler, Jeffrey S. "Murder, North and South: Violence in Early-Twentieth-Century Chicago and New Orleans." *Journal of Southern History* 74, no. 2 (2008): 297–324.

Alexander, Barbara. "The Rational Racketeer: Pasta Protection in Depression Era Chicago." *Journal of Law and Economics* 40, no. 1 (1997): 175–202.

Alvarez, Robert R. "The March of Empire: Mangos, Avocados, and the Politics of Transfer." *Gastronomica* 7, no. 3 (2007): 28–33.

Amundson, Richard J. "Oakley Plantation: A Post–Civil War Venture in Louisiana Sugar." *Louisiana History* 9, no. 1 (1968): 21–42.

Anderson, Brett. "The Natural." In *Cornbread Nation 4: The Best of Southern Food Writing*, edited by John Shelton Reed, Dale Volberg Reed, and John T. Edge, 53–66. Athens: University of Georgia Press, 2008.

Anderson, Oscar E. *Refrigeration in America: A History of a New Technology and Its Impact*. Princeton: Princeton University Press for the University of Cincinnati, 1953.

Arend, Orissa, Curtis J. Austin, and Charles E. Jones. *Showdown in Desire: The Black Panthers Take a Stand in New Orleans*. Fayetteville: University of Arkansas Press, 2009.

Armstrong, Louis. *Satchmo: My Life in New Orleans*. New York: Prentice-Hall, 1954.

Baiamonte, John V. "Community Life in the Italian Colonies of Tangipahoa Parish, Louisiana, 1890–1950." *Louisiana History* 30, no. 4 (1989): 365–97.

———. *Spirit of Vengeance: Nativism and Louisiana Justice, 1921–1924*. Baton Rouge: Louisiana State University Press, 1986.

———. "'Who Killa de Chief' Revisited: The Hennessey Assassination and Its Aftermath, 1890–1991." *Louisiana History* 33, no. 2 (1992): 117–46.

Bailey, John. *The Lost German Slave Girl: The Extraordinary True Story of Sally Miller and Her Fight for Freedom in Old New Orleans*. New York: Atlantic Monthly, 2005.

Bailey, Liberty Hyde, and Wilhelm Miller. *Cyclopedia of American Horticulture*. Vol. 2. New York: Macmillan, 1910.

Bakker, H. *Sugar Cane Cultivation and Management*. New York: Kluwer Academic/ Plenum, 1999.

Barbas, Samantha. "Just Like Home: 'Home Cooking' and the Domestication of the American Restaurant." *Gastronomica* 2, no. 4 (2002): 43–52.

Basile, David G. "Agricultural Sicily." *Economic Geography* 17, no. 2 (1941): 109–20.

Bauer, Craig A. "From Burnt Canes to Budding City: A History of the City of Kenner, Louisiana." *Louisiana History* 23, no. 4 (1982): 353–81.

Beahrs, Andrew. *Twain's Feast: Searching for America's Lost Foods in the Footsteps of Samuel Clemens*. New York: Penguin, 2010.

Beck, Bernard. "The Myth That Would Not Die: The Sopranos, Mafia Movies, and Italians in America." *Multicultural Perspectives* 2, no. 2 (2000): 24–27.

Becnel, Thomas. "Review." *Louisiana History* 28, no. 3 (1987): 337–38.

Beebe, Lucius. *The Lucius Beebe Reader*. Selected and edited by Charles Clegg and Duncan Emrich. Garden City, N.Y.: Doubleday, 1967.

Berger, Molly W. *Hotel Dreams*. Baltimore: Johns Hopkins University Press, 2011.

Bethune, Brian. "Was Pasta the Original Fusion Food?" *Maclean's*, January 21, 2008, 58.

Blount, Roy, Jr. "The Food Music Pantheon: Louis, Louis, Louis, Fats, and Slim." *Gastronomica* 8, no. 2 (2008): 13–16.

Blumenthal, Ralph. *The Stork Club: America's Most Famous Nightspot and the Lost World of Café Society*. Boston: Little, Brown, 2000.

Bonanno, Joseph, with Sergio Lalli. *A Man of Honor: The Autobiography of Joseph Bonanno*. New York: Simon and Schuster, 1983.

Booth, Philip. "French Quarter Fest Features Locals." *Downbeat* 70, no. 7 (2003): 22.

Bordman, Gerald Martin. *American Musical Theatre: A Chronicle*. Oxford: Oxford University Press, 2010.

Boskin, Joseph, and Joseph Dorinson. "Ethnic Humor: Subversion and Survival." *American Quarterly* 37, no. 1 (1985): 81–97.

Botein, Barbara. "The Hennessy Case: An Episode in Anti-Italian Nativism." *Louisiana History* 20, no. 3 (1979): 261–79.

Boulard, Garry. *Just a Gigolo: The Life and Times of Louis Prima*. Lafayette: Center for Louisiana Studies, University of Southwestern Louisiana, 1989.

Bourguignon, Erika. "Memory in an Amnesic World: Holocaust, Exile, and the Return of the Suppressed." *Anthropological Quarterly* 78, no. 1 (2005): 63–88.

Brandenburg, Broughton. *Imported Americans: The Story of the Experiences of a Disguised American and His Wife Studying the Immigration Question*. New York: Stokes, 1904.

Brothers, Thomas David. *Louis Armstrong's New Orleans*. New York: Norton, 2006.

Broughton, John Cam Hobhouse. *A Journey through Albania, and Other Provinces of Turkey in Europe and Asia, to Constantinople*. London: Cawthorn, 1813.

Brouillette, Frenchy, and Matthew Randazzo V. *Mr. New Orleans: The Life of a Big Easy Underworld Legend*. Beverly Hills, Calif.: Phoenix, 2010.

Bruner, Robert F., and Sean D. Carr. *The Panic of 1907: Lessons Learned from the Market's Perfect Storm*. Hoboken, N.J.: Wiley, 2009.

Brunn, Harry O. *The Story of the Original Dixieland Jazz Band*. Baton Rouge: Louisiana State University Press, 1960.

Bucheli, Marcelo. *Bananas and Business: The United Fruit Company in Colombia, 1899–2000*. New York: New York University Press, 2005.

Burton, Nathaniel, and Rudy Lombard. *Creole Feast: 15 Master Chefs of New Orleans Reveal Their Secrets.* New York: Random House, 1978.

Campanella, Catherine. *Legendary Locals of Metairie.* Charleston, S.C.: Legendary Locals, 2013.

Campanella, Richard. *Bienville's Dilemma: A Historical Geography of New Orleans.* Lafayette: Center for Louisiana Studies, University of Louisiana at Lafayette, 2008.

———. *Bourbon Street: A History.* Baton Rouge: Louisiana State University Press, 2014.

———. *Geographies of New Orleans: Urban Fabrics before the Storm.* Lafayette: University of Louisiana at Lafayette, Center for Louisiana Studies, 2006.

Carnevale, Nancy C. "'No Italian Spoken for the Duration of the War': Language, Italian-American Identity, and Cultural Pluralism in the World War II Years." *Journal of American Ethnic History* 22, no. 3 (2003): 3–33.

Catanzaro, Raimondo. *Men of Respect: A Social History of the Sicilian Mafia.* New York : Free Press1992.

Chapman, Peter. *Bananas: How the United Fruit Company Shaped the World.* Edinburgh: Canongate, 2007.

Charters, Samuel. *A Trumpet around the Corner: The Story of New Orleans Jazz.* Jackson: University Press of Mississippi, 2008.

Chase, John Churchill. *Frenchmen, Desire, Good Children, and Other Streets of New Orleans.* 3rd ed. New York: Collier, 1979.

Chesen, Judy Arlis. "It Was More Than Nourishment, It Was More Than Sustenance: A Study of the Importance of Food to the Lives of Southern Italian Immigrant Women in Chicago, 1880–1930." PhD diss., Miami University, 1999.

Christovich, Mary Louise, and Roulhac Toledano. *New Orleans Architecture: The American Sector.* Gretna, La.: Pelican, 1998.

Cinotto, Simone. *The Italian American Table: Food, Family, and Community in New York City.* Urbana: University of Illinois Press, 2013.

———. "Leonard Covello, the Covello Papers, and the History of Eating Habits among Italian Immigrants in New York." *Journal of American History* 91, no. 2 (2004): 497–521.

Ciongoli, A. Kenneth, and Jay Parini, eds. *Beyond The Godfather: Italian American Writers on the Real Italian American Experience.* Hanover, N.H.: University Press of New England, 1997.

Clark, Emily. *The Strange History of the American Quadroon: Free Women of Color in the Revolutionary Atlantic World.* Chapel Hill: University of North Carolina Press, 2013.

Clark, Francis E. *Our Italian Fellow Citizens in Their Old Homes and Their New.* Boston: Small, Maynard, 1919.

Cohen, Hennig. "The History of 'Poor Boy,' the New Orleans Bargain Sandwich." *American Speech* 25, no. 1 (1950): 67–69.

Collin, Richard H. *The Revised New Orleans Underground Gourmet*. New York: Simon and Schuster, 1973.

Collins, R. *New Orleans Jazz: A Revised History: The Development of American Music from the Origin to the Big Bands*. New York: Vantage, 1996.

Coons, George H. "The Sugar Beet: Product of Science." *Scientific Monthly* 68, no. 3 (1949): 149–64.

Cordasco, Francesco, ed. *Studies in Italian American Social History: Essays in Honor of Leonard Covello*. Totowa, N.J.: Rowman and Littlefield, 1975.

Crist, Raymond E. "The Citrus Industry in Florida." *American Journal of Economics and Sociology* 15, no. 1 (1955): 1–12.

Dal Cerro, Bill, and David Anthony Witter. *Bebop, Swing, and Bella Musica: Jazz and the Italian American Experience*. Chicago: Bella Musica, 2015.

D'Amato, Gaetano. "The 'Black Hand' Myth." *North American Review* 187, no. 629 (1908): 543–49.

Davis, John H. *Mafia Kingfish: Carlos Marcello and the Assassination of John F. Kennedy*. New York: McGraw-Hill, 1989.

Davis, Marni. *Jews and Booze: Becoming American in the Age of Prohibition*. New York: New York University Press, 2011.

Dawdy, Shannon Lee. *Building the Devil's Empire: French Colonial New Orleans*. Chicago: University of Chicago Press, 2008.

Denker, Joel. *The World on a Plate: A Tour through the History of America's Ethnic Cuisines*. Boulder, Colo.: Westview, 2003.

Depew, Chauncey Mitchell. *1795–1895: One Hundred Years of American Commerce*. New York: Haynes, 1895.

Dickie, John. *Blood Brotherhoods: A History of Italy's Three Mafias*. New York City: PublicAffairs, 2014.

———. *Delizia!: The Epic History of the Italians and Their Food*. New York: Free Press, 2008.

Diner, Hasia R. *Hungering for America: Italian, Irish, and Jewish Foodways in the Age of Migration*. Cambridge: Harvard University Press, 2001.

Di Renzo, Anthony. *Bitter Greens: Essays on Food, Politics, and Ethnicity from the Imperial Kitchen*. Albany: Excelsior Editions/State University of New York Press, 2010.

DiStefano, Joe. "Joe's Vastedda: A Treat for Old School Sicilians and Offal Lovers Alike." *Chopsticks and Marrow*, March 19, 2014. http://chopsticksandmarrow .com/2014/03/joes-vastedda-a-treat-for-old-school-sicilians-and-offal-lovers -alike/.

Doorley, Michael. "Irish Catholics and French Creoles: Ethnic Struggles within the Catholic Church in New Orleans, 1835–1920." *Catholic Historical Review* 87, no. 1 (2001): 34–54.

Elliott, Maud Howe. *Sicily in Shadow and in Sun: The Earthquake and the American Relief Work*. Boston: Little, Brown, 1910.

Ellis, Scott S. *Madame Vieux Carré: The French Quarter in the Twentieth Century*. Jackson: University Press of Mississippi, 2010.

Evans, Clement Anselm, ed. *Confederate Military History: A Library of Confederate States History*. Atlanta: Confederate, 1899.

Faber, Eberhard L. *Building the Land of Dreams: New Orleans and the Transformation of Early America*. Princeton: Princeton University Press, 2016.

Fairall, Herbert S. *The World's Industrial and Cotton Centennial Exposition, New Orleans, 1884–1885*. Iowa City: Republican, 1885.

Fenton, Roy. *Tramp Ships: An Illustrated History*. Barnsley: Seaforth, 2013.

Fentress, James. *Rebels and Mafiosi: Death in a Sicilian Landscape*. Ithaca: Cornell University Press, 2000.

Fertel, Rien. *Imagining the Creole City: The Rise of Literary Culture in Nineteenth-Century New Orleans*. Baton Rouge: Louisiana State University Press, 2014.

Fitzmorris, Tom. *Hungry Town: A Culinary History of New Orleans, the City Where Food Is Almost Everything*. New York: Stewart, Tabori, and Chang, 2010.

Foerster, Robert F. *The Italian Emigration of Our Times*. Cambridge: Harvard University Press, 1919.

Fortier, Alcée, ed. *Louisiana: Comprising Sketches of Parishes, Towns, Events, Institutions, and Persons, Arranged in Cyclopedic Form*. Vol. 3. New Orleans: Century Historical Association, 1914.

Freedman, Paul. "American Restaurants and Cuisine in the Mid-Nineteenth Century." *New England Quarterly* 84, no. 1 (2011): 5–59.

———. *Ten Restaurants That Changed America*. New York: Liveright, 2016.

Freeman, Mike. *Clarence Saunders and the Founding of Piggly Wiggly: The Rise and Fall of a Memphis Maverick*. Charleston, S.C.: History Press, 2011.

Funkenstein, Amos. "Collective Memory and Historical Consciousness." *History and Memory* 1, no. 1 (1989): 5–26.

Fussell, Elizabeth. "Constructing New Orleans, Constructing Race: A Population History of New Orleans." *Journal of American History* 94 (2007): 846–55.

Gabaccia, Donna R. *Militants and Migrants: Rural Sicilians Become American Workers*. New Brunswick, N.J.: Rutgers University Press, 1988.

———. *We Are What We Eat: Ethnic Food and the Making of Americans*. Cambridge: Harvard University Press, 1998.

Galloway, J. H. "Botany in the Service of Empire: The Barbados Cane-Breeding Program and the Revival of the Caribbean Sugar Industry, 1880s–1930s." *Annals of the Association of American Geographers* 86, no. 4 (1996): 682–706.

Gambino, Richard. *Vendetta: A True Story of the Worst Lynching in America, the Mass Murder of Italian-Americans in New Orleans in 1891, the Vicious Motivations behind It, and the Tragic Repercussions That Linger to This Day*. Garden City, N.Y.: Doubleday, 1977.

Gauthreaux, Alan G. "An Inhospitable Land: Anti-Italian Sentiment and Violence in Louisiana, 1891–1924." *Louisiana History* 51, no. 1 (2010): 41–68.

Gennari, John. "Passing for Italian." *Transition* 72 (1996): 36–48.

Germany, Kent. *New Orleans after the Promises: Poverty, Citizenship, and the Search for the Great Society*. Athens: University of Georgia Press, 2007.

Giunta, Edvige, and Samuel J. Patti, eds. *A Tavola: Food, Tradition, and Community among Italian Americans : Selected Essays from the 29th Annual Conference of the American Italian Historical Association, 14–17 November 1996, Pittsburgh, Pennsylvania*. Staten Island, N.Y.: American Italian Historical Association, 1998.

Guste, Roy F.. *Antoine's Restaurant, since 1840, Cookbook: A Collection of the Original Recipes from New Orleans' Oldest and Most Famous Restaurant*. New Orleans: Carbery-Guste, 1978.

Haas, Edward F. "New Orleans on the Half-Shell: The Maestri Era, 1936–1946." *Louisiana History* 13, no. 3 (1972): 283–310.

Hair, William Ivy. *Bourbonism and Agrarian Protest: Louisiana Politics, 1877–1900*. Baton Rouge: Louisiana State University Press, 1969.

———. *Carnival of Fury: Robert Charles and the New Orleans Race Riot of 1900*. Baton Rouge: Louisiana State University Press, 1976.

Haley, Andrew P. *Turning the Tables: Restaurants and the Rise of the American Middle Class, 1880–1920*. Chapel Hill: University of North Carolina Press, 2011.

Halpern, Rick. "Solving the 'Labour Problem': Race, Work, and the State in the Sugar Industries of Louisiana and Natal, 1870–1910." *Journal of Southern African Studies* 30, no. 1 (2004): 19–40.

Hanna, Stephen P. "A Slavery Museum?: Race, Memory, and Landscape in Fredericksburg, Virginia." *Southeastern Geographer* 48, no. 3 (2008): 316–37.

Hastings, Robert W. *The Lakes of Pontchartrain: Their History and Environments*. Jackson: University Press of Mississippi, 2009.

Hearn, Lafcadio. *Inventing New Orleans: Writings of Lafcadio Hearn*. Edited and introduction by S. Frederick Starr. Jackson: University Press of Mississippi, 2001.

Hearn, Lafcadio, and William Head Coleman. *La Cuisine Creole: A Collection of Culinary Recipes from Leading Chefs and Noted Creole Housewives, Who Have Made New Orleans Famous for Its Cuisine*. New York: Coleman, 1885.

Heitmann, John A. "Organization as Power: The Louisiana Sugar Planters' Association and the Creation of Scientific and Technical Institutions, 1877–1910." *Louisiana History* 27, no. 3 (1986): 281–94.

Hellman, Geoffrey T. "Directed to the Product." *New Yorker*, October 17, 1964, 59.

Hémard, Ned. "Jockey Shorts." *New Orleans Nostalgia*, 2012. http://www.new orleansbar.org/uploads/files/JockeyShortsArticle.6-20.pdf.

Hortis, C. Alexander, and James B. Jacobs. *The Mob and the City: The Hidden History of How the Mafia Captured New York*. Amherst, N.Y.: Prometheus, 2014.

Huber, Leonard Victor. *New Orleans: A Pictorial History*. Gretna, La.: Pelican, 1991.

Hughes, Nathaniel Cheairs. *Yale's Confederates: A Biographical Dictionary*. Knoxville: University of Tennessee Press, 2008.

Hunt, Thomas, and Martha Macheca Sheldon. *Deep Water: Joseph P. Macheca and the Birth of the American Mafia*. New York: iUniverse, 2007.

Hyman, Gwen. "The Taste of Fame: Chefs, Diners, Celebrity, Class." *Gastronomica* 8, no. 3 (2008): 43–52.

"Immigration into the United States." *Journal of the American Geographical and Statistical Society* 1, no. 3 (1859): 90–92.

Isenberg, Michael T. *John L. Sullivan and His America*. Urbana: University of Illinois Press, 1994.

Jackson, Joy. "Prohibition in New Orleans: The Unlikeliest Crusade." *Louisiana History* 19, no. 3 (1978): 261–84.

Jacobs, James B., and Lauryn P. Gouldin. "Cosa Nostra: The Final Chapter?" *Crime and Justice* 25 (1999): 129–89.

Jacobson, Matthew Frye. *Whiteness of a Different Color: European Immigrants and the Alchemy of Race*. Cambridge: Harvard University Press, 1998.

Johnson, Walter. *Soul by Soul: Life inside the Antebellum Slave Market*. Cambridge: Harvard University Press, 2000.

Jung, Moon-Ho. *Coolies and Cane: Race, Labor, and Sugar in the Age of Emancipation*. Baltimore: Johns Hopkins University Press, 2006.

Karnes, Thomas L. *Tropical Enterprise: The Standard Fruit and Steamship Company in Latin America*. Baton Rouge: Louisiana State University Press, 1978.

Kelley, Laura D. *The Irish in New Orleans*. Lafayette: University of Louisiana at Lafayette Press, 2014.

Kendall, John Smith. *History of New Orleans*. Vol. 3. Chicago: Lewis, 1922.

Key, Pierre Van Rensselaer, and Bruno Zirato. *Enrico Caruso: A Biography*. Boston: Little, Brown, 1922.

Kniffen, Fred. "The Outdoor Oven in Louisiana." *Louisiana History* 1, no. 1 (1960): 25–35.

Kolb, Carolyn. *New Orleans Memories: One Writer's City*. Knoxville: University of Tennessee Press, 2013.

———. "Virgilians: The Krewe with a Difference." *New Orleans Magazine*, February 2011. http://www.myneworleans.com/New-Orleans-Magazine/February -2011/VIRGILIANS/.

Kurlansky, Mark. *The Big Oyster: History on the Half Shell*. New York: Ballantine, 2006.

———. *Salt: A World History*. New York: Walker, 2002.

Landau, Emily Epstein. *Spectacular Wickedness: Sex, Race, and Memory in Storyville, New Orleans*. Baton Rouge: Louisiana State University Press, 2013.

Latrobe, John H. B. *Southern Travels: Journal of John H. B. Latrobe, 1834*. Edited and introduction by Samuel Wilson Jr. New Orleans: Historic New Orleans Collection, 1986.

Laughlin, Clarence John. *Ghosts along the Mississippi: An Essay in the Poetic Interpretation of Louisiana's Plantation Architecture*. New York: American Legacy, 1961.

Levenstein, Harvey A. *Paradox of Plenty: A Social History of Eating in Modern America*. New York: Oxford University Press, 1993.

———. *Revolution at the Table: The Transformation of the American Diet*. New York: Oxford University Press, 1988.

Lewis, Peirce F. *New Orleans: The Making of an Urban Landscape*. Cambridge, Mass.: Ballinger, 1976.

Lewis, Richard Anthony. *Robert W. Tebbs, Photographer to Architects: Louisiana Plantations in 1926*. Baton Rouge: Louisiana State University Press, 2011.

Lobel, Cindy R. "'Out to Eat': The Emergence and Evolution of the Restaurant in Nineteenth-Century New York City." *Winterthur Portfolio* 44, nos. 2–3 (2010): 193–220.

Logsdon, Joseph, and Arnold R. Hirsch, eds. *Creole New Orleans: Race and Americanization*. Baton Rouge: Louisiana State University Press, 1992.

Long, Alecia P. *The Great Southern Babylon: Sex, Race, and Respectability in New Orleans, 1865–1920*. Baton Rouge: Louisiana State University Press, 2004.

Long, Lucy M. Review of *Bitter Greens: Essays on Food, Politics, and Ethnicity from the Imperial Kitchen*, by Anthony Di Renzo. *Italian American Review* 4, no. 1 (2014): 57–59.

Louisiana Writers' Project. *Gumbo Ya-Ya*. Boston: Houghton Mifflin, 1945.

Lovrich, Frank M. "Work among the Yugoslavs on the Mississippi Delta." *American Journal of Economics and Sociology* 27, no. 2 (1968): 133–46.

Lowe, John. "Theories of Ethnic Humor: How to Enter, Laughing." *American Quarterly* 38, no. 3 (1986): 439–60.

Macaluso, Joseph N. *Italian Immigrant Families: Grocers, Proprietors, and Entrepreneurs: The Story of the Italian/Sicilian Corner Grocers and Markets of Algiers, Louisiana*. Pittsburgh: RoseDog, 2004.

MacCurdy, Rahno Mabel, V. A. Lockabey, and Richard H. Barker. *Citrus Roots— Our Legacy: Selling the Gold ; History of Sunkist and Pure Gold*. Upland, Calif.: Upland Public Library Foundation, 1999.

Magnaghi, Russell M. "Louisiana's Italian Immigrants prior to 1870." *Louisiana History* 27, no. 1 (1986): 43–68.

Margavio, Anthony V., and Jerome J. Salamone. *Bread and Respect: The Italians of Louisiana*. Gretna, La.: Pelican, 2002.

Mariani, John F. *America Eats Out: An Illustrated History of Restaurants, Taverns, Coffee Shops, Speakeasies, and Other Establishments That Have Fed Us for 350 Years*. New York: Morrow, 1991.

———. *How Italian Food Conquered the World.* New York: Palgrave Macmillan, 2011.

Marler, Scott P. *The Merchants' Capital: New Orleans and the Political Economy of the Nineteenth-Century South.* Cambridge: Cambridge University Press, 2013.

Marquis, Donald M. *In Search of Buddy Bolden: First Man of Jazz.* Baton Rouge: Louisiana State University Press, 2005.

Masson, Ann. "J. N. B. de Pouilly." *Encyclopedia of Louisiana,* June 4, 2013. http:// www.knowlouisiana.org/entry/j-n-b-de-pouilly.

Matsumoto, Nancy. "The Legacy of Joe Baum: The Original Renegade Restaurateur." *Edible Manhattan,* August 2010. http://www.ediblemanhattan.com /magazine/the-legacy-of-joe-baum/.

Matthews, Bunny. "Chris Owens." *OffBeat Magazine,* February 1, 2004. http://www .offbeat.com/articles/chris-owens/.

May, Stacy, and Galo Plaza Lasso. *The United Fruit Company in Latin America.* Washington, D.C.: National Planning Association, 1958.

McCann, Thomas P., and Henry Scammell. *An American Company: The Tragedy of United Fruit.* New York: Crown, 1976.

McDonald, John P. *Flameout: The Rise and Fall of Burger Chef.* N.p.: CreateSpace Independent Publishing Platform, 2011.

McGirr, Lisa. *The War on Alcohol: Prohibition and the Rise of the American State.* New York: Norton, 2016.

McNamee, Thomas. *The Man Who Changed the Way We Eat: Craig Claiborne and the American Food Renaissance.* New York: Free Press, 2012.

Mixon, Gregory. *The Atlanta Riot: Race, Class, and Violence in a New South City.* Gainesville: University Press of Florida, 2004.

Morrison, Andrew. *The Industries of New Orleans: Her Rank, Resources, Advantages, Trade, Commerce and Manufactures, Conditions of the Past, Present and Future, Representative Industrial Institutions, Historical, Descriptive, and Statistical.* New Orleans: Elstner, 1885.

Mortara, Giorgio. "The Economic Revival of Messina." *Economic Journal* 23, no. 91 (1913): 438–42.

Mudu, Pierpaolo. "The People's Food: The Ingredients of 'Ethnic' Hierarchies and the Development of Chinese Restaurants in Rome." *GeoJournal* 68, nos. 2–3 (2007): 195–210.

Nau, John Fredrick. *The German People of New Orleans, 1850–1900.* Leiden: Brill, 1958.

Nelli, Humbert S. *The Business of Crime: Italians and Syndicate Crime in the United States.* New York: Oxford University Press, 1976.

———. *From Immigrants to Ethnics: The Italian Americans.* Oxford : Oxford University Press, 1983.

Nesbit, Darin. "Bourbon House: New Orleans." *Gastronomica* 9, no. 1 (2009): 96–97.

Neu, Irene D. "An English Businessman in Sicily, 1806–1861." *Business History Review* 31, no. 4 (1957): 355–74.

Niehaus, Earl F. *The Irish in New Orleans, 1800–1860*. Baton Rouge: Louisiana State University Press, 1965.

Nitti, Francesco Fausto. "Prisoners of Mussolini: Part II." *North American Review* 229, no. 3 (1930): 263–70.

Nystrom, Justin A. *New Orleans after the Civil War: Race, Politics, and a New Birth of Freedom*. Baltimore: Johns Hopkins University Press, 2010.

Ochester, Ed. "Pasta." *Ploughshares* 32, no. 4 (2006): 93.

O'Neal, Marion S. "Growing Up in New Orleans: Memories of the 1890's." *Louisiana History* 5, no. 1 (1964): 75–86.

Osźuścik, Philippe. "Louis Sullivan's Ocean Springs Cottages: A Vernacular Perspective." *Material Culture* 41, no. 2 (2009): 38–56.

Paddleford, Clementine. "Food Flashes." *Gourmet*, May 1950.

Parker, Walter. "Facilities of the Port of New Orleans." *Annals of the American Academy of Political and Social Science* 86 (1919): 188–98.

Paterson, Seale. "Grocery Matters: The History of Solari's." *St. Charles Avenue*, December 2013. http://www.myneworleans.com/St-Charles-Avenue/December -2013/Grocery-Matters-The-History-of-Solaris/.

Perkins, Paula Pomaro. "Southern Italian Foodways in the United States: Symbols of Ethnic Identity." Master's thesis, DePaul University, 1997.

Peters, Martha Ann. "The St. Charles Hotel: New Orleans Social Center, 1837–1860." *Louisiana History* 1, no. 3 (1960): 191–211.

Pillsbury, Richard. *From Boarding House to Bistro: The American Restaurant Then and Now*. Boston: Unwin Hyman, 1990.

Plummer, Brenda Gayle. "Restaurant Citizens to the Barricades!" *American Quarterly* 60, no. 1 (2008): 23–31.

Pontchartrain, Blake. "What Is the History of the Beverly Casino/Country Club/ Dinner Theater?" *Gambit*, October 20, 2014. http://www.bestofneworleans .com/gambit/what-is-the-history-of-the-beverly-casino-country-club-dinner -theater/Content?oid=2517689.

Powell, Lawrence N. *The Accidental City: Improvising New Orleans*. Cambridge: Harvard University Press, 2012.

Pozzetta, George E. *Immigrants on the Land: Agriculture, Rural Life, and Small Towns*. New York: Garland, 1991.

Pratt, Henry J. "Our Passion for Pasta." *Saturday Evening Post*, January 1994, 20–84.

Presley, Delma Eugene. *Piggly Wiggly Southern Style: The Piggly Wiggly Southern Story, 1919–1984*. Vidalia, Ga.: Piggly Wiggly Southern, 1984.

"Production of Essence of Lemon in Sicily." *Science* 14, no. 341 (1889): 108–9.

Raeburn, Bruce Boyd. *New Orleans Style and the Writing of American Jazz History*. Ann Arbor: University of Michigan Press, 2009.

Rao, Tejal. "Spleen Sandwiches: An Italian Tradition." *The Atlantic*, May 3, 2010. https://www.theatlantic.com/health/archive/2010/05/spleen-sandwiches-an -italian-tradition/39761/.

Ray, Krishnendu. *The Ethnic Restaurateur*. London: Bloomsbury Academic, 2016.

Reardon, Joan. "Review: Sex, Death, and Oysters: A Half-Shell Lover's World Tour by Robb Walsh." *Gastronomica* 10, no. 1 (2010): 165.

Rees, Jonathan. *Refrigeration Nation: A History of Ice, Appliances, and Enterprise in America*. Baltimore: Johns Hopkins University Press, 2013.

Roahen, Sara. *Gumbo Tales: Finding My Place at the New Orleans Table*. New York: Norton, 2008.

———. "Red Gravy." *Gastronomica* 8, no. 1 (2008): 56–65.

Roediger, David. "Guineas, Wiggers, and the Dramas of Racialized Culture." *American Literary History* 7, no. 4 (1995): 654–68.

———. *The Wages of Whiteness: Race and the Making of the American Working Class*. London: Verso, 1991.

Roland, Alex, and Alexander Keyssar. *The Way of the Ship: America's Maritime History Reenvisioned, 1600–2000*. Hoboken, N.J.: Wiley, 2008.

Romero, Ginger. *The Louisiana Strawberry Story*. Natchitoches, La.: Northwestern State University Press, 1984.

Sabatini, Nadia, and Vincenzo Marsilio. "Volatile Compounds in Table Olives (Olea Europaea L., Nocellara Del Belice Cultivar)." *Food Chemistry* 107, no. 4 (2008): 1522–28.

Sanchez, Tanya Marie. "The Feminine Side of Bootlegging." *Louisiana History* 41, no. 4 (2000): 403–33.

Sauder, Robert A. "The Origin and Spread of the Public Market System in New Orleans." *Louisiana History* 22, no. 3 (1981): 281–97.

Scarpaci, Jean Ann. "Immigrants in the New South: Italians in Louisiana's Sugar Parishes, 1880–1910." *Labor History* 16, no. 2 (1975): 165–83.

———. *Italian Immigrants in Louisiana's Sugar Parishes: Recruitment, Labor Conditions, and Community Relations, 1880–1910*. New York: Arno, 1980.

Schafer, Judith Kelleher. *Brothels, Depravity, and Abandoned Women: Illegal Sex in Antebellum New Orleans*. Baton Rouge: Louisiana State University Press, 2009.

Scheib, Flora K. *History of the Southern Yacht Club*. Gretna, La.: Pelican, 1986.

Schlesselman, G. W. "The Gulf Coast Oyster Industry of the United States." *Geographical Review* 45, no. 4 (1955): 531–41.

Schneider, Jane, and Peter Schneider. *Culture and Political Economy in Western Sicily*. New York: Academic, 1976.

Schwartz, Arthur. "Mangled Menus." *Gastronomica* 1, no. 2 (2001): 20–21.

Scora, Rainer W. "On the History and Origin of Citrus." *Bulletin of the Torrey Botanical Club* 102, no. 6 (1975): 369–75.

Scott, Rebecca J. *Degrees of Freedom: Louisiana and Cuba after Slavery*. Cambridge: Belknap Press of Harvard University Press, 2005.

Seftel, Howard. "Government Regulation and the Rise of the California Fruit Industry: The Entrepreneurial Attack on Fruit Pests, 1880–1920." *Business History Review* 59, no. 3 (1985): 369–402.

Shanabruch, Charles. "The Louisiana Immigration Movement, 1891–1907: An Analysis of Efforts, Attitudes, and Opportunities." *Louisiana History* 18, no. 2 (1977): 203–26.

Shifman, Limor, and Elihu Katz. "'Just Call Me Adonai': A Case Study of Ethnic Humor and Immigrant Assimilation." *American Sociological Review* 70, no. 5 (2005): 843–59.

Sinclair, Andrew. *Prohibition, the Era of Excess.* Boston: Little, Brown, 1962.

Smith, Roy J. "Economics of the Lemon Industry." *Economic Botany* 10, no. 1 (1956): 66–74.

Sokolov, Raymond A. *Fading Feast: A Compendium of Disappearing American Regional Foods.* New York: Farrar Straus Giroux, 1981.

Sonneman, Toby F. *Lemon: A Global History.* London: Reaktion, 2012.

Souther, J. Mark. "The Disneyfication of New Orleans: The French Quarter as Facade in a Divided City." *Journal of American History* 94, no. 3 (2007): 804–11.

———. *New Orleans on Parade: Tourism and the Transformation of the Crescent City.* Baton Rouge: Louisiana State University Press, 2013.

Stanonis, Anthony. *Creating the Big Easy: New Orleans and the Emergence of Modern Tourism, 1918–1945.* Athens: University of Georgia Press, 2006.

Suhor, Charles. *Jazz in New Orleans: The Postwar Years through 1970.* Lanham, Md.: Scarecrow, 2001.

Sullivan, Mary Louise. "Mother Cabrini: Missionary to Italian Immigrants." *U.S. Catholic Historian* 6, no. 4 (1987): 265–79.

Swanson, Betsy. *Historic Jefferson Parish: From Shore to Shore.* Gretna, La.: Pelican, 2003.

Theophano, Janet. "'It's Really Tomato Sauce but We Call It Gravy': A Study of Food and Women's Work among Italian-American Families." PhD diss., University of Pennsylvania, 1982.

Thompson, Brian C. "Journeys of an Immigrant Violinist: Jacques Oliveira in Civil War–Era New York and New Orleans." *Journal of the Society for American Music* 6, no. 1 (2012): 51–82.

Tipton-Martin, Toni. *The Jemima Code: Two Centuries of African American Cookbooks.* Austin: University of Texas Press, 2015.

Tolkowsky, Samuel. *Hesperides: A History of the Culture and Use of Citrus Fruits.* London: Bale and Curnow, 1938.

Trautmann, Frederic. "New Orleans, the Mississippi, and the Delta through a German's Eyes: The Travels of Emil Deckert, 1885–1886." *Louisiana History* 25, no. 1 (1984): 79–98.

Tregle, Joseph G., Jr. "Early New Orleans Society: A Reappraisal." *Journal of Southern History* 18, no. 1 (1952): 20–36.

Trillin, Calvin. "No Daily Specials: Customs of a New Orleans Roadhouse." *New Yorker*, November 22, 2010, 60–64.

Tucker, Susan. *New Orleans Cuisine: Fourteen Signature Dishes and Their Histories.* Jackson: University Press of Mississippi, 2009.

Twain, Mark. *Life on the Mississippi.* New York, Harper, 1950.

Van Syckle, Katie. "Preserving the Louisiana Heritage Strawberry." *Gambit*, March 1, 2010. http://www.bestofneworleans.com/gambit/preserving-the -louisiana-heritage-strawberry/Content?oid=1256857.

Vincent, Charles. "Booker T. Washington's Tour of Louisiana, April, 1915." *Louisiana History* 22, no. 2 (1981): 189–98.

Violi, Patrizia. "Trauma Site Museums and Politics of Memory: Tuol Sleng, Villa Grimaldi, and the Bologna Ustica Museum." *Theory, Culture, and Society* 29, no. 1 (2012): 36–75.

Virgets, Ronnie. "Postcards from Ustica." *Gambit*, August 23, 2005. https://www .bestofneworleans.com/gambit/postcards-from-ustica/Content?oid=1244761.

Vujnovich, Milos M. *Yugoslavs in Louisiana.* Gretna, La.: Pelican, 1974.

Vyhnanek, Louis Andrew. *Unorganized Crime: New Orleans in the 1920s.* Lafayette, La.: Center for Louisiana Studies, University of Southwestern Louisiana, 1998.

Warner, Coleman. "Freret's Century: Growth, Identity, and Loss in a New Orleans Neighborhood." *Louisiana History* 42, no. 3 (2001): 323–58.

White, Geoffrey M. "Is Paris Burning?: Touring America's 'Good War' in France." *History and Memory* 27, no. 2 (2015): 74–103.

Williams, Elizabeth M. *New Orleans: A Food Biography.* Lanham, Md.: AltaMira, 2012.

Witt, Doris. "The Larder: Food Studies Methods from the American South." *Journal of Southern History* 81, no. 1 (2015): 258–60.

Wolfert, Paula. "Food: A Dish of Sicilian History." *New York Times Magazine*, December 15, 1985. http://www.nytimes.com/1985/12/15/magazine/food-a -dish-of-sicilian-history.html?pagewanted=all&mcubz=0.

Wright, Gavin. *Old South, New South: Revolutions in the Southern Economy since the Civil War.* New York: Basic Books, 1986.

Wurgaft, Benjamin Aldes. "Stardom and the Hungry Public." *Gastronomica* 5, no. 3 (2005): 121–24.

Zanini De Vita, Oretta. *Encyclopedia of Pasta.* Berkeley: University of California Press, 2009.

Zenner, Walter P. "Joking and Ethnic Stereotyping." *Anthropological Quarterly* 43, no. 2 (1970): 93–113.

Ziegelman, Jane. *97 Orchard: An Edible History of Five Immigrant Families in One New York Tenement.* New York: Smithsonian/HarperCollins, 2010.

Index

SOUTHERN FOODWAYS ALLIANCE
STUDIES IN CULTURE, PEOPLE, AND PLACE

*The Larder: Food Studies Methods
from the American South*
EDITED BY JOHN T. EDGE,
ELIZABETH ENGELHARDT, AND TED OWNBY

*Hog Meat and Hoecake: Food Supply
in the Old South, 1840–1860*
BY SAM BOWERS HILLIARD

*To Live and Dine in Dixie: The Evolution of
Urban Food Culture in the Jim Crow South*
BY ANGELA JILL COOLEY

Still Hungry in America
TEXT BY ROBERT COLES;
PHOTOGRAPHS BY AL CLAYTON;
INTRODUCTION BY EDWARD M. KENNEDY;
WITH A NEW FOREWORD BY THOMAS J. WARD JR.

*Catfish Dream: Ed Scott's Fight for
His Family Farm and Racial Justice in
the Mississippi Delta*
BY JULIAN RANKIN

*Creole Italian: Sicilian Immigrants and the
Shaping of New Orleans Food Culture*
BY JUSTIN A. NYSTROM

Printed in the United States
By Bookmasters